Cue Tears

Cue Tears

On the Act of Crying

daniel sack

University of Michigan Press
Ann Arbor

For questions or permissions, please contact um.press.perms@umich.edu

Published in the United States of America by the
University of Michigan Press
Manufactured in the United States of America
Printed on acid-free paper
First published July 2024

A CIP catalog record for this book is available from the British Library.

Library of Congress Cataloging-in-Publication data has been applied for.

ISBN 978-0-472-07690-1 (hardcover : alk. paper)
ISBN 978-0-472-05690-3 (paper : alk. paper)
ISBN 978-0-472-22213-1 (ebook)

DOI: https://doi.org/10.3998/mpub.12713735

Contents

Digital materials related to this title can be found on the
Fulcrum platform via the following citable URL:
https://doi.org/10.3998/mpub.12713735

Acknowledgments

If crying is contagious, then talking about crying also provokes tearful tales from others. Often, when I have mentioned that I was writing on tears in performance, I have found myself witness to the most poignant of recollections and wondrous of anecdotes. I cannot name all these interlocutors but let me extend a heartfelt thank you to anyone who spent a few minutes pondering this matter with me. This would be a much richer volume if I had included everything I heard.

Writing much of this book in isolation, I have relied on friends who supported me from afar in writing groups and zoom gatherings: Rachel Anderson-Rabern, Kyle Gillette, Yelena Gluzman, Michael Hunter, Rachel Joseph, Dominika Laster, Kris Salata, and Keren Zaiontz. Closer to home, David Rodríguez-Solás, Jane Hwang Degenhardt, Asha Nadkarni, and my colleagues in the English Department at the University of Massachusetts Amherst have provided vital friendship, feedback, and community. Sections were shared at Performance Studies international, at several working groups associated with the American Society for Theatre Research, at UMass's Interdisciplinary Studies Institute, and the Center for European Studies at the University of Wisconsin, Madison (thanks, Nils and Sarah). Financial support was provided by the Office of the Vice Chancellor for Research and Engagement and the College of Humanities and Fine Arts at the University of Massachusetts Amherst. A fellowship from the George A. and Eliza Gardner Howard Foundation provided time away from other responsibilities when I needed it most.

My thanks to the artists and their representatives for the rights to reproduce the images included in these pages. To Chris Wilson for his design work. To Cheryl Bowman, Marcia LaBrenz, Haley Winkle, and the entire production team at the University of Michigan Press. My thanks, too, to the anonymous reviewers of this manuscript, whose commentary provided guidance and captured my intent with an eloquence I've strived to deserve. Above all, I am grateful for the editorial acumen of LeAnn Fields. Since I first mentioned the possibility of this peculiar project years ago, she has been a resolute believer in its promise. She encouraged my departures from scholarly norms, and offered precise suggestions that enlivened cluttered passages, or opened dead ends out to new vistas. It has been a great privilege to work with such an exemplary editor on one of her final projects.

Thanks to my extended family: to Rebecca and Alex, to Cora and Raz, to Nancy and Victor, and to Quince. If one strand of this book concerns children and parents, I have been fortunate to study under the most inspiring of teachers. I acknowledge my mother, Deborah, for her lasting devotion: who else would read the final draft of a book on her phone while flying across country and offer useful comments on the other side? My wife, Alex, for the gift of her dramaturgical insight, her care for our little muse of comedy, Thalia, and her general exuberance, which made an extended quarantine and my reclusive tendency cause for daily celebration.

And, finally, a special word of thanks to my father, Robert, whose study of the biochemistry of tears unintentionally planted the seeds for this project a very long time ago. His willingness to let me theatricalize him into an occasionally humorless scientist speaks to his actual character—far more playful and inventive than the cardboard cutout presented here. This book is some measure of my indebtedness to his model and a very pale imitation of his life's work.

Learning How to Cry

Who will write the history of tears?
—ROLAND BARTHES[1]

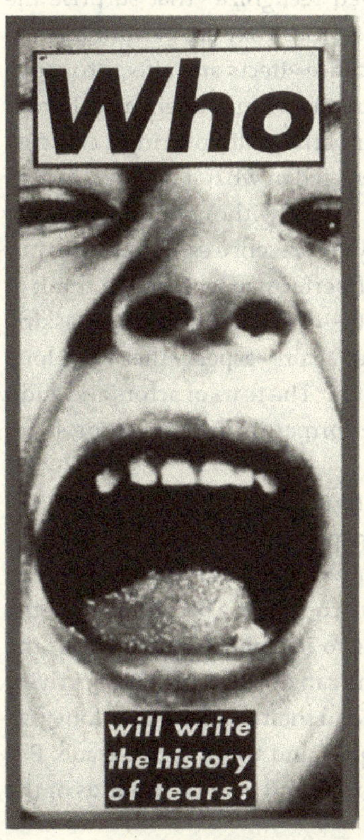

Figure 1 Barbara Kruger, *Untitled* (*Who will write the history of tears?*), 1987, Gelatin silver print. 78 3/4 x 39 3/8 inches. Courtesy of the artist and Sprüth Magers.

My father laughed aloud when he came across a postcard of an artwork by Barbara Kruger with Barthes's words—*Who will write the history of tears?*—printed in black and white atop the face of a crying child. He bought one for his office. I'd never seen him buy a postcard, nor show anything but skepticism toward conceptual art. For him, tears were material of the immediate present. He saw them as consequences of the body's biochemical tides; the event of crying didn't matter much. A scientist, my father conceived of tearful performance in the way that one thinks of a machine or athlete doing their thing.

He spoke with admiration of the virtuosity of one of his co-workers who could cry prodigiously on cue.

I am also interested in tearful performance, though not with the scientist's regard for the composition of tears and their role in the function of the eye. Reading scripts for plays, first as an actor and now as a theorist of performance, I have often wondered at stage directions that state *he weeps* or *her eyes fill with tears*: how do performers cue their tears? Unlike my father's fabled colleague, I cannot turn on my tears with a simple thought. For me, like many others, crying is an act beyond willing—indeed, contrary to willing. If I try to cry, I am quite certain that no tears will come; and if I try to stop crying, I am nearly as certain that my tears will only flow more forcefully. My tears act alongside me. Sometimes unbidden, they give expression to my most intimate sentiments—perhaps those I cannot articulate or even recognize—that surprise me with their call for attention. Tears are cues, too. They are performative in the sense that they do something; they cause effects and affects to move between bodies. When I see the tears of others, I cannot help myself from reacting, perhaps in line with my will, or perhaps discovering a compassion to which I had been blind. I am interested in what it means to watch another cry, to cry alongside them, or to cry without them—in other words, how tears knit together the bodily co-presence essential to performance.[2] But to think of tears in terms of performance is also to think of their potential discrepancy, their duplicity—the crocodile's tears masking a vicious bite, or the boy crying wolf, yet again—aspects that have long invited the scorn of antitheatrical prejudice.[3] The tears of actors and audiences flow through arguments about performance and have done so for a very long time.

I will not write the history of tears, though I will touch on some of the many different contexts that have shaped their usage. I will as often write the memory of tears, how I have found myself crying or unable to cry in this house built for tears that I have chosen as a second home—the theater—and in those spaces contiguous to it—the lobby or gallery, the street. Indexes to one's secret nature, tears can draw on memory's private reservoir of experience, a fact that actors and their teachers have long recognized and utilized in various techniques and tricks of the trade. But there are other forms of memory's tears that spill over the bounds of the private subject.

An installation-performance by the Slovenian artist Janez Janša maps the interplay between tears and different forms of memory in instructive ways.[4] *Camillo Memo 4.0: The Cabinet of Memories—A Tear Donating Session* (1998) asks its participants to individually progress through a series of three chambers, each intended to provoke a liquid response. One first enters "The Cabinet of Individual Memory," a small chamber masked with celestial blue satin where a mirror affords the only view. There one can stay if one wishes, engaged in personal reflection to incite the intended tears. Should this not prove effective, one passes into the next chamber, "The Cabinet of Collective Memory," where an archive of emotionally laden video footage is on hand as an aid. These include excerpted scenes from fictional films (tearjerkers or sentimental tragedies), as well as clips of documentary interest (rousing moments of national pride or dismay, glorious sporting triumphs and public disasters). Janša curated the archive anew for each installation to respond to the attachments of his intended subjects. In Slovenia at the turn of the millennium, one would find "CROATIA VS. GERMANY FOOTBALL GAME THAT RESULTED 3–0 for Croatia; CHILDREN STARVING TO DEATH IN SUDAN; EXODUS FROM VUKOVAR, from the war in Croatia (1992–1994); EXODUS FROM SREBRENICA, from the war in Bosnia and Herzegovina (1993–1996); TITO'S DEATH in 1980; DEATH OF PRINCESS DIANA," and the films *Dead Poets Society, Imitation of Life, Who's Singin' Over There? (Ko to tamo peva)*, among others.[5] Should this assisted endeavor too fail to deliver, the final chamber, "The Cabinet of Physiological Memory," offers a more certain impetus: the cutting of an onion. Here it is the bodily eye itself that acts, recalling evolutionary memory to perform the appointed task. The fumes released from a cut onion produce sulphuric acid when they contact the water in the eye, prompting our tear ducts to flood over and wash out the offending chemical. The three cabinets neatly register the memories of the personal self, the public culture, and the species stretching back beyond a generation's repertoire of events.

Camillo Memo 4.0 is a private theater; there is no audience to witness its dramas. Participants wear specially designed eyeglasses fashioned with funnels that collect the tears produced to provide material evidence, a contemporary version of the lacrimarium or lacrimatory, those ancient tear-shaped vessels purported to store the tears of mourners or absent lovers.[6] The second chamber may recall how we find license to cry in darkened auditoriums among others caught up in a common current, but even this is a solitary act in Janša's configuration. And the mirror in the first chamber stands as a reminder: if anyone is watching it is the crier themselves, attending to the production as both participant and spectator.[7] In this, the cabinet recalls the fact that we are always also witnesses to our own tears, at times only discovering an affect when we feel our dampened cheeks, and, our view hazing over, we find ourselves asking: why am I crying? William James claimed that we know all our emotions retrospectively, that the body reacts and then the feeling follows: "I am sad because I cry."[8] But crying is a universal sign not because it signals transparently, but because it can mean any number of things. It shows us that something is happening even as the cause itself is obscured, blurred.

Camillo Memo 4.0 is also a pseudo-scientific laboratory, established to dissect the means by which that private show takes place. This is in keeping with the nature of cabinets, in the archaic sense of a cabinet of curiosity; as a representative text from the *Oxford English Dictionary* put it in 1796, "the generality of cabinets are schools of study, rather than exhibitions."[9] The pleasures of categorization, of the example: these are the draws of the cabinet. (It is an appeal that my own writing embraces in the many leaky boxes that fill these pages.) Janša plays with and mocks the researcher's desire for objectivity when confronting affective production. Gold certificates are offered to those who manage to produce tears in the first chamber; silver for the second chamber; and bronze for those reliant on the third's more mechanical and automatic means. These certificates authenticate and adjudicate the quality of the tears, but we would have a harder time distinguishing an "authentically felt" gold tear from an ersatz bronze tear after the fact. Neither sight, smell, nor taste can help us to decide whether this vial's contents issued forth from joy or sorrow or mere irritation. Chemical composition is no better guide, since studies are inconclusive at best when it comes to differentiating the variety of human tears.

The conceptual and semiotic ambivalence surrounding crying is reflected in the scientific literature on the subject. From Charles Darwin to William James to the specialized focus of more recent scientific research, modern theories about the production of emotional tears contradict one another as often as not. Part of this stems from the difficulty of conducting research on emotions in a laboratory setting; what are the ethics of making someone cry heartfelt emotional tears for a research experiment? (Which raises the concomitant question: what are the ethics of making someone cry emotional tears for a performance experiment?) Part of it stems, too, from the fluid nature of the subject itself: while most emotional tears convey a negative affect, tears can express practically any emotion. One cries in joy, in wonder, or for reasons that remain obscure to the crier even as the tears roll down their cheeks. One has to agree with Tom Lutz's assessment from his wide-ranging book *Crying: The Natural and Cultural History of Tears* that, "[o]ur best understanding of tears comes not from the medical and psychological sciences, but from the innumerable poetic, fictional, dramatic, and cinematic representations of the human proclivity to weep."[10] In the pages of this book, it is my hope to leverage the extensive, millennia-old knowledge that performance in particular offers to understand how and why we cry—and simulate crying—and what it means to witness another person crying.

Aesthetic performance is awash with tears. Think of the double emblems of the theater: that pair of masks showing the broad grin of comedy alongside the grimace of tragedy. The latter often streams tears through half-closed eyes; occasionally the comedic too joins in with ecstatic tears of its own. As expressed by these conjoined twins, crying figures as perhaps the central emotion of the theatrical endeavor. Shakespeare's Hamlet begins his famous reflection on the nature of acting by considering tears as the metonym for all acting: ". . . What would [the Player] do / Had he the motive and the cue for passion / That I have? He would drown the stage with tears . . ."[11] Many Oscar-winning acting performances prominently feature episodes of weeping, suggesting that the entertainment industry thinks a good cry makes a good actor.[12] The notion of the "ugly cry" arose in the mid-2000s as a mark of admiration and of ridicule to describe celebrities and movie stars—mostly women—who abandon their cultivated grace to contorted collapse, and thereby appear to reveal an unguarded self.[13] The crying of an audience is also considered a measure of successful performance; as Sarah Bernhardt put it: "When a popular audience is moved to tears by the anguish of the actor, when forgetting theatrical convention it imagines that it is present at a real drama, the actor will know that he has achieved the object of his art."[14] I recall a certain strand of Broadway television ads from the 1980s that featured testimonials from audience members, breathlessly exclaiming in the lobby post-show: "I laughed! I cried!"[15] This carries over to the cinema, especially in the domain of the melodrama, where Linda Williams writes of "the long-standing tradition of women's films measuring their success in terms of one-, two-, or three-handkerchief movies."[16] In the visual arts, when the performative turn of the post-WWII period brought the body of the artist into the gallery and museum, it brought an ample supply of tears with it.[17]

The tendency to weigh the efficacy of drama by the volume of tears produced stretches back to the earliest formulations about the theatrical endeavor. Writing the first and most influential work of dramatic theory, Aristotle proposed *catharsis* (generally interpreted as purgation) as the keystone of the tragic experience. In the only passage in his *Poetics* that references the term, he writes that tragedy "achieves through the representation of pitiable and fearful incidents, the catharsis of such pitiable and fearful incidents."[18] Debates about the function of catharsis already fill whole library shelves and would require far more space to elucidate than I can offer here. In his influential treatment of Aristotle's *Poetics*, Stephen Halliwell delineates three general interpretations of this purgation: a medical reading, which sees the purgation of pent-up emotion as a release that returns one to a healthy homeostasis; a moral reading, popularized by neoclassicists, that sees the cleansing aimed at maintaining moderation as a good; and a structural reading, where, as Marvin Carlson puts it, the catharsis "occurs not in the spectator but in the plot, as it harmonizes disruptive elements within [the tragedy] itself."[19] The first two of these interpretations conceive of catharsis as an event that begins onstage, and then is realized in the audience either affectively or intellectually. In other words, it is an essentially relational proposition in which an audience's tears can be readily imagined as the physical manifestation of this purgation. More broadly, tears are the only bodily substance that have been characterized as clean and cleansing—even holy or purifying— across different time periods, cultures, and belief systems.[20]

The interpretation of the salubrious aspects of tragic catharsis only took hold in the mid-sixteenth century, but it adheres to a longer-standing belief that the expression of an emotion relieves its disturbing pressure, allowing one to return to a healthy state of equilibrium, calmed and in balance with oneself and the world.[21] Hippocrates (460–370 BC) and Galen (129–201 AD) offered versions of a humoral theory, where the balance of four cardinal bodily fluids ensured mental and physical well-being, that grounded understandings of the body through the nineteenth century. Even as medical and anatomical study has shown the inadequacy of these theories, their imprint is still evident in the widespread belief that shedding emotional tears is a cathartic act.[22] Ovid wrote that "it is some relief to weep; grief is satisfied and carried off by tears"; in the twentieth century, American psychiatrist Karl Menninger could echo that weeping is "perhaps the most human and most universal of all relief measures."[23] Even tears shed in positive moments have been characterized in these terms. In the 1950s, the psychoanalyst Joseph Weiss argued that tears of joy might derive from a release of pent-up affect, the easing of repressed grief that has been held in check producing positive feeling.[24]

The pioneering work of William H. Frey, whose early research on the chemical composition of tears became the basis for the mass-market book *Crying: The Mystery of Tears* (1985), has had an outsized effect here. As the first major account of the subject written for a broad readership, Frey's writing popularized the theory that tears, like other bodily excretions, contain toxic substances and thus regulate the system by excreting its excesses. This argument developed out of his findings that emotional tears contain twenty percent more proteins than reflexive or basal tears, as well as increased levels of prolactin, a hormone released by the pituitary gland during times of stress. Subsequent studies were unable to reproduce these findings and have raised major questions about his claims.[25] In a review of the state of the field in the late 1990s, several prominent tear researchers wrote:

> the hypothesis that crying generally results in some form of catharsis or positive change in health status could not be verified. Crying in response to a sad film in a controlled setting does not appear to lead to any appreciable decrease in emotional tension or distress, or to an improved psychobiological functioning. Indeed, results of various studies seem to point in the opposite direction, relating crying to increases in arousal, tension, and negative affect.[26]

Nonetheless, Frey's work and its derivatives continue to impact the social imaginary. As one of countless examples, Sigrid Nunez's novel of mourning *The Friend*, winner of the 2018 National Book Award for Fiction, repeats the claim that "in humans, the chemical makeup of emotional tears is different from that of tears that form in order to cleanse or lubricate the eye, say because of some irritant. It is known that the release of these chemicals can be beneficial to the weeper, which helps explain why people so often find that they feel better after they've had a good cry, and also, perhaps, the reason for the enduring popularity of the tearjerker."[27] Many tear researchers would disagree with all of these claims, but they do make for good fiction. These scientists would say that there is no appreciable difference in the chemical composition of tears whether they are caused by a physical irritant or an emotional one.[28] At least, that is what my father continues to aver.

Until his retirement several years ago, my father was a biochemist who studied human tears. Like many tear researchers, he was not interested in emotional crying; his particular fascination was the changing production of tears throughout the diurnal cycle, how their composition altered when the eye was closed during sleep, as well as related concerns about dry eye syndrome and the effects of contact lenses. Human tears are 98 percent water, with trace amounts of more than forty proteins and immunoglobulins in varying proportions, many with salutary effects; he sought to analyze these shifting tides and understand their causes and effects. On and off during my childhood, when an experiment required additional samples, he would collect my tears and those of my mother for study. I was paid for each sample I produced—and, while uncomfortable, and perhaps alienating in ways I'll discuss below—it was not an especially onerous task. He could only use one sample from each crying session, but during especially diligent and productive weeks I would come away with upwards of twenty dollars through this peculiar form of allowance.

My father was after two different kinds of tears. The first, *basal* tears, are an ever-present lubricant that facilitates vision by preventing abrasions and distributing the healing qualities of tears across the surface of the eye. Since the eyes of fish need not be concerned with the danger of drying out, basal tears evolved in reptiles and are found in all land animal species as a means of maintaining ocular function. They form a continuous film over the eye and every blink redistributes this protective layer, making the collection of these ever-present fluids a rather straightforward affair, at least in small doses. As my father described the process in one of his papers, "donors were trained to collect their tears by facing a mirror, cocking their head to the side, and holding open the lower lid with their nondominant hand."[29] There was a catch: in order to better understand the sleeping eye, and what happened during this long period uninterrupted by the distributive power of blinking, my father sought basal tears from when the eye was closed. This presented a challenge for collection. On first waking in the morning, with one eye squinting open, I would stumble to the mirror. Only then would I open the other eye, letting in light for the first time that day, while immediately placing the end of a needle-thin capillary tube along my lower eyelid. In this manner, I gathered the liquid clouded with sleep.

The second type of tear, the *reflex* tear, is most often produced when some irritant disturbs the eye. These tears issue from the lacrimal glands on the outer portion of each eye's orbit and flow toward the inside of the eye and bridge of the nose, where small openings, or lacrimal puncta, drain into the tear ducts. Reflex tears perform the essential task of washing clear and protecting the eye from injury caused by a physical disturbance. Think of the mote of dust in the eye, the sting of cut onions, the automatic overflow of the body reacting to intrusion. Collecting this second type of tear was a more involved and active affair: "*reflex tear* stimulation was carried out nontraumatically by holding open the upper lid to prevent blinking, a procedure that eventually stimulated a heavy production of reflex tears."[30] Other methods were even more effective at prompting the flow of tears: a cotton swab up the nose, a hair pulled from the same. Like Janša's first chamber with its mirror and masking, these performances were solo affairs, but where the installation relied on the gold standard of personal memory and feeling, these turned to an entirely mechanical approach more in line with the bronze certificate of "physiological memory." Looking into the bathroom or bedroom mirror, I would stretch my face into uncomfortable contortions, watching patiently as my eyes reddened and each precious drop accumulated.

As it happens, just as our kitchen's freezer filled with plastic vials archiving days of tearful collection, I also began taking my first acting classes at a barn theater down the road. I was trying to learn how to cry onstage. At the time, I believed weeping to be the mark of the true actor and watched with awe my fellow students who were reduced to tears with a cue from a script.[31] Such fluency did not come easily to me. In my first professional role—which I am now ashamed to relate was as the Siamese heir to the throne in Rodgers and Hammerstein's *The King and I*—I sat staring wide-eyed as my onstage father (another white actor in yellowface) lay on his deathbed. I remember feeling torn between maintaining the stoic expression presumed suitable for the boy-who-would-be-king and wanting to show some vulnerability for this most affecting scene. There were nights where I stared fixedly into the stage lights, watching the shafts of dust shifting and trying not to blink so as to force my tears to come reflexively, borrowing the technique I had practiced in front of the mirror for long hours, capillary tube in hand. What I really wanted to produce was a third type of tear, the *emotional* or psychogenic tear, which my father's research could not, and did not want to, approach. I was in good company, for as Nunez continues in her book: "Laurence Olivier was said to have been frustrated because, unlike many actors, he could not make tears on demand. It would be interesting to know about the chemical composition of the tears produced by an actor and to which of the two types [reflexive or emotional] they belong."[32] I was no Olivier, but I share Nunez's curiosity about the murky distinction between actor's tears cued on demand and those that require a more direct intervention to pour forth.

Emotional tears remain a great mystery, resistant to scientific analysis. When he turned to the subject in his 1872 volume *The Expression of the Emotions in Man and Animals*, Charles Darwin could not conceive of an evolutionary value for such tears—a remarkable departure from his overriding theory of use guiding evolution. Some claim that emotional tears are not far removed from reflex tears, only that the impetus of pain is a psychological rather than physical spur.[33] Indeed, cognitive scientists have discovered that social pain stimulates the same parts of the brain as physical pain.[34] Whatever its evolutionary purpose, Darwin thought that such crying "must have been acquired since the period when man branched off from the common progenitor of the genus *Homo* and of the non-weeping anthropomorphous apes."[35] Most mammals and a few reptiles have reflex tears, but only humans seem to express emotional tears.[36] Chimpanzees and other animals cry vocally when they want attention, but—unverified tales of weeping deer, turtles, dogs, and elephants notwithstanding—emotional tears arguably mark the human as distinct from other animals, which has led some writers on the subject to suggest that crying makes us human. They say that tears are a universal language, recognizable around the world, while also noting that different cultures at different historical moments have various grammars for communicating this language. At root, a common conviction holds that one shows the potential to suffer—and to suffer alongside another—by crying. Indeed, this explicitly and implicitly directs many understandings of animal consciousness; their lack of emotional tears or tears of pain signify the supposed shallowness of their affective range.[37]

But the idea that emotional tears prove an emotional being carries with it a range of problems. There are physical conditions like dry eye that restrict or prevent the flow of tears or, contrarily, produce too many tears. One's tear glands may not produce enough of the lipid basal layer to lubricate the eye, so watery tears keep coming in an endless stream, or one's tear ducts may not sufficiently siphon away the basal flow, causing tears to brim over the lid. There are neurological injuries that can alter or suppress tearing entirely; neurodiversity entails lachrymal diversity.[38] Even when sensitive to contextual and communal distinctions, claiming crying as the unalloyed mark of authentic feeling can readily reinforce troubling notions of proper and improper forms of behavior. Anecdotal and experimental evidence shows that fluency with tears is disciplined by gender expectations (The Cure reminds us "Boys don't cry") and judgments of maturity and self-control (Fergie answers "Big girls don't cry"). Many narratives of racist dehumanization describe people of color as thick-skinned, unfeeling, or less susceptible to pain, or contrarily too expressive and excessive in their display. José Esteban Muñoz wrote of "brown feeling" to describe "the ways in which minoritarian affect is always, no matter what its register, partially illegible in relation to the normative affect performed by normative citizen subjects."[39] The expectation for well-regulated expressiveness privileges an "affective performance of normative whiteness [that] is minimalist to the point of emotional impoverishment."[40] Too much crying or too little crying marks a departure from proper (read "straight white") subjectivity. If Muñoz's late writing explored the political potential of affective excess in queer Latinx aesthetics, other scholars of queer and minoritarian subjectivities have turned to the potential in the dry eye. Uri McMillan has drawn out a tradition of Black women performance artists stretching over the last one hundred and fifty years who have embraced positions of passive objecthood, and Tina Post has written evocatively of a deadpan aesthetics attached to Blackness, while Xine Yao mines the potential of disaffection for a range of minoritarian subjects in the 19th century.[41] This is to say that tears (and their absence) convey multiplicitous affects, altered by culture and context, and variously freighted with gendered, raced, and normative signification, a panoply behind that uniform transparent appearance.

At least in its vocal formulation, crying is easier to place. Infants cry for attention, out of need or distress. Here, the animal kingdom offers antecedents in calls, barks, or howls intended to reach caregivers and those in the larger family of whatever species. Psychotherapist Judith Nelson writes that "crying is an interpersonal rather than strictly individual behavior: crying and caregiving go hand-in-hand."[42] Long before they learn to shape sounds into words, crying engages the full apparatus of the voice and breath, essentially allowing a speechless infant (from the Latin *infans*, meaning "unable to speak") to rehearse vocal mechanisms before language. For a largely immobile baby, the act of crying is tiring work and good exercise. When Darwin's first child was born, he thought the occasion a singular opportunity to test the development of emotional display in humans. Ever the scientist, Darwin found the perfect experimental subject in this readily available infant body—another father-son research team. He noted that while his son wailed and screamed in his first months, he did not produce emotional tears until he was some 4–5 months old (139 days to be precise). Darwin reported other infants crying at 20 days and another at 104 days old, and more recent studies have confirmed this delayed production: we have basal tears before birth; reflex tears arrive a few weeks after birth; and emotional tears within a few months.[43] The assumption is that we somehow learn to cry psychogenic tears in that intervening time, making weeping one of the earliest manifestations of the *homo imitans*. In a not-so-subtle misogynistic aside, referencing how women in particular might develop the ability to tear up voluntarily, Darwin argued that crying "required some practice" and that "the power of weeping can be increased through habit."[44] Such a claim bears some weight when it comes to acting, where one's weeping might accordingly become "more powerful" with practice, though evidence throws doubt on this supposition—if Olivier couldn't do it, then practice does not make perfect. As they grow older, children learn to weep without vocalizing, such that many crying episodes in adulthood are silent affairs. This development may be a protective measure. Vocalized crying is like an emergency beacon, alerting friends and potential enemies alike that one is in distress and vulnerable. Such a signal would generally be reserved for instances of genuine need, for fear of drawing unwanted attention, perhaps contributing to the idea of crying as an honest expression.[45] Leading tear researcher Ad J. J. M. Vingerhoets writes that "infant crying has been referred to as the 'acoustical umbilical cord,' because it serves to establish and maintain a close connection between the infant and the caregiver, although it will also stimulate adult non-parents to provide care and protection."[46] Tears that persist without vocal accompaniment, or with only minimal sound, can communicate this relation on a more local level, directly signaling to those closest without alerting the whole neighborhood.

This signaling also works self-reflexively. When crying, I become aware of my feeling body as separate from the subject who says, "hold it together." These tears tell me something significant is happening, even when I cannot place the event passing through me. And in recognizing these tears, I find myself inevitably recognizing a potential other, witnessing my weeping. Can I ever cry alone? By which I mean, can I ever cry without presuming someone who sees me crying or wanting someone to see me? Are all my tears wept in some kind of theater with its attendant double?[47] Here is Barthes again:

> By weeping, I want to impress someone, to bring pressure to bear upon someone ("Look what you have done to me"). It can be—as is commonly the case—the other [. . .] but it can also be oneself: I make myself cry, in order to prove to myself that my grief is not an illusion: tears are signs, not expressions. By my tears, I tell a story, I produce a myth of grief, and henceforth I adjust myself to it: I can live with it, because, by weeping, I give myself an emphatic interlocutor who receives the "truest" of messages, that of my body, not that of my speech: "Words, what are they? One tear will say more than all of them."[48]

That query at the end and its voluminous response belong to the composer Franz Schubert, but he might speak on behalf of any number of other writers on the subject. Emotional tears are frequently called forth as an assertion of the inexpressible or the excessively expressive. Indeed, for cultural theorists writing over the last century or so, it seems that tears become cyphers where letters cease to make a meaningful imprint. There are longer histories at play here, where the pages of the 18th century sentimentalist or 19th century romantic were often inscribed and underlined with their invisible, yet indelible, ink. What are called "emotional" tears in the literature might be better served by the name "affective tears," since these can index sentiments that move through us in far more complicated and complex ways than a word like "sadness" can suggest. Teresa Brennan writes that affects sit uncomfortably outside or between many names, while more definite feelings are "sensations that have found the right match in words."[49] Asked why you are crying, how often you've responded: I don't know. Of course, you know if a fly is in your eye or a speck of dust, but internal obstacles and meanings are harder to extract.

Tears also always carry with them their homonym, implying a force that ruptures, as one might speak of a tear in fabric. This connection is apparent in the oldest etymological hypotheses, even outside the English language. In 636 BC Isidore of Seville posed that *"lacrimae"* comes from *a laceratione mentis*, meaning "from the wound of the soul."[50] Tears derive from a tear in the soul. The metaphors, images, and words attached to crying convey this instability and fracture. They speak of dissolution or collapse, of breaking down or out, but they also frequently turn in the opposite direction: one can be filled up with tears, come to the edge or verge of crying, find oneself brimming over. This captures a contrary aspect of crying, how it offers a fullness as if to compensate for lack or incapacity. My tears often gather to witness that which exceeds my capacity to contain an experience—what might otherwise be called the sublime. To cry in this manner is to feel along the threshold where I become other than myself; I exceed the definitions of the language that I use, just as the world I see hazes over at the edges. I think of crying in these moments as a moving tension, my depth surfacing and touching the world, the other. A shared translucent skin forms, a window or passage opens, between those self-sustaining fictions of interiority and exteriority, of private and public sentiment, that normally keep me comfortably grounded as a subject among objects and distinct from other subjects. The literary theorist Peggy Kamuf wonders if weeping could "be said to be proper to man since it erupts as a dispossession, non-self-possession, or possession by some other? It would perhaps make more sense to say that humans are beings who must try to learn to stop weeping."[51] Weeping, we lose ourselves to another not-quite-human self. Alongside other ecstatic experiences like sex or experiences of abjection like nausea, this counters the idea of an "out-of-body" transcendence with a sense of the body escaping the self or asserting volition unconsciously. According to Kamuf, you'd best be able to stop crying if you want to return to the conversation. We become "human" in our mastery of the inarticulate just as articulation gathers force through its entwinement with the inarticulable.

At the limits of our expression, we pass over into tears, whether in sobs or bouts of laughter. Indeed, tears point to the strange confluence between these outbursts usually situated at either end of the human field of feeling. Both crying and laughing manifest themselves in similar fashion—interrupting the breath in gasps, in an audible cascade of sound. Darwin noted that heavy laughter constrains the muscles around the eyes to extrude tears in much the same way as violent crying. Their aftereffects, he continues, are equally muddled, so that "it is scarcely possible to point out any difference between the tear-stained face of a person after a paroxysm of excessive laughter and after a bitter crying-fit."[52] This shared vocabulary can lead to confusion. James Joyce wrote of "laugh-tears" in *Finnegan's Wake*; Samuel Beckett's Molloy confronts this hazy common ground when he inadvertently strikes and kills a dog with his bicycle and observes its owner's reaction. "I thought she was going to cry, it was the thing to do, but on the contrary she laughed. It was perhaps her way of crying. Or perhaps I was mistaken, and she was really crying, with the noise of laughter. Tears and laughter, they are so much Gaelic to me."[53] I recall watching a scene in Jacques Rivette's dream-like film *Celine and Julie Go Boating* (1974) and facing a similar conundrum. I saw Celine (or was it Julie?) laughing hysterically over the infanticide that both main characters are forced to witness day after day, then a second later I could have sworn she was weeping. Or watching the short video *Hysteria* (1999) by the artist Sam Taylor-Johnson (previously Taylor-Wood), showing a woman in closeup, her head thrown backward against a black abyss, as wide-eyed and wide-mouthed she casts herself into an endless stream of laughter that slowly transitions into full body sobs and back again.

Look back at the paired emblems of theatrical performance, those twin masks of the drama, never seen in isolation from one another. An equally

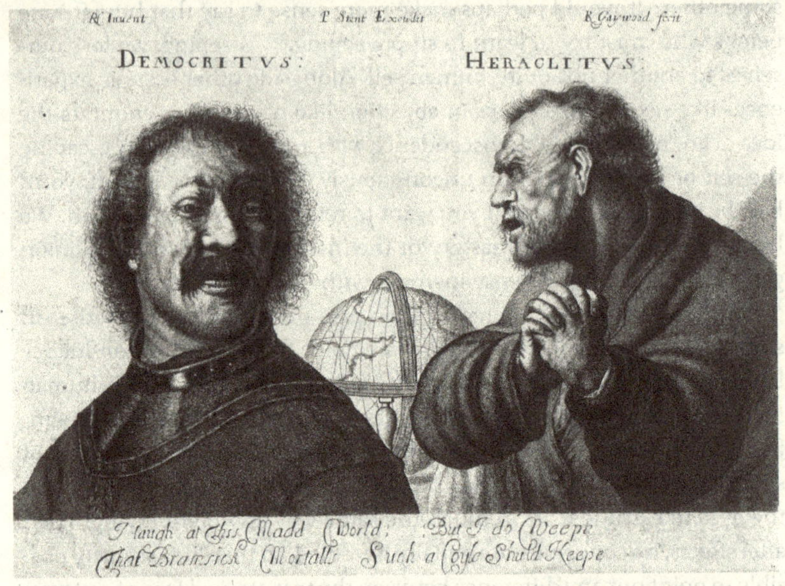

Figure 2 *Heraclitus and Democritus.* Etching by Richard Gaywood, after a design by Jan Georg (Joris) van Vliet. Formerly attributed to Wenceslaus Hollar. Circa 1650–1660. © The Trustees of the British Museum.

long-standing tradition depicts the pre-Socratic philosophers Democritus of Abdera and Heraclitus of Ephesus in partnership and opposition: two sides of the same coin, Democritus ceaselessly laughs at the world, while Heraclitus cannot stop crying at it.[54] Like the emblematic masks of the theater, fixed for eternity in their paroxysms, both philosophers are trapped in a problem of time. In an etching of the pair from the mid-17th century, a caption underneath states: "I laugh at this Madd World; But I do Weepe / That Brainsick Mortalls Such a Coyle Shuld Keepe," clearly recalling Hamlet's "shuffle off this mortal coil."[55] According to Lucian's satirical reading of the pair, Heraclitus's tears are inspired by his recognition that the world is in constant flux, that nothing is fixed and certain, as all forms decay, decompose, collapse into formlessness.[56] Heraclitus's tears (themselves falling in a constant flux) exemplify the very nature of the live arts, their living so often coupled with dying, or at least with perpetual change and variability. As that old chestnut from the philosopher has it: you cannot step into the same river twice. Even if the word "river" remains the same, the waters that pass through the stream move on otherwise. You can cry me a river, but you can never cry me the same river.

Laughtears erupt out of speech and take the body over against our control. One of my friends growing up was a very neat and contained young woman, her speaking voice always measured and authoritative, while her laugh boomed out like the guffaw of Santa Claus and seemed to take her by surprise as much as those around her. Hand to mouth, she would visibly try to contain the full-throated intrusion, but it would rise up and overwhelm her. We break down in tears or crack up into peals of laughter, our proper form collapsing under an uproarious surge.

Many contemporary theorists and philosophers follow the paired Heraclitus and Democritus to reflect upon the significance of this common escape from sense. A few examples should suffice. In *The Tears of Eros*, his final book on eroticism's play with death in the history of visual art, Georges Bataille writes that "the object of laughter and the objects of tears are always related to some kind of violence which interrupts the regular order of things, the usual course of events."[57] Judith Butler has, following the work of Helmuth Plessner, said that both laughter and crying show how "the person is overwhelmed by its expression."[58] She distinguishes between the language of parliamentary politics, which relies on and acknowledges only those who speak from an authorized subject position, and the "noise" of those who are excluded from subjecthood in the modern democratic state—the logorrhea of laughtears. Giorgio Agamben writes that "laughter and crying are the two ways in which humans experience the limits of language: while in crying the impossibility of saying what one wants to express is painful, in laughter this passes over into joy. Ultimately, however, in the sudden collapse of the facial features and the breakdown of language and voice into gasps and hiccups, laughter and crying seem to blur into each other."[59] In this understanding, the interruption breaks down two registers of language: semiotically, tears and laughter often exceed naming, a boundless liquid depth without sign for anchor; phenomenologically, they also disrupt the oral flow of clear speech, jamming phonemes together into hard guttural hacks or dissolving into open-mouthed vowels—aaahhhh/hahahaha— those places where writing too must disaggregate itself from words.[60] In her translations of the Greek tragedies of Euripides, the poet and classicist Anne Carson leaves the wails of characters as streams of Greek or conglomerations of vowels that show a whole field of sense inaccessible to contemporary audiences who do not know the language. (Punctuation also delineates this threshold of writing, thus the role of the dash and the ellipsis in the writing of emotion and the writing of tears.)

These reflections and their variants that recur throughout philosophy primarily regard the effects of crying on breath and voice as an aural phenomenon. In English, the word "crying" refers to both the production of tears and to purely vocal events like a call, alarm, or shout; any parent will agree, with regards to a crying child, the sound often takes precedence. As noted in Darwin's observations above, tears are an expected though not required accompaniment to some of these outbursts. Behavioral psychologist Debra Zeifman writes that "[w]hereas crying is primarily an acoustical signal in infancy, it may be primarily a visual one in adulthood; most adult crying appears to be simply tearing."[61] Neuroscientist Robert Provine adds that "the developmental shift from vocal crying to visual tearing favors the face-to-face encounters of an intimate setting."[62] "Crying" and many of its cognates ("sobbing," "wailing," "keening," etc.) disturb the flow of smooth speech and breath, and therefore work on the register of sound. Breath for the crier can become an obstacle, in heaving exhalations that drain the lungs and leave one gasping for air, or sputtering in and out in short rhythmic spells. I can hear someone crying as a sudden stoppage of speech, or, at the other extreme, as a non-verbal wail that swallows speech under its wave. As the poet Ann Lauterbach notes, tear is "a neat little word, a single syllable, with 'ear' tucked within, mingling two senses, seeing and hearing."[63] But not all tears trouble verbal communication in the same manner. There are, for example, tears that arise over calm and steady breath, as in the silent tears suggested by the word "weeping." Throughout this book I move freely between these various names, rather than applying an artificial taxonomy to delineate such a variable landscape. Yet it bears consideration here: if crying is, as so many philosophers have proposed, primarily a problem of sound and speech, are tears primarily a problem of sight?

Apart from the rheum of sleep, the sediment of the sandman which is itself a discharge of the tear film, tears are the only substance excreted from the seat of sight, our eyes. There is the old saying that the eyes are the window to the soul; or from a different angle, as Italo Calvino writes, "the retina is a peripheral portion of the cerebral cortex. In short, the brain begins in the eye."[64] Whether a window to the spiritual or the beginning of the biological core of a thinking, feeling being, looking in the eyes of another can be an intimate experience, even an intrusion. Tears underline, and undermine, this passage into the heart of another. If I am crying, my own sight and my position as spectator are compromised. I blur with the world and lose distinctions. This is not to say that my sight fails so fully that I cannot see, for if my vision falters under this translucent veil, I will blink my way toward transparency.

The world I see through tears is haloed with a feeling made manifest in several senses. My feeling state appears before me and frames my sight. Unless the saying is accurate and rage literally clouds sight for some or casts it in a red-tinged haze (in my experience, it does not), there is no other affect that makes its presence visible to me when it passes through me. Tears cast my feeling like a mesh over the world seen, altering all upon which my attention alights. Here is one tangible proof of sentiment. Here is another: whether I see or not, whether I cry in darkness or blindness, I feel the actual disturbance of these tears as a touch upon the eye, an irritation that draws my attention. The tears feel my eyes, run sensation along the outer curve of this sensory surface. Through tears, I see myself feeling and feel myself seeing, a chiasmatic proposition that twins and twines the self and world. I've written elsewhere about Aristotle's rumination on the eye staring in the pitch dark as a means of discovering the faculty of sight itself, how there is nothing to look at in this pit of blackness but the potential to see.[65] Perhaps tears, too, are a way of encountering the complexity of our potential sight—both as a seeing and as a being seen.

If, on the other hand, you are the one crying, you offer an image to my sight that compels an affective change. Psychological experiments have shown that people pre-cognitively recognize and respond to the tears of another. Subjects who were shown the image of a tear-stained face for the smallest fraction of a second—a flicker too fast for conscious recognition—expressed an impulse to approach that other, even if they could not say what inspired the impulse. Another experiment comparing photographs of weeping people to the same photographs with the tears digitally removed found that the presence of tears seemed to inspire viewers to approach rather than avoid the person encountered.[66] The biologist Oren Hasson argues that tears compromise vision in a manner that is sufficiently visible to others as a way of communicating that one is no longer aggressive.[67] They act as a white flag of surrender. A theater of tears is one that addresses and distresses spectatorship.

To say that tears are a problem of sight is not to suggest that they are *only* visual obstacles or acts. Tears link the body in a chain of autonomic responses: swollen throat, runny nose, quivering mouth, a confusion of facial contractions, not to mention that ragged breath, that cracking voice. My tears show that my sight manifests in an eye that belongs inextricably to my feeling body as much as to the larger world. When I cry, I become aware of my eyes as a threshold between myself and the world. This is no floating transcendent eye mastering the scene from a timeless distance, as certain modernist critics like Clement Greenberg averred.[68] Rather, the tearful eye is a part of a complex of gestures, rhythms, reactions, flows, and stoppages that together comprise the field of crying. Actors in many traditions have often used the body's associated symptoms and elaborate traditions of gestural vocabulary as a way of triggering or simulating tear production. A dab of a handkerchief, a shudder of the shoulders, or arhythmic breathing might create the semblance of a tearful act, and even activate an actor's dormant lachrymal glands. *Cue Tears* is concerned with some of these habits and styles of crying, as represented onstage or in performance, but people cry in such different ways across times, places, and communities that I inevitably can only address a small fraction of this multi-textured field.

As I wrote above, this is no history of tears, but a writing beholden to memory. Looking back once more at the multi-chambered installation with which I began this discussion, recall that Janša is interested in tears as the material evidence of memory's recurrence. Both the first two chambers rely on recollection of the past—personal or collective, respectively—to produce the present episode. (The third chamber stretches further still to the biological memory shared by a species.) As Marina Grzinic puts it in her account of the installation, "the participant has to prove his or her successful achievement of memories by crying."[69] In other words, to "successfully" remember the past is to feel in the present and to make a show of it. In this, Janša's cabinets recall that other cabinet of curiosity, that other memory machine, the theater. Here the past's conflicts, its heroes and its dead, come to life again nightly; here, in a more mundane manner, a monumental task of memory is communicated to an audience with every performance in lines and choreography. (What actor has not been asked that deflating post-show question: How do you remember it all?)[70]

If the theater is a place for, and reliant upon, memory's recurrence, then memory can rely in turn on the theater. The full title of Janša's work, *Camillo Memo 4.0: The Cabinet of Memories—A Tear Donating Session*, draws the connection overtly: the Camillo in question is the Italian philosopher Giulio Camillo (1480–1544) who proposed a "theater of memory" that promised the storage and immediate recollection of all manner of data and experience. In her book *The Art of Memory*, Frances Yates describes how a long history of mnemonics stretching back thousands of years modeled its techniques for retaining the past on the theatrical situation. Many of these techniques direct one to wander room by room through an imagined house associating this arrangement of furniture with that arrangement of time, as if architecture were the objective correlate for a set of memories, as if the spatial could be translated into the temporal. But Camillo proposed a theater in place of a house. By arraying an auditorium with rows and rows of memory triggers, signs and statues in place of the audience, one could rehearse the recollection of each lived event in succession. Such a theater is constructed around a single life: the one who sits at centerstage and looks out to where the audience should be, but where instead the panoply of chosen memory triggers stare back from the seats, opening windows to that one private past. This is a theater that reverses the direction of the gaze: seated onstage, the one who remembers breaks the fourth wall and willfully stares at each visage in that private audience to isolate that face's specific trigger; it fragments the gaze from that silent gathered mass into its individuated stare. To remember is to have the world oriented toward me, looking back and acknowledging me as the subject and center of time's passage.

There is another side to my story, one that perhaps borrows from fiction the promise of a narrative resolution. During those adolescent years, when fumbling through various techniques in the laboratory and theater, I stopped crying in my everyday life. In my recollection, I didn't shed a tear for close to fifteen years, maybe more, though there were many moments where I thought I should be crying or wanted to break down. I remember a numb remove when told that my beloved dog had been hit by a car and died. I remember not crying at my grandmother's funeral, even as the sight of so many aunts and uncles weeping unmoored me. This was, of course, my own tutelage in a rumored masculinity. The pride I felt when a friend called me stoical, distant, as if I had finally conquered my more feeling self. It had been different earlier, in another life.

He was a sensitive boy. A slight pressure and the scene would cloud before his eyes and suddenly there were fingers pointing and children laughing at how he was crying. He would duck away but the sentiment lingered and somehow the occasional comments consolidated into an image: sensitive, particular, delicate. On one hand these seemed marks aligned with his sensibility and desires—to submerge himself in the world and suffer its affects as his own—but the social surround proclaimed this course etiolated, minor, compromised, effeminate, weak, soft. He became an artist and aesthete, but kept himself removed, analytical. By the time he started collecting tears he was caught in a bind. He wanted to maintain himself, to restrain these emotions with their attendant threat of ridicule, their awkwardness in public settings. And yet, he began seeking out tears in controlled avenues. There was the theater, with its reassuring encouragement that this was all a game, that whatever poured forth had been authorized and justified by the part played. Here, what remained of that sublimated emotional streak could break forth under the guise of another character, not himself. And there was the laboratory, where his tears would be quantified and formalized as part of an economy that did not include emotion.

I think I felt this way for a long while, far past the time I knew I upheld a deeply suspect ideal. It took a genuine rupture in my life—the end of a ten-year relationship—to shake those foundations loose. In the months after that loss, I would well up in tears not at the memory of my absent partner, but at the very texture that surrounded me, catching on sharp angles of perception. A simple appearance: the wind would pick up across a field, churning the trees, and I would find myself crying; a certain turn in the singer's cadence, the way their breath caught in the throat between phrases; subtle variations, flares and flickers, gaps and hesitations, a change was enough to send me over the edge. These were not tears of sadness, but what I'd venture to call ecstatic tears, in the sense of "an exalted state of feeling which engrosses the mind to the exclusion of thought; rapture, transport."[71]

That summer I went to the Edinburgh Fringe Festival for the first time and spent three weeks seeing as many performances as I could. Such vulnerability carried over to the theater, where I gave way to tears with striking ease. I had often played the analytic viewer, weighing formal compositions, structural and conceptual arrangements, while admiring the technique of performers as they cheated tear-streaked faces into the light, but I now found myself exposed to sensation and committing to the fiction with no critical remove. I fell wholly into the story's sentiment. I wept with abandon.

This shift in my private experience of spectatorship also altered the currents of feeling in the theater at large. Perhaps a transparency showed in my face, illuminated even when the tears had long since dried up, for something novel followed: any time a performance involved some form of participation, I found myself called up, selected from out of the dark mass of the audience. Here I was on stage not three or four times, but many, many more. I saw five or six performances each day over the course of three weeks, and again and again I found myself drawn into the fold as I gave myself over to whatever event. I had attended countless performances and many theater festivals in the past; not once had I been selected for these tasks. Indeed, I had always looked on the prospect of audience participation with no small terror. Perhaps in those past occasions performers could sense my critical eye from afar. Perhaps my tendency to furrow the brow whenever listening created a barrier to the proceedings. I later asked one of the performers why they'd elected me among so many others. You were present to me, she said. It was as if the tears had exposed me to sight or had made me a problem of sight. It was remarkable—strangers and friends alike made mention of my recurring role as a member of the supporting cast, how fully I gave myself to my nascent part—and it was short-lived. While I still cry with some regularity, the tide of my tears receded after that summer and I too receded from attention, once again comfortably apart from the proceedings. Crying is an offering of oneself in relation to another, and this meeting at the threshold of sight's fragile vulnerability is one of the most vital the theatrical endeavor can provide.

In his essay "Of the Power of the Imagination," Montaigne posits the imagination not in terms of the capacity to conceive the impossible or fantastical, or to project a possible future action, so much as a capacity to be affected by others. To empathize is to imagine ourselves into the position of another. "I am one of those who are very much influenced by the imagination," he writes. "The sight of other people's anguish causes very real anguish to me, and my feelings have often been usurped by the feelings of others. [. . .] I catch the disease that I study, and lodge it in me."[72] He quotes from Ovid's *Remedy of Love*: "by looking at sore eyes, eyes become sore: / from body into body ills pass o'er." (Or in Nahum Tate's even more relevant translation of these same lines: "By looking on sore eyes, our own we wound; / Dry lands are oft by neighb'ring rivers drowned."[73]) If tragedy's catharsis unleashes pent-up pressures, it also, according to neoclassical readings, teaches us how to imagine feeling with others through the pity and terror that it arouses, those "neighb'ring rivers" from the weeping actor drowning our own.[74] Indeed, mimesis within the aesthetic frame seems to lubricate these imaginative transfers, perhaps too readily. Many have noted the ease with which an audience feels alongside theatrical or cinematic suffering, or in response to the tribulations of a sentimental novel's hero or heroine, when they would coldly observe the same in everyday life. In his discussion of how many readers stained the pages of *Uncle Tom's Cabin* with their tears, while turning a cold eye to the racism that suffuses American society, James Baldwin cuts to the marrow of such aesthetically sanctioned and contained sympathy: "Sentimentality, the ostentatious parading of excessive and spurious emotion, is the mark of dishonesty, the inability to feel; the wet eyes of the sentimentalist betray his aversion to experience, his fear of life, his arid heart; and it is always, therefore, the signal of secret and violent inhumanity, the mask of cruelty."[75]

Just as Montaigne's imagination invited empathetic infection from another's suffering, his susceptibility to the things and affects he studied brought disparate elements into his personal orbit. His essays are mobile constellations of association that he discovers in the process of writing; they are networks that essentially rewrite his conception of self. As he put it in another essay, "I have no more made my book than my book has made me—a book consubstantial with its author, concerned with my own self, an integral part of my life."[76]

Montaigne began writing his essays in his 38th year, having retired from public life and secluded himself in his library. Outside a plague raged across the land, killing a third of the population of Paris, including his best friend, Etienne de La Boétie. While I am no Montaigne, I did begin this work in my 38th year and I occasionally worry that I have also retired from public life, a sense only exacerbated by the pandemic through which I've written many of these words. Secluded on the outskirts of a small town in the center of Massachusetts, my time in the theater has been greatly reduced over the past three years and I miss that space in ways my body knows even better than myself. Crying and performance are strong antidotes to this tendency to retreat since both require, and even constitute, relations with others. The many op-eds and articles published on Montaigne during the last few years of our pandemic confirm I'm not alone in turning to the inventor of the essay genre. I have found solace there, and also a form for this book to emulate, if only loosely. Tear-like, each of the essays in *Cue Tears* functions as a discrete drop in a longer stream of queries into the nature of performance. For, across many languages, tears are never referred to in the singular, but always as plural, to mark a timebound succession or multiplicity.[77] The book flows from an analysis of tears and their meanings to the internal and external means of their production, before addressing how tears constitute different subjects in performance, and, finally, in the academy.

I begin by relying on my father's expertise to try to make sense of the biology and anatomy of tears, staging a lesson via a fictional dialogue. Where every other essay in the book circles around a set of theatrical and paratheatrical events, this dramatization compensates for the lack of a performance text grounding its discussion by inventing one in its place. "On the Nature of Tears: A Semi-fictional Dialogue" consolidates several zoom conversations conducted during the pandemic into a single script, adding a liberal dose of imaginative play to stake out two different perspectives on crying: that of the scientist and that of the performance theorist. The resulting scene attempts to present the facts about the structure and function of tears, while also enacting the fundamental relationship between parent and child that undergirds any discussion about crying. As autotheory/autotheater, writing the self and the fact of its own making, the dialogue crosses into the terrain stretching between facticity and fictionality that tears stream across. All to say that the versions of the two of us represented here are fantasies that borrow from actuality—I'm grateful that the real Robert Sack was willing to play along.

Tears seem to give us access to an affect before and beside language, for even if crying can be a private performance, enacted (for some) exclusively in seclusion, it begins its life as a communicative act. The next chapter, "I'm Too Sad to Tell You: On the Private Language of Tears," looks at how the tear is a prism, clarifying or distorting the relation between a statement and its inciting affect. I pair Bas Jan Ader's laconic set of works *I'm too sad to tell you*, which feature the conceptual artist crying silently and without explanation, with a text that is shared between the neurodiverse poet and disability rights activist Mel Baggs and the artist Wu Tsang. The resulting video performance, *The Shape of a Right Statement*, directly challenges the idea of speech and comportment as means of rendering divergent subject positions legible and culminates in a single strand of tears that descends like a tangential remark on the spoken text. A final glance at one of the hundreds of screen tests that Andy Warhol produced—in which a stock-still Ann Buchanan stared unblinking at the camera, streaming tears—rounds out this series of performance portraits that break open any easy identification of crying with a definitive emotional statement.

One assumes that the tears of Ader, Tsang, and Buchanan belong to them as expressions of some private self, however inscrutable. But what of the actor who cries on behalf of a character? The next two chapters focus on some of the techniques that might be used to produce and inspire tearful performances: through internal and then external means. The memory triggers of Camillo's theater mentioned above perform the same function as the remembered details that inspire the affective or emotional recall employed by actors trained in the Method, consolidating memory so that they might perform a feeling again and again. I follow this strand further in "Learning How to Cry (Again): Or, How Actors Keep Feeling the Past," by looking at works by the British artists Sam Taylor-Johnson and Gillian Wearing, two women who interrogate the terms of the Method and masculinity. If the other essays in this book tend to embrace the more esoteric world of performance art, conceptual art, and experimental theater, these artists cross over into more popular media of film and television, of everyday people and celebrities.

In "The Weeper's Toolbox: An Incomplete Catalog of Prosthetics, Props, and Prompts," I offer a guided tour through another kind of cabinet of curiosity, devoted to those objects that inspire an actor's tears from the outside in. The essay imagines a toolbox or prop closet organized according to a jerry-rigged taxonomy: 1) *prosthetics* that replace tears with artificial substitutes; 2) *props* that represent tears; and 3) *prompts* that physically motivate tears. Like the drawers or divisions that might segment a display case, this essay is composed of smaller chambers, subsidiary mini-essays that detail exemplary tools—the handkerchief, the onion, etc.—and their use in a range of contemporary performance-based artworks.

As tools, these external objects have a distinct purpose in provoking tears from human actors, but what would it mean for a tool itself to break from its presumed utility, and burst into tears? Crying things recur across a range of literary genres, from the fairy tale and folk tale of early childhood to the speculative fictions of late capitalism. Riffing off the idea that humans are the only creature capable of tearful crying, "On Getting Water from a Stone: Or, Do Androids Weep Electric Tears?" takes up tales that explore a chiasmatic relationship between the object world and the anthropocentric, as in the trope of the weeping statue or puppet brought to life. These leaky things collapse two distinguishing presumptions of the anthropomorphic perspective on the world of objects: their permanence (or extensive duration) and their lack of interiority or sensibility. Here I am less interested in the mechanisms that puppeteers, animators, or (in the many cases of miraculous weeping statues) charlatans utilize to give this impression than I am in the consequences of such an expression. While I touch on the actual practice of puppetry, I will intentionally blur the distinction between a performing object's tears and a fictional object's tears to focus instead upon why the weeping thing recurs with such regularity in the cultural imaginary of the West. I conclude by considering crying machines in Karel Čapek's play *RUR*, where the robot first found its name, and in the two *Blade Runner* films, examples of a widespread trope in science fiction of a tearful epiphany from para-human constructs. My subtitle for this essay answers Philip K. Dick's question *Do Androids Dream of Electric Sheep?* with a question of my own: "Do Androids Weep Electric Tears?"

By way of conclusion, I reflect on my own profession and its discomfort with tears. "Teaching How to Cry" briefly looks at breaking down *in* the lecture hall as a means of breaking down its staid proprieties. Inspired by a moment when I unexpectedly and inexplicably found myself tearing up while delivering a guest lecture, I ask how embodied affect figures in the largely disembodied structures of knowledge production and transmission, and in the lecture theaters in which academic performance plays out its routines.

Writers of essays frequently hail the etymological root of the word "essay" as an attempt or an effort, in order to emphasize its contingent and performative thrust.[78] Each of the texts in this book is an act in a larger drama, following its own slight formal divergence, its ending only an intermission; each is a partial (in both senses, as incomplete and completely biased) response to a provocation, a reflexive and at times emotional outpouring. As Adorno writes of the essay: "It thinks in fragments, just as reality is fragmentary, and finds its unity in and through the breaks and not by glossing them over. [. . .] Discontinuity is essential to the essay; its subject matter is always a conflict brought to a standstill."[79] An essay rambles on and wanders off course, occasionally following a well-trammeled path before treading new ground. Is it too much to suggest that these words fall like tears themselves, streaking across the face of the page along paths illuminated by previous currents, pooling in cracks well-lined by smiles and frowns, or limning new lines along this map of my past and present expression? And yet, if a book about the performance of crying knows anything, it is the fact that the grooves in which its words may gather belong to another mask, a second skin of papier-mâché, as much as any dream of an authentic face. And so, I begin by donning the masks of father and of son.

On the Nature of Tears
A Semi-fictional Dialogue

Curtains rise on an empty black box. The words "Robert Sack" in white projected at center. Muffled sounds in the dark.

DANIEL SACK: Can you hear me?

ROBERT SACK: Yes, I can hear you. Can you hear me?

DS: Yes. Can you see me?

RS: Yes, I can see you. Can you see me?

DS: Not yet. You need to turn on the video. It's in the lower left corner of the screen. Click that box.

The lights come up on a man in his early eighties. He has a halo of sparse dark hair floating overhead, untamed eyebrows, a prominent nose, and olive skin. In the past he was often mistaken for a man much younger than his years. He loved to tell the story of the time he took his daughter to the open house at an art school and the staff thought that he was an applicant.

DS: Alright. There we go. Are you ready for this? As I said, I'm hoping you can talk with me a little about the science of tears and that this can be the basis of a chapter in the book. I'm recording everything and will probably go back to make edits, so don't worry if something goes wrong. I can fix it later.

RS: Ok. But I'm not sure what you want me to say. There are a number of really smart people I'd like to connect you with that can give you a lot of information.

DS: I know, but I want to talk with you.

RS: I should connect you with X at Oxford. He's fascinating. Has an encyclopedic knowledge about music and has some fantastic slides—

DS: You can send me his contact information and maybe I'll talk to him later, but—

RS: And then there's Y, who you remember from Thailand, how we took that long walk in Bangkok with him. He practiced orienteering. He's much clearer about these things.

This goes on for some time. A veritable who's who of ophthalmologists and biochemists from the 1980s, 1990s, and early 2000s.

DS: I know, I know, but I want to talk to you. Didn't you used to teach these things? We can pretend that we're back in the lecture hall, covering the fundamental aspects of tear production. I want to use this conversation to get some basic building blocks in place.

RS: I hated lecturing. All those grants let me pay someone else to lecture in my place so I essentially stopped teaching in the early 1990s.

DS: Well, here the roles are reversed—I'm asking you to teach the things you take for granted, on my behalf. Besides, it won't be a lecture since I'll interject questions and comments along the way. In keeping with the book's focus on performance and drama, it will be more of a dialogue. I can supplement with footnotes and other references if we go too far astray. I'll even make some stuff up after the fact.

RS: What kinds of things? Can you give me an example?

DS: Well, that for instance. You didn't say it, but I added it to make a point that I forgot to make in the moment.

RS: Ha!

DS: I'll also take things out, move them around. Don't worry. I'll just supplement with a few elaborations that will make us both look a little better or at least a little more put-together.

The lights flicker. RS reappears in a clean pressed dress shirt. He has a real haircut now, as opposed to the self-inflicted pandemic variety he previously sported. Close-cropped and shaven, the resemblance between father and son is amplified.

RS: A button up shirt? So this isn't really me up here, is it?

DS: You're a projection in at least two senses of the word.

RS: At least . . . ?

DS: Let's just say that I'll be writing a fictional version of you, of both of us, accentuating some features to make us more representative of opposing viewpoints, but it will all be based in the past circumstances of this conversation. Kind of like an actor relying on their private memories to act a part. That's something I'll be discussing in a later chapter that I can send you to read sometime if you're interested.

RS nods (noncommittally?).

DS: Now then. Let's start by providing some anchor points: the anatomy of the eye and the system of tear production. What are tears? What do they do?

RS: Well, with the cornea you have a window that is always exposed to bacteria, to noxious agents, to abrasion. Its transparency and optical clarity can be lost through infection or scarring. How do you protect that surface and its attendant vision? Without skin, the eye needs this fluid shield as protection.

DS: The eye is the most exposed part of the body, where inside and outside share a common surface and touch each other. Tears are a kind of liquid skin, a moving point of contact.

RS: I guess so. The skin itself is a three-layer substance. There's a lipid-type of outer layer—a secreted oil which functions as a lubricant and to some extent prevents the tear's evaporation and the desiccation of the cornea. Then there's an aqueous layer. It contains many things but is primarily water.[1] Finally, there's a mucus layer that extends down to the surface of the ocular tissue and helps maintain viscosity.

DS: When you say that there are three layers, does this mean that each of these different components can be isolated? Can you skim off the lipid layer, say?

RS: No, not at all. This is just the classical way of conceiving their composition. In reality, these three layers are all intertwined, but each comes primarily from a different source. The mucin is produced by the surface of the cells of the eye. Some of it is released, some of it is intertwined with the cell to form a protective layer under the eyelid. This outer surface is continually being regenerated and shed to release any bound potential pathogen. The lipid layer is produced by the meibomian and Moll glands that line the rim of the eyelid, where your eyelashes are found.

DS: Maybe it would be helpful if I had a diagram here to show what you're talking about. I glaze over a bit whenever I hear meibomian glands.

RS rummages about, then produces a diagram with the various parts of the eye labeled.

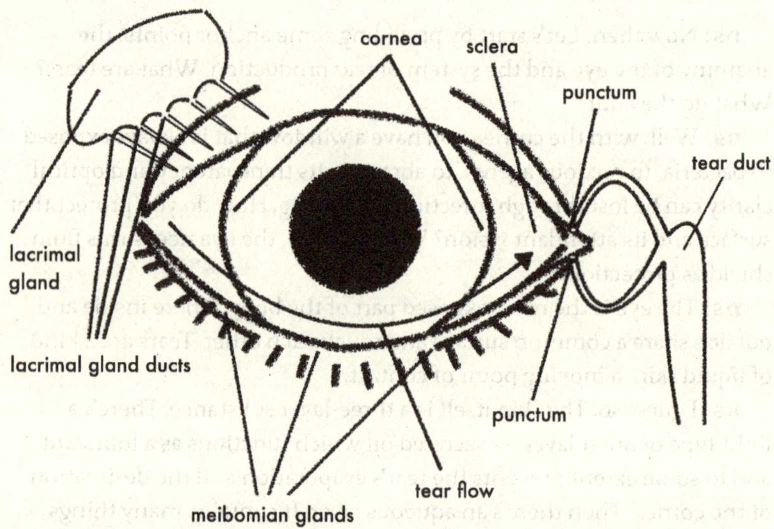

Figure 3 Diagram of the eye, drawn by the author.

RS: As I was saying, the aqueous layer is produced by the main and accessory lacrimal glands, which are located on the outside of either eye. These more liquid and flowing tears collect in the lower lid and exit through small openings, called "puncta," located where the eye meets the nose. So the tears are carried out of the eye during waking hours and into the tear ducts.[2]

DS: This theorist Roland Barthes—the one who posed that question

"Who will write the history of tears?"—he also wrote about how most photographs present an organized view of the world. They reproduce a scene we know and can read, as part of a uniform and meaningful visual fabric. But when facing certain photographs that move us inexplicably, each of us is struck by some accident that speaks to us and us alone. This accidental detail can't be accommodated into the organized visible order; it can't be named. It just is. He calls these little points *puncta*— well, *punctum* in the singular. He says: "A photograph's punctum is that accident which pricks me (but also bruises me, is poignant to me)."[3] I wonder if he was thinking of those small openings in the eye, the passages for tears to flow out of. The kinds of photos he describes as having a *punctum* are often the ones that would bring tears to someone's eyes. His prime example is an otherwise unexceptional photograph of his dead mother that he never shares with us. Facing his absent parent once more, he'd feel the swell of tears, their sudden change, but he couldn't put his finger on why this particular picture moved him more than any others.

RS: (*after a pause*) Hm. I'm not sure I see how they're connected apart from the fact that they share the same name.

DS: Well, that creates a kind of family relation, even if they are referring to different things. But you're probably right: it's a stretch. Anyway—sorry to interrupt. You were talking about how tears are always moving.

RS: Yes, tears are in constant flux. They flow through or across the eye—you might consider it a kind of canal system that is constantly being washed. Or you can think of the eye as a swamp, in which the aqueous layers flow through and exit out the tear ducts, while the lipids stay on the top and the mucins cling to the cells of the eyes. If you stimulate the lacrimal glands to produce excess fluid, you're going to have an increased flow, or an overflow: crying.

DS: So when we see someone crying we're primarily seeing the flow of aqueous tears from the lacrimal glands—those are the tears that would matter for performance. The mucins and lipids may get caught up in the flow, but they generally stay in place. They have no affective or social bearing, but they're important for other reasons. What kinds of things are in tears?

RS: Well, water accounts for about 98 percent—with trace amounts of more than forty different proteins.[4] They also contain immunoglobulins, antibodies which are produced by the body during an immune response. This suggests that tears have a function in fighting infection, viruses, and bacteria.[5] The aqueous layer carries proteins that provide nutrients to protect the ocular surface from infection and inflammation. It's a fail-safe system because any damage to the cornea threatens vision.[6]

DS: So there is some truth to the idea that tears are healing, or at least, the proteins and antibodies they carry contain some healing properties. I wonder if that has any connection to the idea that having a good cry will make you feel better?

RS: I don't know anything about the psychological or emotional effects.

DS: (a pause) I'm really interested in that, but let's hold off discussing it for a moment anyway. As I understand it, there are three kinds of tears: basal tears, which are present at all times to lubricate the eye. Reflex tears, which flow in response to some physical or neurological irritation. And emotional tears, which flow in response to a psychological irritation. Each of these has this same three-layer structure, though the proportions of their composition vary. People are familiar with the reflex and emotional forms of tears, but I read that basal tears were only discovered in the late 18th century.[7] These are also less central to my discussion, so we only have to touch on them here.

RS: Ah, but basal tears are incredibly important! You can't just brush them off like that. They form a protective film that covers the eye and lubricates it to facilitate blinking. This film creates a more uniform surface for the refraction of the light entering the eye, since the surface of the eye is not sufficiently smooth on its own. It's irregular because it is constantly shedding cells.[8] The tears are there to wash away any pathogens or particulate matter introduced from the air, to wash away inflammatory and noxious agents, and to smooth over roughness.

DS: So the basal tear film actually helps us see more clearly? It's only when we start to weep in earnest that things begin to blur.

RS: You can't see without tears. Other species have evolved different ways to create a reliably smooth surface for eyesight. Some birds have developed a third eyelid that is almost transparent and that allows them to see underwater. Since the cornea, unlike other parts of the eye, doesn't have a blood supply, basal tears also play the communicating role that blood plays in the body, providing oxygen and transmitting nutrients to protect the eye. They communicate between different tissues that need to function together: (*referring to the diagram*) the *corneal surface*, which is the clear dome that lets light into the retina; the *conjunctiva* that covers the sclera—the white—of the eye and the inner surface of the eyelids, essentially extending from the lids to the edge of the cornea. The cornea also has some of the most dense nerve tissue in the body, making it painful to touch or scratch. Reflex tears are primarily used to wash away irritants that might be felt in the eye.

DS: Those were the tears you had me collect as a kid. Did you know that Darwin also relied on his son's tears for his study of the evolution of expression? Most of this was purely observational; he recorded when his son first produced tears. But to test when humans developed reflex tears, he ran his shirt sleeve against his son's open eye. Rather nasty.

RS: I'd never have done that. We used methods that wouldn't have any risks attached. It was entirely safe, just a little uncomfortable.

DS: Which I greatly appreciate. And no matter how strange it sounds to an outsider whenever I bring up the fact, I always insist that there was nothing remotely traumatic about the tear collection. It was just an unusual childhood occupation. Besides I was doubly paid for my labors. Not only did I receive pocket money, but I also got some material for this book. Darwin's son didn't even get a mention in the acknowledgments. In any case, I bring it up to say that there are other ways to produce reflex tears, apart from irritating the eye directly. I'm thinking of how I used to collect tears for you—by sticking a cotton swab up my nose and making my eyes water.

RS: That's because the internal nasal nerve is connected to the trigeminal nerve, which is heavily involved in the production of reflex tears. Its upper portion is in the ocular region, so if you press on your eye you'll also increase tearing. There's some belief that this is why we unconsciously rub our eyes when we get up in the morning: to get the tears going. Another branch of the trigeminal relates to the back of the mouth, which might be why yawning can produce tears. An injury or pathology anywhere along the path of the trigeminal can lead to spontaneous crying.

DS: The cotton swab technique has little use for an actor, otherwise I would have been an expert, but I know that some people use yawning to get their tears going. There's this episode of *Conan* where Bryce Dallas Howard tries to teach him how to cry by yawning. It doesn't go well.

RS: I'm not sure I know who that is.

DS: She's the daughter of Ron Howard and appeared in a bunch of movie sequels you probably didn't see: the second *Twilight* movie, *Spiderman 3, Jurassic Park X, Terminator Y* . . . ?

RS: I must have missed those.

DS: Do those different causes—the yawning, the cotton swab—do they produce differences in the tears?

RS: Not in those tears, exactly, but if you look at it there are three or four sources for tears. Say, if there's an inflammation you are going to see certain types of cells, which are called PMM cells, recruited in. These cells clean up debris and digest and dispose of bacteria. And the composition of basal tears will change according to different conditions—time of day, age, and so on.[9] Again, it's a complex and dynamic system.

DS: So the composition of a tear does change in response to the state of the person who cries it, but primarily from physical conditions, not emotional ones. In a way, a tear could communicate something to us, if we only had the means to read that message.

RS: Tears are a record of the moment. There isn't a reservoir holding your tears ready for release. They are produced as needed and vary in composition based on how and when they are required. For example, basal tear production is minimal earlier in the morning and increases as the day goes on.

DS: I like that: tears are a record of the moment. Let's keep that. In broad strokes, I know that you were interested in tracking the changes of tears over the course of a day, but beyond that it still gets a little confusing for me. You didn't really talk about it much in detail as I was growing up. Am I right in thinking that your late work focused on the possibilities of tears not only to communicate the state of a body *outward*—looking for ways that the glucose levels in tears might be measured for a diabetic, say—but also as a means of communicating *into* a body—delivering treatments as an alternative to the bloodstream?

RS: Well, yes, when I found out your sister had Type 1 Diabetes, I wanted to see if there were a way for her to measure her glucose without having to prick her skin several times a day.

DS: She got used to it, but it was hard to witness her sticking those needles in again and again.

RS: Yes, and the injections. I wondered, too, whether it was possible for insulin to enter the bloodstream via tears.

DS: It strikes me that your sense of the communicative possibilities of tears is quite different from the kind of social signaling that most people would associate with tears, and that I'm most interested in exploring in this book. Yours is a matter of how the tear functions as part of the biological whole, not how crying feels or how seeing someone cry makes us feel. There are numerous psychological studies focused on how crying impacts social relations, signaling surrender, or need for care, or whatever. Did you ever wonder about how different emotions might alter the chemical composition of tears?

RS: I don't think the differences between emotional and reflex tears are materially significant, but I wasn't really interested in emotional tears.

A pause. DS briefly considers pursuing this line of thought again but decides on a different course.

DS: Did you ever make use of emotional tears in your studies or were all your experiments reliant on physically inspired tears?

RS: Well, when I used to collect tears, I had one person who was a kind of tear cow. This woman who would think a sad thing and she would fill capillary tube after capillary tube just by thinking about something. Some people can induce emotional tears at will. Other people have a very hard time.

DS: Ironically, back when I used to act, I really struggled to cry onstage. You'd think that fluency with reflex tears would translate to emotional tears, but it wasn't so. I'd be curious to know what your tear cow thought about to inspire those tears—some memory or a general state of affairs or just a tv show she'd watched recently. Perhaps she had an especially active imagination. Was it the same impetus every time? Was she depressed?

RS: She seemed a happy person most of the time.

DS: I know you don't know the answer to these questions, and it would have been improper to ask why she was crying so much, but you must have been curious. *(No response.)* What was this term "tear cow"?

RS: Well, you'll have to change that. She was paid per ml of tear. Like you'd have milk from a cow. Whenever I needed a large amount. She'd just think of something. She worked in the one of the offices near me. Some people have the ability to do that and cry frequently. I wonder . . . probably a lot of it has to do with ethnicity, sex. In some cultures people have learned to cry. You know in ancient Greece, they had vials for collecting tears and they had slaves who would produce large amounts, probably for the antibacterial activity. So they would store them. You can do that yourself, see for yourself. You can make a petri dish with agar, an ideal environment for bacteria growth. If you put the tears in it and then you add bacteria—certain types of bacteria—they won't grow.

DS: Wasn't this the basis for that science experiment we ran for my school science fair? I'd completely forgotten about this until just now. Remember how we used to have to create a science experiment at home and then illustrate our findings with these posterboard displays? It was clearly evident which of the projects had been a joint parent-child venture, especially for those children whose parents worked at the lab: the scientists. It must have been right after you started collecting my tears, so my last science fair in 5th grade. I placed some of my tears in those plates of agar and recorded the growth of bacteria over several days, then compared them with the growth on another agar plate with some other substance in it—plain water, maybe? It was a real experiment—not one of those homemade volcanoes—but I'd clearly borrowed the idea from your work. I can't remember the outcome, but I do remember displaying those tiny glass capillary tubes that we'd use for collecting the tears—the ones that looked like syringes. Everyone was weirded out. I think that this was my final act on the scientific stage, but it was likely just a coincidence.

RS: Creative writing already had its grip on you. You were making those books—remember the one about the fragment of the mirror? You stayed up all night working on it, which you never did with your other homework. As for the experiment, there would have been less bacteria on the plates with tear samples than on the agar plates treated with plain water.

DS: Are there other bodily secretions that have that property or is it just tears?

RS: Oh, they all have it. But it is more concentrated in tears. With saliva you don't have the same problem—if there's scarring in the throat or mouth it is not as dire as in the cornea, where lasting injury would threaten vision. The tears don't function in isolation. They coordinate with cells that are part of the immune system.

DS: To go back to the tear cow woman. Would her tears have been different from those obtained by other means?

RS: There would be some differences. What she would be producing is something which is predominantly from the lacrimal gland. Basically, she would cry so much that everything got diluted out. But in the lab, we didn't approach them differently from the reflex tears that were produced by an external irritation.

DS: I've read that this is contested territory. There was a widely read book in the mid-1980s by William Frey in which he reported a study he conducted showing that emotional tears had higher concentrations of proteins than other kinds of tears. It is my understanding that this has been called into question by other researchers since, but the idea still captures the public imagination.

RS: It's not reproducible. Actually, there are probably fewer proteins in emotional tears because they're more diluted. You have certain types of proteins which are pretty consistent, others which will be lessened through dilution.

DS: Was she the only person who you worked with who could produce tears in this way?

RS: No, but she stood out as an extraordinary producer.

DS: So there are a lot of reasons that one might cry, but you were less interested in *why* than in *how* the crying happened.

RS: Well, we're always producing tears. The basal flow is continually occurring.

DS: So when I am just sitting here looking at you, my eyes are crying slowly; if I start to weep, it is still the same material, just the flow is speeding up.

RS: It is basically the same. The reflex flow occurs more quickly if you stimulate it; that stimulation could be emotional, neurological, it could be from a foreign body sensation or inflammation. The more it flows, the quicker you get rid of something that is annoying—be it a thought or bacteria, what have you.

DS: In other words, tears are a cleansing mechanism to move the things that get caught in our eye and the ideas that get caught in our attention. Tears are agents of change. In a way they do function as a release valve, as a kind of cathartic measure, if we think of catharsis as change from a place of discomfort. In a way, it makes sense that a notion of tragedy that relies on purgation would use tears to do its work.

RS: I'm not sure how any of that is verifiable. On one hand, the movement of reflex tears comes from their higher concentration of water and lower viscosity. On the other hand, the movement of the basal tears is driven by the blinking. Every time you blink it pushes the tear fluid into motion and redistributes the tear film. Animals don't have to blink as often because the higher concentration of lipids in their tears prevents evaporation. Rabbits, for example, only blink every four or five minutes. If you close your eyes and go to sleep there's no blinking, meaning there's a different composition of the tears as you shift into night. Basal tear flow decreases dramatically when the eye is closed and you're asleep.

DS: Growing up, one of the types of tears you'd have me try to collect were those that I produced while I slept. What were you looking for?

RS: Well, when I started doing my work, it was unclear what happened during sleep, not only with tears, but also with the eye more generally. Nobody knew that tears were relatively still during sleep. I came up with a technique to measure the proteins in the tears that allowed me to show that tears did not move much when the eye is closed.

DS: We're looking through the same tear for the duration of our sleep?

RS: Without the blink of the eye, the tears sit suspended and are unable to cleanse the eye of any intrusions. I found that the eye introduced different levels of proteins into the tear film to accommodate these conditions and to provide more robust cleansing and antibiotic protection while in stasis.[10]

DS: While I have sharper memories of the discomfort of collecting reflex tears, I only have a hazy sense of those "closed eye" tears, collected in the very moment of coming to consciousness. You'd wake me in the blue light of dawn, and I would stumble to the mirror, while holding one eye closed. I'd only open it once I had a capillary tube in hand, ready to draw out the night's production before it could see the light of day. I never mentioned this to you, but at the time, I had this crazy thought that these might be the residue of my crying from that night's dreams— not that I remembered crying in dreams, but I felt this sediment might indicate something I could no longer see. A kind of forensics for the imaginary. I'd wondered if especially vivid nightmares were somehow visible in the tears that following morning. Like how I'd imagined those diagrams of the chemical composition of the tears were some map to the experience that had provoked them.

RS: Which diagrams?

DS: Those mysterious figures that you crafted to accompany your papers. I'll pull one up from the files you sent me. Any chance you can explain these to me so that they finally make some sense?

Another slide fills the back wall. Off to one corner, one can just make out the heads of father and son watching on, as the tone shifts to a more speculative night space. It is as if they were sitting in a darkened classroom, the fan of a slide projector lulling them in and out of sleep. The digital screen up here is suffused with memories of its own technological childhood, the carousel of glass slides slipping each scene into place with its signature "clack." Like how RS would set up the projector in the long hall of the kitchen, and we'd all sit around watching the past come alive again, saturated in amber light.

The figure is taken from one of the many, many papers that RS published in the 1990s. Even back then I associated their photographic grain with that of the moon landing, communications from some distant place. He had to design the slides himself, learning how to work with early graphics software programs on the desktop computer that churned away at all hours, bringing up the contrast or exposure to make these ghost lines visible. That is what

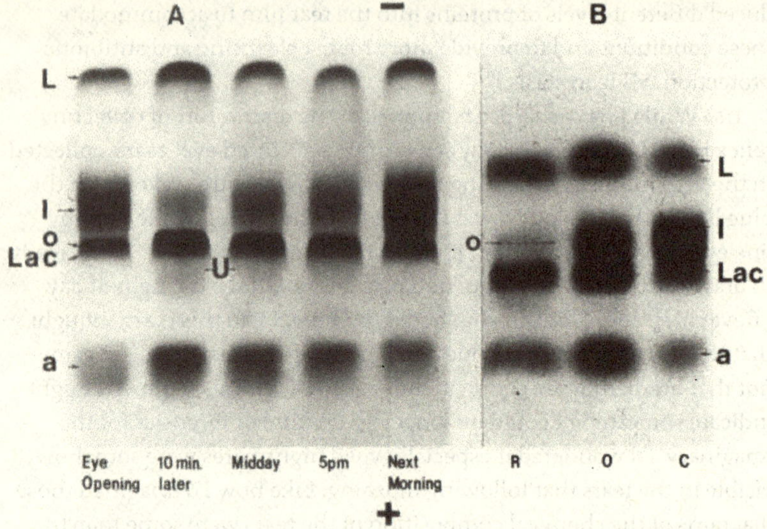

Figure 4 Illustration accompanying article by Robert Sack, circa 1995.

they seemed to my eye—ethereal traces, hazy spots like belly buttons or closed eyes, shadows marking a passage to another dimension, now foreclosed. In the back room of the house, long after everyone had gone to sleep, he'd annotate charts with an arrow indexing this point, a jumble of letters in boldface laid atop the image. Like some prophet reading the signs, an arcane knowledge, hieroglyphic. Back then, I believed in the spirit of science more than any holy word; we'd had no church or synagogue, only visits to the lab.

A strange association, but I also connected these figures with the large canvas that hung in my bedroom, which he had painted in the lone art class he took in college. An abstract expressionist field of greens and blues showing cellular proliferations stretched edge to edge, or the dapple of evening light through leaves, Monet's lily pads. A remarkable piece of work, showing some other promise beyond the analytical frame—the staff at admissions had been correct: he could have been a painter!—a dormant aesthetic intelligence that manifested now in these more functional figures. He happened into graduate school as a way to avoid the draft, then happened into tears when his advisor moved in this direction. A series of fortunate encounters. He only applied for the one job during his career. Though he was headhunted by rival labs, he stayed at the same institution from beginning to end.

RS goes on to explain that these pockets of black depict various protein levels in tears, one small facet of the substance translated into definition. He'd developed a technique to run an electrical charge through the proteins that would separate them into distinctly visible bands to record the relative presences of each component. The method had drawn the interest of other researchers in the field and led to a few years of international attention, when he was sought out as a prized collaborator on industry projects funded by the leading contact lens producers in the world—"the boondoggle years," as he called them. In a way these were indeed pictures of tears, but only a fragmentary view; like a cross-section of the ground beneath one's feet, they offered a very partial view of the landscape. I had thought of them as portraits in the entirety. I believed that my collected tears would be dissected in the lab and later unfolded into a map of feeling. If affects can be pictured, if they can be held for an instant, this is what I imagined they looked like: dark clouds clustered on a plain. A weather system with concentrations of pressure where the sense is heaviest, surrounded by more diffuse peripheries of feeling. One cannot say with precision where a cloud begins or ends.

Was there a part of me that wondered if these tears might reveal too much? My secret self suddenly shown, tabulated, diagnosed? Kierkegaard says that the aesthetic is the interior, hidden individual, and the ethical brings that individual into the light of the universal moral. Is it surprising these concerns weighed on me around the same time that I felt myself coming into a private self, found myself worrying about how to convey or obscure this interiority? Found myself acting?

Those night-time tears were like the rheum of sleep, residue from the night's dreams stilled in the corner of the eye. I recall tales of the sandman sprinkling sand in the eyes of children to put them to sleep. Hans Christian Andersen named the Sandman "Ole Lukøje," the Danish for "close eye," and tells of how he lulls children to sleep, then opens an umbrella with pictures on it over them so that "they dream the most beautiful stories all night long."[11] What traces might remain from those nightly performances—fluid tears or their distillate sand from the shores of sleep?

The slide changes to show a second ghostly abstract image; if the previous figure seemed to show a cross-section of a landscape, this one pulls out far

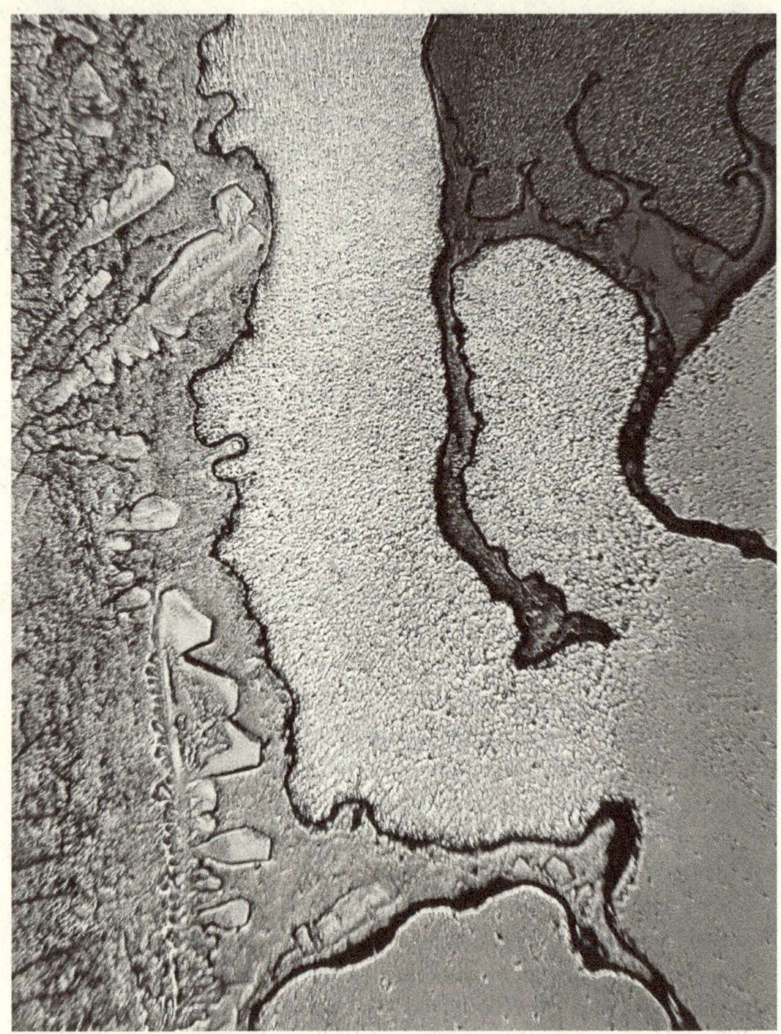

Figure 5 Rose-Lynn Fisher, *Catharsis*. From *The Topography of Tears* © Rose-Lynn Fisher, published by Bellevue Literary Press, 2017.

overhead to take in a whole field. When she first learned I was interested in tears, a friend sent me an article about the photographer Rose-Lynn Fisher's book The Topography of Tears; *over the coming years, several other people directed me to her wondrous work. Fisher dried tears on slides and then viewed them under the magnification of an optical microscope. As she describes her process, "I wander in search of a 'region of interest' and then photograph it with a specialized microscopy camera."[12] She casts herself as a peripatetic drifter collecting such "regions of interest," the topographies of her title, and each photograph seems to show a different geographic form. Organic and inorganic at once, here are floodplains and plateaus, or the labyrinthine architecture of some forgotten civilization to get lost in. If we could only get close enough, they seem to say, we might find a way through this alien land, comprehend its logic, or name it properly. Could the scientist read these signs too, mark them up with his seer's boldface?*

DS and RS resume their conversation over this image of a wasteland. In the half-light cast by the projector they look more ragged now, more deconstructed, like two tramps beside a road going nowhere. They are both there and not there. It is a fiction and the truth.

DS: What do you make of Fisher's photographs?

RS: It's a gimmick. They're no different from any substance you'd see under a microscope at that level. A turnip or a carrot would look as interesting up close.

DS: Well, I love a good gimmick. It is the frame of reference that makes the show. Knowing that we are looking at tears suggests that these images hold some secret meaning. Fisher gives each photograph a title that refers directly or obliquely to an episode of weeping: "After the sun came the tears," for example. This one is fittingly titled "Catharsis." I think these striking images are especially appealing because we all wish that our tears were uniquely beautiful, like the proverbial snowflake. A liquid fingerprint scattered with "regions of interest."

RS: I see what you're doing: setting up a comparison between my diagram as an analytical tool and this photograph as an affective one. But like the *puncta* you mentioned above, the parts only align so far.

DS: I think your diagrams are also aesthetically pleasing, even if they weren't intended that way. They just need better titles. I guess I'm also thinking how all the tears we cry look the same. And, if I correctly understand your hesitations about research that proclaims a noticeable chemical difference between emotional and non-emotional tears, all tears are essentially chemically the same, too. I mean they vary slightly according to the occasion, but not in any way that corresponds to a feeling. At least in their basal and reflexive forms, tears are involved with cleansing and repair—they play a purely functional role. To recognize someone as "crying" or "weeping" is to recognize tears as emotional productions, for it is here that the cultural, psychological, symbolic, and aesthetic enter the scene. Reflexive tears produced from an onion or a grain of sand only gather cultural portent through an error of understanding, a mistaken impression about their cause. We think that something is amiss when it's just a mote of dust. I want to get at the thought behind the tears, how varied the causes and contexts that might lead one to cry. The tears, in this sense, are a relatively uniform medium that poorly transmits an infinitely various message. If I've been drawn to tears, it is precisely their relationship to this expression that matters to me, the cultural meaning, feeling, and power of tears; for you, this was their least remarkable aspect. In a way the blind spot of your research has shown me my subject. Perhaps all children play out such a dialectical relationship with their parents.

RS: Is this your way of justifying the fact that the objective and scientific understanding of tears remains your blind spot?

DS: Well, your work was interested in what tears communicate on the biological level. I suppose I'm interested in what they communicate as a social signal. But I do find it striking that your work never broached the subject of emotions, when surely this was the first thing that came to someone's mind whenever you mentioned that you researched tears. I know you weren't alone here, that so much of tear research at the time avoided the subject or thought it suspect. I believe that is changing now, but the point remains valid. How did you feel about working on something so full of feeling?

RS: To my mind, you are once again avoiding the assignment and trying to do something creative instead of actually doing your homework. When you were in high school you never wanted to learn about the structure of the cell or how calculus worked. You'd construct elaborate frames to avoid the labor of doing the work you'd been assigned, or doing anything practical really.

DS: Well, yes, I suppose this is why I liked the theater so much, nothing ever gets made—not materially anyway—though plenty happens.

RS: So many diversionary tactics. Like when you used to ask your grandmother a question right before bed so that you could trick her into staying up later.

DS: Ha! She overheard me explaining my methods to the cousins and she was not amused.

RS: All this meta-stuff. You're doing the same thing again. Asking me to come in and explain to your reader how the eye works, instead of doing it yourself.

DS: But I had to learn all this information to write this dialogue, Dad. I've written all of this.

RS: Except for the things I've said. Why not just write a nice, carefully crafted chapter on the science of tears? How is this going to help your book? What does this have to do with tears and anatomy?

DS: I'm hoping that the dramatic aspects of our dialogue might engage the reader and keep them reading what is essentially the driest section of the book. I mean, why come to a book on performance if you want to learn about the anatomy of eyes? No, I think I overstated that— but a basic sense of this immensely complex system should do.

RS: Do you think we've accomplished that?

DS: No, not really, and this hasn't been especially dramatic . . .

RS: (*with mock disappointment, seeking to draw out some drama*) I thought you really cared about tears.

DS: Oh, but I do! In another life I could have seen myself as a tear researcher, too. But I can only get so close to the science, especially since—as you note—I have no background there. I mean I have your background, but not my own. I am an inveterate pretender. When I took my first acting class at the Red Barn—I must have been nine or ten—we went around the room and had to mime a gesture to show what we wanted to be when we grew up. I held my hand to my eye and looked down as if into a microscope, then raised my head again to look out to the rest of the group, my hand still glued to my eye, as if the mimed microscope had become a kind of telescope. (*He demonstrates the gesture.*) I already had the mechanics wrong: bringing the instrument up to survey my larger surroundings rather than regard the specimen before me. Perhaps that was some kind of juncture, a split from the dream of being a scientist to playing one on stage—and poorly at that. It certainly speaks to my tendency to play fast and loose with the details in favor of some imagined bigger picture.

You changed the subject though and didn't answer my question.

RS: I don't remember that—What was your question again?

DS: Actually, I kind of answered it for you anyway. You'll note, though, that even as you were describing my pattern of avoiding the assignment when it comes to science, you yourself were "avoiding the assignment" when it comes to your relationship to the feelings associated with tears. We both create frames to avoid that side of thought from which we feel most alienated.

RS: I find it amusing that you've chosen this moment to elaborate on our conversation with your fictions. I mean, I didn't say any of this. It plays into your desire for symmetry and order, how, when you were a kid, you would never let the colors of different foods touch each other when you ate, how upset you were if your shoelaces were uneven. Seeing resemblances everywhere, especially between forms and their subjects. Foucault, whom I've never read, would talk about this as a perspective indebted to the classical order of things where everything stands in for something else.

DS: You're right. But, in that case, what conversation is this conversation standing in for? Perhaps the one where I truly understand what you did for all those years, secreted away in labs, and written up in the arcane complexities of grammatically dubious articles thick with multisyllabic words and chemical compounds. Perhaps the one where you understand what I'm trying to do, or where I finally understand it myself? Or perhaps the one where all the subtext migrates from silent stage directions and parent(hetical)s to lucid spoken dialogue? Wouldn't tears be a sufficient and appropriate shorthand for those things that are too much to say?

RS: You're right. Let's both cry now.

DS: Yes, let's.

They do not move. The projection blurs to darkness.

I'm Too Sad to Tell You

On the Private Language of Tears

> There is a sacredness in tears. They are not the mark of weakness, but of power. They speak more eloquently than ten thousand tongues. They are the messengers of overwhelming grief, of deep contrition, and of unspeakable love.
>
> —"WASHINGTON IRVING"

Google these lines and you will find them everywhere: in books and listicles, on Instagram or Pinterest, laid atop any number of photographs of misty trees and soothing ocean vistas. You will find them attributed to Washington Irving, to Dr. Johnson, to Rumi. The deeper you descend into the rabbit hole of the internet, the more variants you will unearth scattered widely across repositories for quotations that stretch from the mid-19th century to the present—some of them blossoming from four lines into a full half-page.[1] You will not find an original source.

Somewhere in this freefall you will grasp a handhold on a website managed by one "Dr. Boli" who has attempted a similar traverse. The earliest reference he can find is a miscellany from *The American Masonic Register*, published on February 6, 1841, where the quoted passage is anonymously posted. "Was it made up by the editor of a Masonic newspaper in Albany to fill a couple of column inches, and then picked up by other editors, with 'Dr. Johnson' added to give it weight and authority?"[2] "Dr. Boli" may speak from experience; he claims he is H. Albertus Boli, but is really one of several playful pseudonyms for the writer Christopher Bailey. (The displacement is contagious: Washington Irving also wrote many of his works under various pseudonyms.) In other words, there is no certain source for these words, no root of an authentic subject excessively speaking of the excesses of speech.

Like many quotations that circulate in these online collections and their print antecedents, awaiting reclamation in wedding toasts and graduation speeches, Irving/Johnson/Rumi's words have the weight of wise proclamations, laying claim to "sacred" marks of "unspeakable" "power," even as they bluster like so much hot air. In the four sentences quoted above or in their more voluminous variants, these rote phrases rather neatly support their claim that "tears speak more eloquently than a thousand words." Certainly, one could believe that tears could be more eloquent than this pablum. But what is it that tears say?

Crying begins as an act of communication. Developmental psychologists posit crying as the earliest and most effective means for an infant to express its needs to a caregiver. As children develop speech, they shift from acoustical crying to the production of tears, and generally cry less frequently as they mature. It would be a mistake to assume a directly inverse relationship between crying and language, but, as one psychologist puts it, "the hypothesis that crying is a form of communication is bolstered by the finding that crying declines precipitously with language development."[3] To generalize broadly, most researchers on the subject argue that crying signals powerlessness and surrender. An infant's cries are a clarion call for care and attention; they seem to express need in its purified state, just as tears seem to distill affect to a transparent purity. When my epigraph's pseudonymous words of wisdom speak of a "sacredness" in tears, they recall long-held beliefs that these waters offer a consummate expression of faith more telling than spoken prayer.[4] Early Christians stored what they believed to be the tears of Mary, and any number of saints and martyrs, in reliquaries as material evidence of their statement of faith. Likewise, the tears of lovers and mourners have been treasured in lachrymatories in large part because they seem to distill longing and loss to a liquid essence.

But tears are also sacred, because—in the sense that Durkheim and others have proposed—they stand as the constitutive other to the profane world of language and its everyday uses. They (wordlessly) convey the capacity of that speakable world from the outside. If tears are messengers, as my epigraph suggests, their message is the excessive itself—the "overwhelming," the "deep," the "unspeakable"—an intensity in place of content. And so, we are faced with something of a contradiction: on one hand, tears are considered the transparent, direct, and honest communication of emotions. According to such a view, tears mean more than words because they express need more forcefully and directly than words. On the other hand, tears are the other to language itself, excessive because they are the unspeakable outside of speech.

Do tears underline the truth of whatever statement or do they show what we cannot tell? I can think of no better way to approach this question than to look directly at someone caught in a tearful act to see what their tears say and refuse to say. Rather than attend to a scene excised from the larger drama of a film or play, where a character or framing world might divert my relation to this weeper, I turn to the annals of performance art and video art to watch a person who purports to an appearance unalloyed by those animating fictions. The three performances presented in this chapter are (self-)portraits of the artist in tears, each caught on camera from the shoulders up, and revealing their respective breakdowns in endless loops. Each tackles the dissonance between speech and crying in revealing ways.

But before turning to the first of these works, let me take a brief detour through the relationship between public language and private affect via a thought experiment for the theater. As the editor of the book *Imagined Theatres: Writing for a Theoretical Stage*, I gathered hypothetical performances conceived by makers and thinkers of the stage, proposals that asked what might be possible within the frame of a theater and what that frame allows us to see differently about the world beyond its purview.[5] In one of his contributions to the book, "Private Language Argument II," Andrew Sofer proposes an exercise for a town to perform together and uses the theatrical situation to address the problem of communicating private feeling through language.

> Participants are screened based on their ignorance of beetles.
> A and B walk onstage and are each presented with a small, opaque
> box.
> They are informed that their boxes contain a "beetle."
> Neither is allowed to check the other's box.
> At a signal, each checks his or her own box. They can check it as often
> as they like.

A and B describe their beetles to each other.
Following the performance, every spectator is handed his or her
own beetle-box, along with strict instructions never to reveal its
contents.
Some boxes are empty. Others contain, say: a paper clip, a rose, a
starfish.
The performance continues until everyone in town has received his
or her own box.
The title of the piece is "Pain."[6]

Here is a performance that teaches its audience a new language, or rather reminds them of how their language already works, for each identical box shares the name "beetle" and acts like a word might if it were given physical form. We each point at our own box, repeating, "this is a beetle," when each container holds a private and wild thing within. A linguist or semiotician would tell us that the word "beetle" is the *signifier*; the box is the *signified*, since all references to "beetles" really reference the box; and the actual thing within the box is the *referent*, the actuality to which the idea of the sign corresponds. Following Saussure's model of semiotics, the sign is a linguistic construct that brackets the referent, excluding the actual from its model just as the contents of the box are removed from the act of signification.[7] Even those boxes that are empty—like my epigraph, without a source—can circulate widely. But the last line of Sofer's score shows that this is not merely a question about our private understanding of a word like "beetle." In fact, the beetle stands in for its owner's unique conception of pain: a strange shape, whose singular colors, intensities, and rhythms are condensed into that same four-letter word.

What are words when they pertain to private sentiment? This "private language argument" derives from the *Philosophical Investigations* of Ludwig Wittgenstein, who wrote penetratingly of how language requires that an utterance be legible to a public; it cannot "refer to what can be known only to the person speaking; to his immediate private sensations."[8] An utterance whose reference remains secreted in private cannot participate in language. In a gloss accompanying his imagined theater, Sofer offers a series of haiku—those small poetic boxes of uniform dimension—by way of explication:

A word like "beetle"
can't refer to a critter
that only I know.

So a word like "pain"
must refer to something else
than my sensation.
[...]
Theater as black box:
actors perform how pain feels.
Perhaps they're lying.[9]

Let me offer my own gloss in turn. The word—or signifier—refers to a public or shared version of the signified idea "pain," an ill-fitting container for the actual private affect. Sofer's last haiku adds another layer of complexity specific to the theater, for the "black box" in question refers both to the "beetle" box with its hidden meaning and to the form of mutable theatrical space that can be rearranged for different audiences and stages, available like language itself to an array of possible uses, settings, situations. It is also, finally, the black box of the flight recorder, holding its secret source and history in reserve—the mechanics of the actor's suffering rendered inaccessible. As the next two chapters in this book explore, placing the act of signification in a theater affirms the possibility of simulation and dissimulation. If we cannot know the shape of the feeling inside a beetle box, this uncertainty is even more apparent when that box belongs to an actor.

We can imagine replacing the word "beetle" or "pain" with a simple howl, though a howl of agony might be mistaken for a howl of pleasure. Crying out loud folds into laughing out loud, in keeping with Joyce's neologism *laughtears*. But tears present an even greater ambiguity. Even though different cultures and times register gestures variously, tears signal that something significant is happening with universal clarity, though what exactly is taking place in the crying person is harder to pinpoint. The historian of emotion Thomas Dixon writes that "[a] tear is a universal sign not in the sense that it has the same meaning in all times and all places. It is a universal sign because, depending on the mental, social, and narrative context, it can mean almost anything."[10] The tear looks the same and falls the same no matter what its history, though its constraints may be more or less pronounced depending on so many cultural channels.

There is a tendency to think of tears as signs of emotional states, like the most undiluted words that transparently show the inner core of a being. This is a mistake. Tears are not "beetles" or boxes; they are not signs indicating emotions, but symptoms of an affective event. Or perhaps "symptom" is the wrong word, for it suggests a distinction between the event and the tear that is not tenable. Tears mix with the affective, cueing witness and weeper alike. They do not represent a thing, but are themselves the very movement of affect, the creature in the box on the run, leaking everywhere. Basal tears, constantly flowing in tides along the surface of the eye, are homeostatic liquids contained within the banks of the eye lid. Emotional or affective tears, on the other hand, cannot be held in place—they flood over lids, form passages as transitive acts. Fluid and brimming over the confines that distinguish one sign from another, tears are queer in Eve Kosofsky Sedgwick's oft-cited understanding of the word as an inherently temporal disruption of the spatializing logics that lock identities (of people or whatever) into place: "a continuing moment, movement, motive—recurrent, eddying, *troublant*. The word 'queer' itself means *across* [. . .] Keenly, it is relational, and strange."[11] Tears may be accompanied by words, but they escape their boxes; more eloquently than a thousand words, they show too much to tell.

I. I'm Too Sad to Tell You

The black and white photograph captures a young man head on. His hand rests on his brow; a sheen of tears illuminates one side of his face, a drop clings to his chin. The Dutch artist Bas Jan Ader is looking at the camera and he is crying—or I should say that he is *not* looking into the camera, for Ader's eyes are closed, unavailable. His is a private pain, distanced from the camera's focus, and I am watching him cry from an even further distance, from a span of fifty years away.

On 13 September 1970, Bas Jan Ader sent several friends a postcard with this portrait on the front; no explanation, simply the words "I'm too sad to tell you" scrawled on its back. The still image was taken from a longer film that Ader had recorded of himself weeping, and which he briefly screened in a gallery in Claremont, California in 1971. That footage disappeared, and so Ader recreated the event a year later in Amsterdam, filming himself crying for ten minutes, his longer hair marking the longer passage of time between the two iterations. Edited down from ten minutes to little more than two and a half, a short film also titled *I'm too sad to tell you* completes this series of works. In this last version, the title is hand-written in black against a white background before Ader appears with eyes closed: breathing deeply, he runs his hand across his cheeks. His tongue dabs at the corner of his mouth, which then pulls back in a grimace, a silent seizure or gasp. Surfacing from the grain of the recording from half a century ago, one can just see the tears streaming.

True to his word, the source of Ader's distress was never disclosed, though the legend of this conceptual artist's abbreviated career is overcast in tragedy. A few years later, in 1975, as the second part of a proposed trilogy called *In Search of the Miraculous*, he would set off from the coast of Cape Cod, Massachusetts, in a thirteen-foot boat intending to sail alone to Amsterdam.[12] His empty vessel washed up on the shores of Ireland some weeks later, but he was never seen again. The parallel between his sudden disappearance and his work is hard to ignore. Again and again, Ader's aborted oeuvre worries over suspense and collapse as in a series of filmed falls from trees or into canals, or in his studies of landslides along the west coast of the United States. As with many of the other conceptual artists of the early 1970s, who moved toward an art of the idea in place of its instantiation, Ader's work shows a capacity to do without arriving at a thing done, or what I've elsewhere written about as an exposure of potentiality.[13] Such potentiality holds itself in reserve as a way of keeping the indeterminate future endlessly available in the present.

I'm too sad to tell you holds itself back on multiple levels. The film catches Ader mid-tear and leaves him there unresolved and unexplained at its close. No beginning and no ending to orient his act; no cause and no cure, this is a tragedy without cathartic release and its promise of a return to equilibrium. Without a soundtrack, the film's silence reiterates its incommunicability and distances the weeper from the watcher. It is as if Ader were acting underwater, in another room, on another planet; always too much, always too late, there is no way that these tears can elicit a timely response. The excess its title describes is apparent in the multiple iterations of the work, as if a single avowal were not sufficient and it needed to be repeated across different forms and times. Each repetition reminds us of its insufficiency and, perhaps, suggests that there might be a telling in a time to come, in the next repetition.

One might presume that Ader's original performance of speechless weeping responded to some traumatic episode. That original lost performance now itself plays the part of the traumatic event, absent and inaccessible, doomed to repetition. Freud proposed that one can only be relieved of a traumatic rupture by talking through the cataclysmic event and thereby re-incorporating it into one's narrative of self. There is no talking cure for something too sad to say. Should we take Ader's repeated statement as a mantra describing an essential quality of his very being ("*I am* too sad to tell you")—an isolation from language familiar to anyone who has struggled with chronic depression or melancholia?

Then there is the statement itself, a curiously self-defeating grammatical construction that hollows out its own ability to hold sense or convey meaning. To a certain extent it sets up the expected communicative relationship between a subject "I" and a recipient "you," and—as if in response to that everyday query "how are you?"—seems ready to play the conventional role of publicly describing a private state of feeling. But it steps aside from fulfilling that promise of verbal revelation by telling instead what it cannot do with words. (Here it approaches the rhetorical device of apophasis, in which one raises a point through its negation, as in the phrase "I will not mention x.") The statement appears as an appendix after Ader's crying, the artist's hand-written scrawl atop the photograph or introducing the film only after the fact. Language takes place in a separate time and space from the act of crying.

These words are a proof for the scene that plays out before our eyes, a formula for some essential secret of tears, one that cannot be written or spoken. If his feeling overflows the word or box labeled "sadness," Ader's tears pour forth as a surrogate expression of that excess. I'm thinking here of how the affect theorist Teresa Brennan distinguishes feelings which are "sensations that have found the right match in words"—the "pain" put in its proper box—from the wayward affects that resist the confines of naming.[14] Crying signals an affect that is *not yet* a worded feeling or has overstepped its compass. This too-muchness might spill over to include contiguous or contrary sentiments, shading into joy or wonder or whatever. Ader's excessive affects circulate within a closed and private system; words cannot extend a communicative bridge to allow another entry. This is one way to exhaust language's search for the meaning of tears—standing on the other side of the glass, watching a silent scene divorced entirely from speech or any sound, only being told that this is too much for a named emotion, too much for the entire enterprise of verbal language. Watching Ader and letting him drown over and over, I still feel a need to do something. I confront what Sara Ahmed calls the "sociality of pain," in which "the ungraspability of my own pain is brought to the surface by the ungraspability of the pain of others [. . .] Insofar as an ethics of pain begins here, with how you come to surface, then the ethical demand is that I must act about that which I cannot know, rather than act insofar as I know."[15] Years removed, my inscrutable tears surface to face those of Ader.

Thus far I've performed close readings of three statements that show how crying distresses the presumably stable meaning-making structure of language. Each of the three differently shows how tears interpose a plane of expression that cuts across the one-to-one correspondence that attaches a word to its named emotion:

1) *There is a sacredness in tears*—a source-less statement that uses language to describe tears as the excess of verbal potential;
2) *This is a beetle*—a statement that performs the mismatched semiotics of words and all affects; and
3) *I'm too sad to tell you*—a statement that expresses the power of tears through the negation of language.

All three examples employ verbal language to make a statement about the nonverbal character of tears, about how such language approaches affect but falls short of encompassing it sufficiently. (This resonates with my own challenge here and throughout the essays collected in this book.) If a tear is in fact more eloquent than a thousand words, these inverted statements or paradoxes that dismantle semiotics from the inside are perhaps the proper means to approach a verbal understanding while retaining an adequate distance, not presuming to name too much. And yet, these three examples remain phrases in a verbal conversation. What would it mean to conceive of tears not in terms of a content waiting to be told, withholding the potential to be more than words, but instead as the constitutive outside of a statement? From this perspective, tears do not make a statement; they make, as the title of a work by the artist Wu Tsang puts it, *The Shape of a Right Statement.*

II. The Shape of a Right Statement

Quotation marks always work in pairs.

—JUNE CASAGRANDE, THE BEST PUNCTUATION BOOK, PERIOD[16]

The artist Wu Tsang also often works in pairs, or as more than one. An interdisciplinary trans artist who frequently develops works via collaboration, Tsang's practice integrates both formal and quotidian languages of expression. In her early video performance *The Shape of a Right Statement*, she works alongside the artist and autism activist Mel Baggs to express their shared dislocation from normative language. Over the course of the five-minute piece, a strand of tears sutures together these disparate positions.

The Shape of a Right Statement belongs to a series of performances created for the "Wildness" club night that Tsang hosted in collaboration with friends from 2008–2010 at the Silver Platter, the oldest gay bar in the MacArthur Park neighborhood of Los Angeles.[17] Founded in 1963, the Silver Platter first served immigrant men from Central America and later became a gathering place for the city's trans Latinx community.[18] It was, in an unusually vocal way, the subject of the magical realist documentary *Wildness* that Tsang directed with the Iranian-American filmmaker/scholar/curator Roya Rastegar in 2012. In that film, the bar is a character who narrates its own history via the rise and demise of the eponymous club night that brought a collective of queer, punk, and art communities to the space, but also inadvertently contributed to the gentrification of the neighborhood. Spoken in Spanish by a trans Latinx performer, this voiceover participates in the transposition of voice and language that runs as one strand through Tsang's work. As she put it in an interview with *The Guardian*: "Growing up in a multiracial family, I never learned Chinese, so I was used to having 'conversations' that weren't verbal. When there's an understanding that we can't fully understand each other, that's a better space for me. It's happening all the time, but maybe it's more obvious when we're speaking a different language."[19]

The Shape of a Right Statement shows Tsang from the neck up, staring directly at the camera, her eyes unwavering, even unblinking, as she speaks. Her voice possesses an unusual singsong quality, but the words spoken are unavoidably direct.

> The previous part of this video was in my native language. Many people have assumed that when I talk about this being my language that means that each part of the video must have a particular symbolic message within it designed for the human mind to interpret. But my language is not about designing words or even visual symbols for people to interpret. It is about being in a constant conversation with every aspect of my environment. Reacting physically to all parts of my surroundings. In this part of the video the water doesn't symbolize anything.

It quickly becomes apparent that these words do not belong entirely to Tsang or to this moment, that they perform a disjunction between language and world, speech and body. There is no "previous part of this video," nor is there any water in sight "in this part of the video." In an acting technique she calls "Full Body Quotation," a hidden earpiece feeds the performer the speech of another speaker. Not just the words, for Tsang makes of her voice and breath a playback device, channeling the rhythm, volume, and shape of another's voice through her own body. The text derives verbatim from "In My Language," a video that Mel Baggs posted to YouTube in 2007, explaining their experience as a person who communicates nonverbally in a predominantly verbal world.[20] Typing words into a computer that then generates the speech they cannot say, Baggs crosses the abyss between private and public language, the experience of pain, say, and its description. In Tsang's restaging of the text, the subjects "I" and "we" merge and diverge between two positions outside of normative language.

The source video "In My Language" begins by showing Baggs in their apartment, interacting with their surroundings in what might be read as rhythmic exchanges of sound and gesture. In the first part of the video (the part mentioned in the spoken text above), the camera looks down the telescoping insides of an orange Slinky, its coils unspooling like a mobile tunnel of perspective. It cuts to a hand working a loop of metal around and around the curve of a door handle; to fingers batting at a chain that hangs midair; to something that caresses, brushes against something else—the pixelation of the image confuses analysis, just as the camera brought so close fragments things into disparate parts, those parts becoming new wholes, novel assemblages in movement. My fragmented description here is not unfounded, for Baggs's play de-emphasizes the status of the object as a distinct form or use, instead enacting a visceral and holistic conversation, a dance with the material world.

There are no words in this first section, though the sonic dimension is rich and varied as Baggs sings a clear note above all, an ethereal refrain in a minor key. The video possesses a felt, and felt-like, texture—those percussive sounds and songs overlay shots so proximate they seemingly press against the viewer, involving them too in a haptic space. After several wordless minutes immersed in this environmental play, a title intercuts: "a translation." The scene shifts to a closeup of Baggs's hand playing in and out of a water stream, the liquid running over their fingers as a computerized voice replaces the organic song and speaks the first words in the video:

> The previous part of this video was in my native language. [...] In this part of the video, the water doesn't symbolize anything. I am just interacting with the water as the water interacts with me. Far from being purposeless, the way that I move is an ongoing response with what is going on around me. As you heard, I can sing along with whatever's around me ...

To see the water as symbolic would be to impose a semiotic scission between the sensed thing and its meaning. The whole structure and grammar of normative subjectivity would follow from such a meaningful cut, as the cut would organize and name each thing in terms of its use for, or relation to, the subject. Here, on the other hand, is an interaction with the water as an extension of the body, the body as an extension of the world, a living in and among its forces. Baggs puts it this way: they *sing along with whatever's around*, rather than *speak to (from, by, over, etc.) a specific object*, abandoning all those prepositional relations built upon power differentials or directions. Such a perspective resists "chunking" the world into conceptual parts and instead shows thresholds everywhere, mutual harmonizations. Baggs's play with water, and with the other materialities encountered elsewhere in the video, is an exploration of a means without end, a doing without a thing done.

Compared with the fluid and mobile sensorium of "In My Language," folding self so thoroughly into world, Tsang's restaging in *The Shape of a Right Statement* is spare and static in the extreme. Tsang stays unmoving at the center of the screen for the duration, looking directly at the camera. Her uninflected intonation, borrowed from the computer program that speaks Baggs's words, recalls ableist conceptions of autistic flatness and also resonates along racial lines, where normative whiteness has a long history of remarking upon the supposed inexpressiveness of the Asian body. Both stereotypes presume that this impassivity reflects an inherent diminished capacity to feel and, as a correlate, a diminished access to personhood. Eric Hayot has written about the figure of the "coolie," a derogatory term that refers to South Asian immigrants—in the US context, especially those hailing from China—who were recruited to perform heavy manual labor in the late 19th century:

> The mechanical, automatic, and enduring qualities of the Chinese were explicitly tied to sociological theories of Chinese culture produced by American missionaries. An "absence of nerves," remarkable "staying qualities," and a "capacity to wait without complaint and to bear with calm endurance," were all features of Chinese people in general described by Arthur Smith in his 1894 *Chinese Characteristics*, the most widely read American work on China in the late nineteenth and early twentieth centuries. [. . . T]he coolie's biologically impossible body was the displaced ground for an awareness of the transformation of the laboring body into a machine.[21]

By taking the place of the speech program through which Baggs communicates and converting her own body into a quotation machine, Tsang implicitly invites comparison with this vision of the mechanized Asian laborer, relentlessly working while seeming to possess no awareness of privation or boredom or pain. This seeming disconnect applies to the *mise en scène* as well, for if the spoken words reference "the water that doesn't symbolize anything," all we see is the performer and the Silver Platter's curtain of gleaming sequins framing her head in undulations of slow twinkling light like a spectacular waterfall in drag.[22] Wearing what looks like a leotard and what might be a tight-fitting swimmer's cap, Tsang appears as a Busby Berkeley water nymph perpetually suspended above a glittering artificial lake.

On second thought, there is "real" water here, too, but it takes a quite different course from the endless whorl of fingers in the faucet's stream shown in the original video: as the performance progresses, two additional points of light glint, one in each of Tsang's eyes, collecting into beads until the final passage, when the tears cascade down her cheeks. This is a perfectly choreographed descent, as graceful as any consolidated tear that might underline the climax of whatever actor's performance, though it is impossible to say whether these are planned or happenstance. It would be a mistake, too, to say that Tsang's tears index pain or anger or frustration—they might mark all and none of these at once. Tsang's tears enact an exchange that, like the play between water and hand for Baggs, "doesn't symbolize anything;" it *is* the interaction across differences that stand outside of linguistic normativity, outside of hegemonic perceptions of personhood. The tears fall just as they—Baggs's words through Tsang's mouth—speak:

> In the end I want you to know this has not been intended as a voyeuristic freakshow where you get to look at the bizarre workings of the autistic mind. It is meant as a strong statement on the existence and value of many different kinds of thinking and interaction in a world where how close you can appear to a specific one of them determines whether you are seen as a real person or an adult or an intelligent person. And in a world in which those determine if you have any rights there are people being tortured, people dying because they are considered non-persons because their kind of thought is so unusual as to not be considered thought at all. Only when the many shapes of personhood are recognized will justice and human rights be possible.

In the speech that Baggs must produce to be acknowledged as a person, there cannot be a "right statement" of their being; there can only be the *shape* of a right statement. So, by embodying these words, Tsang draws a connection with her experience as an Asian American trans woman, for whom normative language is also an ill-fitting translation. Writing of the trope of the inscrutable Asian in nineteenth century American literature, Xine Yao poses that "inscrutability might constitute not just an impassive mask indecipherable to Western eyes, but also the signifier of Oriental ontological hollowness."[23] This racist presumption of Asian hollowness corresponds to ableist stereotypes of a similarly emptied autistic being, seeing a person as a shape without sensible content. Where words fall short, tears cling fast to the contours of Tsang's face to describe the outside of such a formulation, like a pair of parentheses or brackets framing a phrase, like a pair of quotation marks.

In a passage from his book *The Language of Tears* that recalls my opening quotation with its celebration of tearful grandiloquence, psychologist Jeffrey Kottler writes: "Tears are often meant for others' view, to say something compelling that words cannot express. They lend an authenticity to communication that words cannot touch. [. . .] They are the punctuation at the end of a statement that gives credence and power to what was said."[24] What if we took Kottler's concluding metaphor seriously? What would we learn by thinking of tears as the punctuation to a statement? Operating alongside the matter of signification, a punctuation mark is an accompaniment that directs the dynamic of a statement's affective force. As Jennifer DeVere Brody puts it, "punctuation performs as a type of (im)material event or, perhaps, as a supplement" to a statement.[25] This supplemental character is often used toward clarifying ends. Manuals on grammar generally focus on how to regulate proper punctuation as a tool for an author to promote ease of reading, for example, by showing places for pause and breath. One could readily imagine tears as exclamation points underlining an utterance's force, or question marks inviting response. Such tearful punctuation is apparent in many crying episodes, where tears supplement the latent intent of the words that they accompany to drive a point home. But what would follow from conceiving of tears as quotation marks, setting off a statement as "scare quotes" might do?

"In their present condition of use," Marjorie Garber writes, "[quotation marks] may indicate either authenticity or doubt. (Make that 'authenticity' or 'doubt.')"[26] In the first case, quotations signal authority and belonging to a certain community. So one peppers a speech with the words of others to establish credibility ("as Shakespeare once said . . .") or to situate the present articulation in dialogue with an "authentic" originary event, laying the foundations of a stable past atop which the present may take shape.[27] But in the second case, Garber writes of the stylistic tendency to use quotation marks in-text to cast suspicion on a statement, marking the refraction of a statement as it moves into the new context of its present speaker. This double act of the quotation mark as both proof of fact and of doubt closely aligns with the divergent roles of theatrical tears as I've characterized them throughout this book: sincere and duplicitous by turns.

Quotation marks are theatrical punctuations; a script's spoken lines are backed by their invisible presence throughout, and the actor is the necessary double to allow those lines their voice. Tsang's method of "full body quotation" may initially recall the techniques that theater directors Elizabeth LeCompte, Marianne Weems, and Annie Dorsen, among others, have explored for decades as a means of dislocating the performer from their role, of highlighting the technology of acting as a perpetually failing copying machine. These overtly theatrical cases give primacy to the doubt Garber sees in the quotation mark, shoring up the distance between speech and speaker as a Brechtian maneuver to create space for critique. But Tsang's enterprise is a different kind of actorly quotation. Baggs's "voice" arrives with an intonation and cadence already filtered through their computerized surrogate device. This machinic performer can claim to be the original "vocal expression" and yet it is always already alienated from Baggs's subject position; Baggs's first speech is a quotation and a peculiar one at that. Peculiar because this "first speaker" performs according to the algorithms its programmers taught it so that it might parse the implicit phrasing and the explicit punctuation of any text that is fed into its reader. Here is a most constrained—quite literally programmed—version of a normative voice, and one that advertises the unwieldiness of such a restrictive confine. Tsang's re-performance, then, lends not just voice and breath, but a full and specific body to what was "originally" disembodied speech. She provides the shape for the right statement. Which is to suggest that—counter to the Brechtian operation of the Wooster Group technique, say—Tsang's *full body* quotation lends her embodied weight to what had been the hollowed mechanics of normative speech. This performative speech act takes over her whole body but does not leave her body behind. Her quotation is not a comparative project, but one that makes present the absences (in normative speech) of both speakers.[28]

Those twin streaks that line Tsang's cheeks as the performance unfolds are visual analogues to the twin strokes of quotation marks, working in pairs. There is no suspicion here—except regarding language itself, with its defunct promise of universal access and applicability. They are, to recall Sedgwick's definition of queerness once more, "a continuing moment, movement, motive—recurrent, eddying, *troublant* [. . .] *across*" differences. As Brody reiterates in her own chapter devoted to the performativity of this form of punctuation, "[q]uotation marks are as queer as they are quotidian. While appearing to bend themselves to the theatrical, the 'meta,' and the excessive, in practice they are part and parcel of habitual, pedestrian behaviors. Their paradoxical presence, even when unscripted, questions the status of that which passes for the natural and the normal."[29] We could say similar things about tears in a broader sense, how the drift between reflexive and psychologically motivated variants prompts questions about that which passes for the natural and the normal. Like quotation marks, tears instigate conversations about theatricality, the "meta," and the excessive. The content of a quoted passage sits within the bounds of normative language, but tears, like punctuation marks, are a visible surplus that marks the outside of language. When Tsang cries, she does not give us the right statement, but the shape itself. A fluid bridge between bodies, a pair of tears.

III. Girl Who Cries a Tear

Let us imagine a tear that could communicate affect transparently, without language's interference and a statement's constrictive norms.

Say the lights rise on a person crying. You don't need to know how or why it began, only that they are there and you are here on the other side of sight: not seen, but looking in. Incrementally, drop by drop, their tears fall, not downward to the raked floor, but outward across the solitude of the boards and over the lip of the stage as if over the lid of an eye, flooding into the throng of the auditorium—spanning from the private to the public. As you watch, you find your own eyes, too, beginning to water, to weep, to meet them there in between. An impossible strand reaches out from their eyes and directly into your own and, like that, a fluid bridge joins disparate bodies in an intermixture so complete that one becomes the other. A web of sensibility hovers in a common time and space. In this imagined theater, tears do not convey words, they illuminate an affect. You see and feel with the eyes of another; another sees and feels with your eyes. Everything happens now in a co-presence that dispels the division between seer and seen.But, I hear you say, this is a fantastical story of the theater, another bridge built of language. You are still turning tears into words. Let's try this again, then, using language only to set the stage before receding and letting tears have their silent say.

It is 1964 and visitors to Andy Warhol's Studio—celebrities and anonymous strangers alike—might expect to find themselves subjected to a "screen test" before the artist's camera. Between 1963 and 1966, Warhol recorded nearly five hundred of these short films, intended to capture a portrait of an individual, not as a means toward some future role or endeavor (as in the screen tests of the cinematic industry) but as an end in itself. The score is as simple as can be: each subject sits still for the duration of a single hundred-foot roll of film (roughly 4 ½ minutes, when slowed slightly to Warhol's preferred tempo), displayed before this recording machine's unflinching eye.[30] With no sound and no speech, the script is simply an open and closed pair of quotation marks that frame a silent appearance. While some of the hundreds of figures featured in Warhol's series bask in the camera's attention, others are uncomfortable under its glare, filling their time with gestures or coy play or trying to avoid this relentless stare. Some submit to the test as if it were something being done to them.

This is the case with the young woman here. She stares squarely at the camera, meeting its obduracy with her own, her hair framing a symmetrical face. Her stillness is so absolute that for a time it seems she has realized the impossible task of turning a film into a photograph. Her eyes do not blink, even as they fill with water, even as the tears begin to fall. She does not move; the water moves over her.

The label on the film canister reads "Girl who cries a Tear." She is Ann Buchanan, though strangely she is named only by her act. Buchanan was involved in the beat poetry scene of the 1960s where she makes occasional appearances along the sidelines—she was briefly married to the poet Charles Plymell, lived in a commune in Berkeley with Allen Ginsberg in the early 1960s (who references her in two of his poems), and can be found in a number of group photographs from that moment—but she is most remembered for this screen test, which Warhol singled out as among his favorite. Strangely, too, the label casts this as a singular tear, as if her ceaseless weeping were caught in a single frame, though one can count the many beads as they slowly drip from her jawline. If the statements I've considered in this chapter borrow from different rhetorical devices, then here we find a synecdoche: the singular tear of the label standing in for all of Buchanan's tears. Indeed, one might say that the screen tests that survive from Warhol's series all propose a synecdochal relationship with their subjects. Each film, portrait-like, stands in for a whole person, just as each screen test stands in for the whole project. A fitting rhetorical pose for Warhol, the master of serial representation.

Buchanan takes her direction seriously and labors to stay too still, to look too hard. It seems that her refusal to blink prompts the flow of reflex tears that her body performs without her and in spite of her. (In a second screen test she filmed for Warhol, Buchanan's eyes slowly converge until they are crossed—another automatic reaction to the camera's durational gaze.)[31] She props her eyelids open and does not blink. She shows us that the external object in the eye is the medium of sight itself: the very air in and through which we see can dry us out and cause a welling up. Such tears provide no access to an inner self, no eloquent message. They mark the fact of being seen, and seeing another, under the pressure of time's passage. In her reading of this scene, Giulia Palladini writes of the potentiality of Buchanan's idle stare: "her tears can be regarded as the excess of her labor of appearing."[32] And perhaps this is an affect we can share, can communicate transparently, like a liquid span joining two people between 1964 and right now: simply the weight of a moment, waiting to pass before our weeping eyes.

Let these two stills from the beginning and end of Buchanan's appearance stand in for this duration: nearly four minutes of silence, too much to tell.

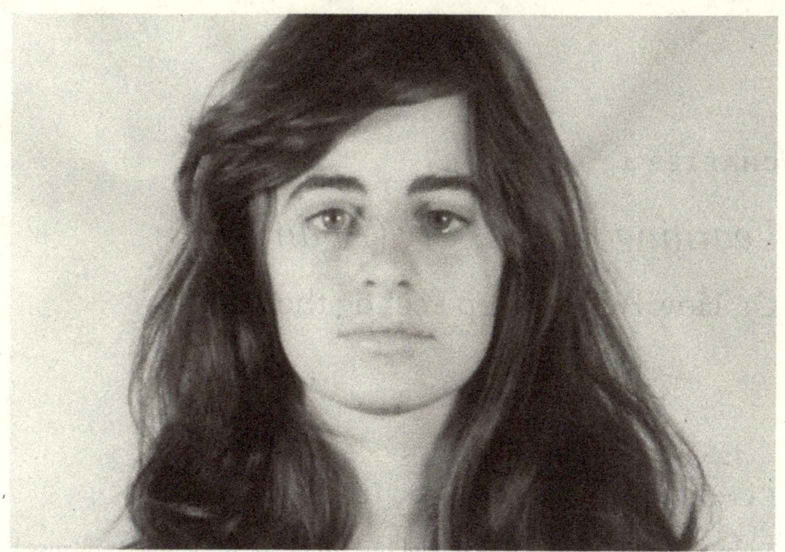

Figure 6 Andy Warhol, *Ann Buchanan* [ST33], 1964 © The Andy Warhol Museum, Pittsburgh, PA, a museum of Carnegie Institute. All rights reserved. Film still courtesy The Andy Warhol Museum.

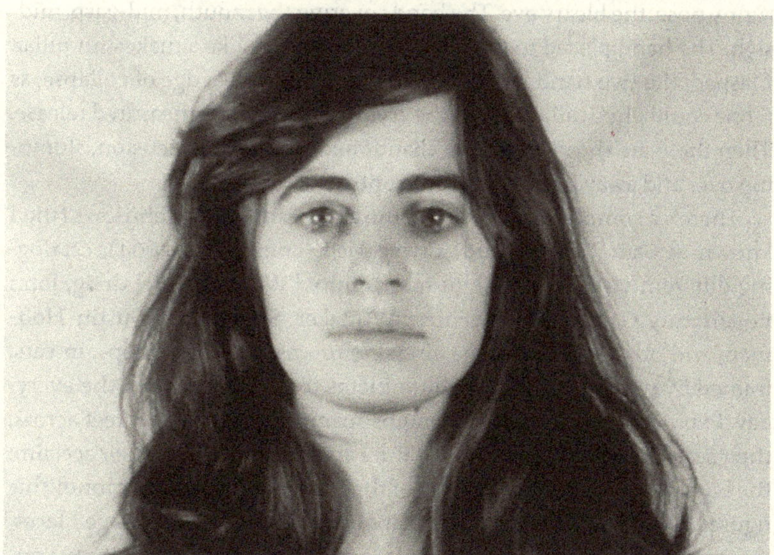

Figure 7 Andy Warhol, *Ann Buchanan* [ST33], 1964 © The Andy Warhol Museum, Pittsburgh, PA, a museum of Carnegie Institute. All rights reserved. Film still courtesy The Andy Warhol Museum.

CHAPTER 4

Learning How to Cry (Again)

Or, How Actors Keep Feeling the Past

I. Crying Men (Crying Actors)

Twenty-eight leading actors model how to perform a studied collapse.[1] They propose various arrangements of their instrument—consider, for example, the techniques of the hand: one pressed to brow, another cradling the forehead, a third shielding the eyes. The hand brushing the runny nose, the bleary eye. The hand covering the mouth, mid-gasp, mid-sigh. The hand placed to crown or planted on jaw like a makeshift pillar. Clasped, the two hands hold the self together on the edge of collapse, as if one could physically restrain the crying or support its measured release. Then there are those who have abandoned all muscular tension, slumping over and away from the actor's control.

There's a comprehensiveness to the artist Sam Taylor-Johnson's (then known as Sam Taylor-Wood) *Crying Men* series (2002–2004), cataloging different visions of straight masculinity.[2] We see Daniel Craig, John Leguizamo, Gabriel Byrne, Forest Whitaker, Sean Penn, Dustin Hoffman, and others in bedrooms, dressing rooms, on front stoops, in cars, framed by windows. Sunlight illuminates them like saints of the everyday. Exposed close-up in photographs spanning three or four feet across, their scale matches the subjects' stature and the medium of their acclaim: the big screen. No hiding here. All of them are pictured alone, monolithic figures filling the frame with their singularly beautiful and ravaged faces, their curated dishevel. We are voyeurs on these scenes of magnificent pri-

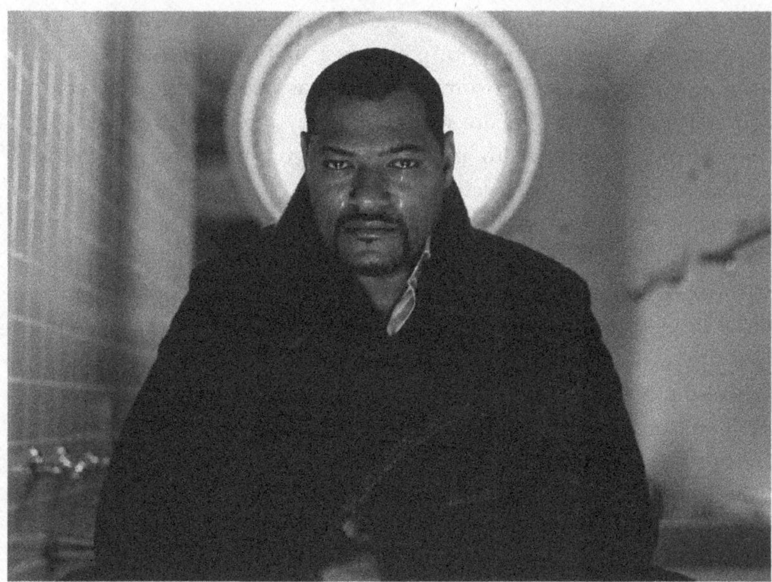

Figure 8 Sam Taylor-Johnson, *Laurence Fishburne*, 2002. C-print. 33 13/16 x 43 13/16 in. (86.2 x 111.7 cm). © Sam Taylor-Johnson. All Rights Reserved, DACS/ Artimage 2023.

vacy; each casts his gaze downward, offstage, pulling inward or drawing focus on that elsewhere beyond the border of our sight.

A lone exception among these many diverted gazes: Laurence Fishburne meets the camera's eye directly, two streams glistening down his cheeks in lush and aestheticized symmetry. In keeping with Taylor-Johnson's penchant for suggestive iconographic play, Fishburne stands in what appears to be a public bathroom—the basest of settings—but his head is perfectly framed by a circular window filled with white light, at once a halo and the aperture of an eye looking back at us. At the time the photograph was taken, Fishburne was reprising perhaps his most iconic role in the sequel to the sci-fi blockbuster *The Matrix* (1999), a film in which his character, Morpheus, unveils the simulated nature of the world we take for reality. Morpheus, sharing his name with the Greek god of sleep, passes weightlessly between the real and virtual world. He is always shown wearing dark sunglasses (as the next chapter shows, a signal prop for crying or covering up crying), so it is as if Taylor-Johnson's portrait were showing the tears of someone who has unveiled his penetrating sight for the first time. We are seen from every angle (from every angel). These tears, like Morpheus in *The Matrix*, give the game away—twin strokes that are almost too reflective, with the gloss of holy or prosthetic tears—as if a reminder were wanting: these men are all only "alone," since there is that necessary other taking the picture and demanding that they perform as "crying men." Cornered by the camera, all these icons perform without the usual garments of a part, bereft of character aside from their public persona. They are men crying; they are actors crying.

These performances don't seem that different from most of the crying men I've encountered in my life—likely an indication of the fact that nearly all my reference points stem from the actors I've seen playing with tears. I don't often witness men crying in my daily routine, nor in my room within the ivory tower (more on that complexity in the final pages of this book). Does this imply that only those men trained in the arts of expression can cry publicly? That only those with firmly established credentials can perform such vulnerability without compromising their masculinity?

Big girls don't cry, but all boys don't cry. Or, at least, they don't cry very much. Studies show that on average adult women cry four or five times per month, while adult men cry once per month, if they cry at all.[3] (It is worth noting that many of these studies rely on a gender binary that feels antiquated in the current moment.) While certainly not an absolute rule, this is a widespread phenomenon: a thirty-nation study from 2001 showed that "there was not one country in which men reported a higher crying frequency than women."[4] A larger survey of the critical literature in tear research reported a general agreement that hormonal factors may influence these discrepancies, but also that there is "large cross-cultural and contextual variance."[5] The authors hypothesize that, if crying signals powerlessness, cultures that align masculinity with dominance and independence would privilege the dry-eyed and unmoved man. Tears may be unruly intruders, but one can learn to suppress them or avoid situations in which they might be provoked, continuously disciplining oneself according to the strictures of gender expectations. Likewise, anthropologists have suggested that the choreographed expressions of ritualistic wailing and keening found in many cultures may encourage women to lean into the release of weeping, often as way of constituting social connection.[6] According to researchers from Tilburg University in the Netherlands, anti-social attitudes conventionally associated with masculinity have been shown to limit tearfulness: "people with 'dismissive' attachment styles—or those who tend to avoid close relationships with others—were less likely to cry and tried harder to inhibit their tears than people with other attachment styles."[7]

Literature shows us that in other times and places the tears of glorified masculinity flowed differently. Let me cite but one example among many.[8] Plato may have imagined his ideal Republic as one in which clear-eyed men could legislate without wayward emotional disturbance clouding their sight, but the French classicist Hélène Monsacré reminds us that the ancient Greek world that preceded Plato embraced other ideals: "The heroes of the *Iliad*, in particular, are very often presented in tears, suffering grief and pain. The tears of Achilles, just as his military exploits, are present throughout the poem, from his first appearance to his last. When he is not fighting, he is crying."[9] This is not the restrained single tear of the laconic American man; heroic masculine tears are active and engross the full body of the weeper. They are vigorous counterparts to his exploits on the battlefield. Indeed, when she first reads *The Odyssey*, choreographer Annie-B Parson is immediately struck by the prevalence of tears throughout the epic; she gathers these instances into a block of text that functions as a kind of textual dance in her book *The Choreography of Everyday Life*:

Dissolving in tears, bursting in tears, indulging in tears,
brushing away tears, tears streamed down his cheek, a flood
of tears, tears flooding his eyes, spells of grief, storms of
tears, tears overwhelm, blinding tears, blinding tears, my
tears, her tears, his tears, shedding tears, wiping his tears
[and on and on . . .][10]

Weepers of heroic stature like Achilles and Odysseus cry vigorously as a counterpart to their world-changing actions. But these photographed men stilled in their grandiose frames are always crying; always acting, they never complete the act and realize the cathartic prospect of "getting over it." Indeed, as this essay will explore, many actors want nothing more than to *not* get over their tearfulness. Melancholic to the core, they want to return to it again and again. For adherents to this method (aka The Method), to act is to feel *again*.

Taylor-Johnson often portrays figures suspended within crisis, outside narrative's comforting logic of beginning and end. "Many of my works are about being placed in difficult positions, which normally aren't public. They are hard to watch precisely because they are not part of a narrative," she has asserted.[11] Again and again, they center on acts of crying without resolution.[12] The year she was diagnosed with colon cancer, Taylor-Johnson's series of self-portraits, *Cry Laughing* (1997), show her face contorted into shapes that might belong to either expression—the *laughtears* of Joyce. She appears possessed by Democritus and Heraclitus by turns. (If the two philosophers are so often depicted together hovering over a globe—the one laughing, the other crying—it is because they face an extinguishing world.) That same year, her short 8-minute film *Hysteria* tracks a woman in closeup wide-eyed and wide-mouthed as she transitions from laughter into full body sobs and back again. Her head floats in a black space, isolated from context and ground, cause and effect; unmoored, her appearance recalls the antiquated conception of hysteria as a condition of the uterus wandering through the body. The artist had the performer recount a recent breakup as fuel for her manic expressions, though the piece leaves such source material undisclosed.[13] The audio track has been removed, abandoning her to sight alone and making it even more difficult to discern the nature of this violent expression. For art critic and novelist Michael Bracewell, this exemplifies how Taylor-Johnson "uses sound as a kind of emotional blocking signal—a further restraint on the relief of catharsis."[14]

While the affective rollercoasters of *Cry Laughing* and *Hysteria* are anchored in the lived experience of the people they depict, many of Taylor-Johnson's works with tears plumb the more uncertain depths of the actor. Taylor-Johnson has frequently collaborated with the most recognizable celebrities, where, as in *Crying Men*, each radiates a signature aura peculiar to his actual person and to the moment of his public acclaim. From the older Michael Gambon—photographed here just having played the quintessential British patriarch in *Gosford Park* (2001) and about to raise the type to its supernatural extreme as a surrogate Dumbledore—to the younger ingenue Hayden Christensen—fresh off his stint in the reboot of the *Star Wars* franchise, but already renowned for his lachrymose talents.[15] The biographies of each actor frame their appearance. Following his well-publicized string of drug-related arrests, Taylor-Johnson had cast Robert Downey Jr. in an Elton John music video—his first acting role post-rehab. The many bleary-eyed and bloodshot mugshots that plastered celebrity gossip shows in the late 1990s find their sacred antithesis in his portrait from *Crying Men*. Flanked by hazy white light cast from a bank of shaded windows, Downey Jr. lies naked on a bed, a sheet draped across his loins: the classical martyr, redemption personified. The actor stares placidly heavenward, a reflection flaring his single tear into a long white stroke down his cheek.[16] Looking back at the portraits now, two decades later, the intervening years convey added significance. Photographs of Philip Seymour Hoffman and Robin Williams, whose untimely deaths were tied to severe depression, confirm what I cannot help but see as evidence of a private pain in these acts.

And yet, as my mention of Fishburne's potential prosthesis suggests, these portraits—inevitably and almost immediately—invite one to look for cracks in the representation. At the time of their first showing, reviews of Taylor-Johnson's series often focused on discerning the authenticity of the act; in a scathing piece for *The Guardian*, Laura Cumming writes that "the whole thing descends into a spot-the-fake contest" and then proceeds to do just that for the latter half of her review.[17] Because we are so used to seeing these actors perform similar moments of tearful exposure, our attention is drawn to the means of making those tears visible or failing to do so. The photographs are not just the statement of a fact—Laurence Fishburne is crying—but they also raise the question of how one is doing that act. On the surface this would also seem to disarm any ethical quandary we might confront if we were facing individuals who had not consigned their expressive potential to public consumption; how suspect these encounters would be if we were not assured that these crises were the work of craft. Ariella Azoulay has written of a "civil contract" that photography poses between the photographed, photographer, and spectator that amounts to a responsibility for what has happened in the image and continues to happen in its viewing.[18] No such contract is in effect here.

Taylor-Johnson provides a stage on which we can admire and study men crying (because they are actors crying). I am interested in that parenthetical gesture, with its pairing of inside and outside, and its focus on how one moves across that unspoken divide. Continuing the previous chapter's somewhat tongue-in-cheek exploration of an analogy between punctuation and tears, this chapter's title and its subsidiary sections each have parenthetical claims nested within them. The doubling of phrase within phrase here corresponds to a certain perspective on the doubling of actor and role that lies at the root of much psychologically realistic acting. Such a view presupposes that to produce "sincere" tears, one must have an interiority separate from, but providing vitality to, an outward facing self. Here I am thinking of sincerity in the terms that Lionel Trilling defined as "a congruence between avowal and actual feeling."[19] In other words, sincerity takes place in the present moment of a speech act (an "avowal") backed by the force of an "actual feeling," but it also assumes that there is a difference between the outer self and an inner self that is brought into alignment through this act. Ernst van Alphen and Mieke Bal emphasize the point:

> In a traditional sense, sincerity indicates the performance of an inner state on one's outer surface so that others can witness it. [. . .] In order for sincerity to come to the surface and, indeed, enter the social realm, a specific notion of subjectivity is necessary. This notion assumes that we, as individuals, have an "inner self" responsible for our conduct, performances, and speeches—in effect, all the ways in which we manifest ourselves for others.[20]

Tears purport to open a passage between such an inner and outer self, between the overt statement and its covert parenthetical force. But acting shows how the relationship between the surface and depth of a feeling is at root a paradoxical one.

II. The Paradox of the (Weeping) Actor

Ask an actor how they cry and you'll likely get dismissed as readily as the rube asking how they remember all their lines. Perhaps this is because both queries presume a reduction of the craft to its most rudimentary ends: on one hand the automatic, on the other hand the studied. I've tried dancing around the question with strangers and friends; in those moments where I've asked directly I've received little useful information. There is the old canard that if you want to make an audience cry, you should yourself retain dry eyes to let those others watching weep for you. (This is not a reliable dictum.) Many actors say that they do not think about crying, that it must arise as it can when it can. Some are able to spontaneously weep, having discovered a physical trick to manipulate their tear glands as one might wiggle an ear. YouTube is full of videos that promise techniques for learning how to cry on cue. And there are those gifted few who have found ways to invoke an affect through imaginative play, just by inhabiting the part, or by thinking the thought.

Studies might be made of the performance histories and characters of all our bodily excretions: tears, sweat, blood, semen, milk. These volumes would sit on the same shelf with surveys of flushed faces and of those drained of all color, the shiver and the hiccup, the sneeze: those unintentional side effects and symptoms to our actions that performers have long worked to simulate convincingly.[21] Further down the shelf might sit an investigation into methods for fainting, the little death of sexual climax, or its bigger brother, playing the corpse. These pass over more fully to the imitation of involuntary action, those acts that—at least in the theater—reassure us that they must belong to the world of pretense. How to cultivate the symptoms of these acts the body performs without our conscious self? Marvin Carlson and Rebecca Schneider draw our attention to a civil war re-enactor who is renowned for his ability to play a bloated corpse, and the decomposition of material form seems the furthest remove from conscious action.[22] How does one choreograph such a symptomatic dance under the full glare of another night's performance? How does an actor perform unintentionally, master the accident?

Many would say that an actor who relies on the accidents of affect is playing with fire, for feeling might flare up incandescently, or as quickly fizzle out. Such unpredictability is dangerous for an artform that so often relies on repetition and that demands its practitioners replay its traumas night after night. Recorded performance, on the other hand, can risk contingency, which is why one hears tales of the cruel and clever tricks that film directors play on their performers, hoping to capture an unexpected breakdown. Those most gullible to the suggestion of the moment offer especially troubling accounts. In his memoir *Please Don't Shoot My Dog,* for example, the former child actor Jackie Cooper recounts filming the sentimental comedy *Skippy* (1931). Unable to bring forth tears for his first of several crying scenes in the movie, the director Norman Taurog (who happened to be the actor's uncle) was finally able to make the ten-year-old boy cry by threatening to have him replaced in his role, even going so far as to dress another child actor in his costume. Having successfully cried and survived this first ploy, Cooper dreaded what trick might be used to provoke his tears for the next big crying scene required by the script. When the boy was once again unable to cry on cue, the exasperated director announced that the policeman on set was going to shoot the child's dog. "I saw [the officer] draw his gun out of the holster," Cooper recounts, "and watched him as he went in the same direction my grandmother had gone with my dog. The set was deathly still. I couldn't see them. Then I heard a single shot. It echoed a moment. Then total silence. [. . .] I began sobbing, so hysterically that it was almost too much for the scene."[23] Even after learning that the dog had not been harmed, the child was inconsolable and required sedatives to sleep that night. Taurog was awarded the Academy Award for Best Director for the film.[24] Recorded performance can rely on one-off tricks to rouse heartfelt tears, but each occasion requires a more extreme provocation, a further abuse manifesting trauma.

The burden of repetition weighs heavily on the actor and forms the basis for what has been termed the "Actor's Paradox." This paradox or dilemma centers upon whether an actor should feel, or be sensible to, that which they represent, or whether they should remain internally impassive while in control of a performance that only gives the outward signs of affect. This is terrain that others have explored in impressive and extensive fashion.[25] Allow me, then, to merely sketch out the role that tears play in such a history, while acknowledging a full treatment would warrant a book itself.

The question of what an actor feels or thinks while engaged in performance makes an early appearance in Plato's dialogue *Ion*. The philosopher's surrogate Socrates confronts the eponymous rhapsode, an interpreter of Homer's epics, and argues that poetry and performance are not arts of knowledge but of divine inspiration. Socrates contends that the performer does not know their own professions, but rather is a medium that allows a feeling its passage from inspiration to audience; performers are caught up in a swell they cannot control, whose currents they cannot even accurately name.[26] Each time that the topic of Ion's emotional technique enters the conversation, tears are brought up first and foremost as the primary example of affect's contagious force in action. For example, Ion says (by which I mean that Plato has Ion say): "Whenever I recite a tale of pity, my eyes are filled with tears, and when it is of horror or dismay, my hair stands on end with fear, and my heart goes leaping."[27] Ion does not know these affects in their Platonic form as an idea, which Socrates sees as a fault. In a roundabout way, one might say that the performer's lack of knowledge about affects points toward a more thorough sense of their operation. As the previous chapter showed, the sentiments that weeping evinces do not behave as ideas or things, they are too sad to tell by that widespread word "sad." The rhapsode knows that he cannot know his feelings fully.

For the modern origins of the debate one might look back to 1750, when John Hill published *The Actor: A Treatise on the Art of Playing*, a translation and extension of the treatise *Le Comédien* by Pierre Rémond de Sainte-Albine (1747), in which he posed sensibility as fundamental to the actor's craft. Sensibility is, in the words of Hill, "a disposition to be affected by the passions," affected in the sense of having *and* showing a passion. In other words, the sensible actor is disposed to the movement of affect and allows its resonance to speak across the greatest extent of their body.[28] They cultivate a fluency and mobility of voice, of breath, of bodily and facial comportment, to let their private experience surface in public visibility.[29] As Sarah Bernhardt, a strong adherent to the ideals of sensibility in a later era, put it, "he who is incapable of feeling strong passions, of being shaken by anger, of living in every sense of the word will never be a good actor."[30]

Hill's treatise inspired Denis Diderot's famous rebuttal, *The Paradox of the Actor*, which drew the outlines of a debate that would be revisited for centuries to come. Taking up Plato's form of the dialogue, Diderot stages a conversation between two speakers about the nature of acting, with the first serving as his mouthpiece and advocating for the art of the detached technician over the passionate one. For Diderot, the true actor is one who masters the art not of being a body, but of having a body, as if it were an object or medium to be worked from without. In the words of one of Diderot's disciples, the French actor Benoît-Constant Coquelin, the ideal actor is "a soft mass of sculptor's clay [. . .] capable of assuming at will any form."[31] Such a performer is a sculptor working their own body as clay, who, like Ion, witnesses the effects of their performance. But where their Greek predecessor gets caught up in a divine inspiration, this technician stands removed and practices an art of knowledge in Socrates's terms.[32] Diderot writes: "He must have in himself an unmoved and disinterested onlooker. He must have, consequently, penetration and no sensibility."[33] The actor's interior self is an "onlooker" that "penetrates" but does not feel what its second external self represents. Or, as Coquelin put it, "[k]eep the control of yourself. Whether your second self weeps or laughs, whether you become frenzied to madness or suffer the pains of death, it must always be under the watchful eye of your ever-impassive first self, and within fixed and prescribed bounds."[34]

Diderot allows his idealized technician-actor of the eighteenth-century to weep, but only if he has pre-arranged "the precise moment at which to produce his handkerchief, the word, the syllable at which his tears must flow."[35] Cue tears, indeed. But unless such an actor possesses the rare gift of well-tuned lachrymal glands, they would struggle to work their tears as readily as their crying. As I've discussed, crying involves breath and voice, both which might be worked manually, but most tears are an unruly supplement. It is certainly the case that manipulation of the former can convey a forceful impression of weeping, especially from the distance of a stage, however clear-eyed and dry-eyed the actor may remain. The painter Charles Le Brun's *A Method to Learn to Design the Passions* (1734), which codified the gestural vocabulary of eighteenth century painting and was influential for actors on the melodramatic stage of France and Britain, barely mentions tears at all under the heading for "weeping." His accompanying graphic representations of weeping do not even show tears.[36] The tragedian François-Joseph Talma, lead actor of the Comédie Francaise in the early 19th century, admits:

I scarcely know how to confess that, in my own person, in any circumstance of my life in which I experienced deep sorrow, the passion of the theater was so strong in me that, although oppressed with real sorrow, and disregarding the tears I shed, I made, in spite of myself, a rapid and fugitive observation on the alteration of my voice, and on a certain spasmodic vibration which it contracted as I wept; and, I say it, not without some shame, I even thought of making use of this on the stage, and, indeed, this experiment on myself has often been of service to me.[37]

Talma's study of his own weeping zeroes in on physical effects like the wavers of voice and breath, the vibrations of musculature, "disregarding the tears" in part because he could not borrow these autonomous productions from everyday life. In some ways, Talma's disregard also resonates with the practice of many actors today. One is encouraged to focus attention on the physical memory of the tearful response, how one's contextual body reacts à la Talma, or to retroactively regard the situational circumstances which inspired the act. One should avert one's eyes from the tears themselves.

In 1888, the theater critic William Archer sought to determine the merits of Diderot's hypothetical claims through reference to the actual practice of working actors. He sent letters of inquiry to many of the leading performers of the English-speaking stage while also scouring diaries and testimony of the historical archive across Europe and the US; the resulting text *Masks or Faces? A Physiological Study of Acting* is remarkable for its research on and treatment of the subject, and also for how tears take pride of place in Archer's consideration.[38]

Archer begins his survey of actors by directly raising the matter of crying: "In moving situations, do tears come to your eyes? Do they come unbidden? Can you call them up and repress them at will?"[39] In part, the priority of tears stems from the researcher's desire for objectivity, to look for the "outward symptoms" of emotion as evidence rather than an internal interpretation: "A tear, a blush, or a tremor is an external, visible, sensible fact."[40] But he also recognizes tears as the reliable "groundwork" upon and from which the expressive architecture of performance is constructed:

> Thus the physical effects of the simple emotions may be regarded as the raw material of expression; whence it follows that the reproduction of these physical effects must be the very groundwork of the actor's art. And of the simple emotions, grief in all of its phases is, to the actor, by far the most important. [. . .] What I mean is that, with the rare exception of terror, which is of comparatively rare occurrence, no emotion manifests itself so directly, so inevitably, and so peculiarly as grief.[41]

For Archer, the tear is this direct and inevitable manifestation peculiar to grief (even as my previous chapter contests the universality of this sign). Other emotional states, he later suggests, are too various in their external symptoms for the actor to benefit from their experience in performance. Love might agitate one person to giggle excessively, another to redden with a sudden flush, a third to slacken into wide-eyed awe.

The first chapter in which Archer discusses his findings is titled "Sunt Lacrymae Rerum" ("There are tears of/for things" or "the world is a world of tears" in Dryden's translation from 1697), a reference he leaves unexplained but which bears consideration. The line is borrowed from a scene in Virgil's *Aeneid* where the hero Aeneas begins to weep profusely before a stone mural of the fall of Troy, the "tears rivering down his face" in a performance akin to that of the actor before the stony silence of his audience. Aeneas relates how the scenes depicted before him recall the horrible destruction of his friends and people, indeed his world; his weeping is rooted in the revelation of a traumatic past.[42] In other words, the mural is his memory made visible, a memory that he himself has not fully processed. Is it too much of a stretch to see a parallel here with that practice of recalling the private past to unleash a present affect?

Actors have long siphoned the raw power of private memory and trauma to fuel their performances, laminating a character's suffering atop their own vibrant pain. Most famously, while playing the role of Electra, the Greek actor Polus reportedly placed the ashes of his own recently deceased son into the urn that Electra imagines contained the ashes of her brother Orestes. Archer's interlocutors speak of bringing private experience forward almost exclusively into tearful depictions of grief; nearly all these occasions, like those of Polus, hinged on the death of a child. The English actress Madge Kendal (née Robertson), for example, had for many years been identified with a particular role that featured a scene in which her character mourned the loss of a child. When she performed the piece a fortnight after the sudden death of her own child, the effect was so distressing for actress and audience alike—a woman in the audience rose mid-performance and called out "No more! No more!"—that the theater was forced to drop the curtain in the third act. Kendal never played the part again. Archer writes that "[t]his was an instance in which acute and present personal sorrow absorbed rather than reinforced the mimic emotion, and changed the imagined heroine's imagined agony into real torture for the real woman."[43] It is unsurprising that the death of a child spurs the emotions of actors.[44] I can only speculate that this premature death, cutting short that emblem of futurity and potentiality, exerts the greatest of pressures on the present. This is a past event that remains vibrantly painful long into the future as the absent child continues to age in the conditional case, an ever-present time where they would have been. Such a traumatic loss is a constant reservoir for tearful performance and, in a cruel way, exemplifies a form of vital and unknowable memory which an actor might use in an array of situations.

Archer's respondents who admitted their private pain into public appearance all relied on a direct parallel between the suffering of their character and the actor themselves. Each began weeping over their lost child when a character they portrayed faced a similar cataclysmic rupture. Conversely, Polus's weeping arrives by analogy: his filial despair stands in for Electra's weeping over a sibling she presumes lost. Brecht used a similar trick of surrogacy in a rehearsal with the great actress Helene Weigel. At a certain point in the scene Weigel had to pick up a framed picture that would move her character. He placed a photograph of their five-year-old boy who she had not seen in years, as a means of instigating her emotions.[45] (Again, a child!) And, indeed, for the acting teacher most famous for advocating the use of one's own experience to produce tears, Lee Strasberg, "[t]he memory event need not directly parallel the event onstage but should stimulate an analogous feeling."[46] In these cases, affect originates in an actual memory belonging to the actor's private subjective experience, which is then repurposed into the external expression appropriate to the character portrayed.

Where the actors Archer interviewed had to learn their trade through apprenticeship or intuitive experimentation, the years immediately following his inquiry saw the establishment of the first modern actor training programs in the West. Most prominently, the Russian director Constantin Stanislavsky's studio work at the beginning of the 20th century came to dominate the popular imagination in the United States and—through the dissemination of the Hollywood film industry—global culture writ large. In the broadest of strokes, on US soil this Russian influence split into three branches during the mid-century, led by the prominent teachers Stella Adler, Sanford Meisner, and Lee Strasberg. Adler and Meisner relied in divergent ways on the power of the actor's imagination to inspire emotion in the middle of performance and these differences ground their respective philosophies of acting. Adler, for example, "was emphatically convinced that by its nature drama dealt with doing, not feeling, and that feeling was a by-product of doing."[47] Or, as filtered through another of Stanislavsky's students-turned-teachers, Yevgeny Vakhtangov, for the actor, "emotion, as well as the means of its expression, is being generated subconsciously, spontaneously, in the process of executing actions directed towards the gratification of a desire. The actor must, therefore, come on the stage not in order to feel or experience emotions, but in order to act."[48] According to such a perspective, one sure way not to weep is to approach it as an objective at the end of an action, to be willed into being again and again. Tears are symptoms of actions and their disappointments; they are not an action in themselves. So one sets out to beg for forgiveness, as an example, and what tears may come arrive as a consequence of this attempt or its frustration.

Strasberg, on the other hand, enlists the private history of the actor to ground their stage life in the present. According to Strasberg's Method, emotional life onstage is a shadow cast by the past: "The basic idea of affective memory is not emotional recall but that the actor's emotion on the stage should never be really real. It always should be only *remembered* emotion. An emotion that happens right now spontaneously is out of control—you don't know what's going to happen from it, and the actor can't always maintain and repeat it."[49] This was accomplished not by focusing on the actual experience of a remembered emotional event, but by a studied recollection of the circumstances of that event. One does not look the memory directly in the face; one takes stock of everything that surrounds its becoming. As Strasberg put it: "You do not start to remember the emotion, you start to remember the place, the taste of something, the touch of something, the sight of something, the sound of something, and you remember that as simply and as clearly as you can. You touch the things in your mind but with your senses alive."[50] The actor rebuilds an imaginary sensory container of the chosen event, rich with what Uta Hagen, working in a slightly divergent manner, would call "release triggers"—those details that might spur on an affective memory.

Strasberg and his followers sought to harness the unruly power of involuntary memory, the flicker of affect that takes us unawares and comes to suffuse our attention. A single strand of sensation pulls at the whole cloth of memory, which blankets one in the enfolding texture of another time and place. The most famous instance of such an upswell of affect derives from Marcel Proust's novel *Swann's Way*, when the taste of a madeleine biscuit dipped in tea unexpectedly throws the narrator back into the full feeling of his childhood. As Samuel Beckett wrote of the episode of the memory-soaked biscuit in his study of the author, the lone scholarly work he produced in an abortive academic career:

> No amount of voluntary manipulation can reconstitute in its integrity an impression that the will has—so to speak—buckled into incoherence. But if, *by accident*, and given favourable circumstances (a relaxation of the subject's habit of thought and a reduction of the radius of his memory, a generally diminished tension of consciousness following upon a phase of extreme discouragement), if by some miracle of analogy the central impression of a past sensation recurs as an immediate stimulus which can be instinctively identified by the subject with the model of duplication (*whose integral purity has been retained because it has been forgotten*), then the total past sensation, not its echo nor its copy, but the sensation itself, annihilating every spatial and temporal restriction, comes in a rush to engulf the subject in all the beauty of its infallible proportion.[51]

Leveraging involuntary memory, the Method brings the "total past sensation" into performance; "not its echo nor its copy" (in other words, not its representation), but the affect itself. It seeks to wrest control of this accidental appearance, normally impervious to "voluntary manipulation," and conjure the spirit of the past into a present act. In other words, the actor's practice simulates the conditions for an affect to reappear of its own accord and to give its lasting liveness free reign. Strasberg puts it this way: "Often we see things going on inside that can't come out—the face contracts, the eyes contract—the emotion isn't let through. The actor feels at times like crying but he can't cry, he can't uncurl the muscles to permit the tears to flow."[52] The actor must learn to relax their control and allow the impulse to pass from private sensibility to public appearance; they must become a transparent and fluid medium for the movement of forces. They must become sincere in Trilling's sense, and allow "a congruence between avowal and actual feeling," between surface and depth.

In Strasberg's formulation, such sincere emotional flow is synonymous with the flow of tears.

In some ways, this conception resembles Camillo's memory theater that I discussed in the opening of this volume. Like that theater in reverse, the details are arrayed around an actor who stands alone at the center of the memory stage, hoping that these recognizable figures might re-release the past into the present. But there are significant differences between the two memory theaters. Camillo's device placed the subject centerstage looking out upon an auditorium filled with things that stood as signs for definite information, each a surrogate representation of a larger field of memory that the mnemonic performer might know. Here, on the other hand, all the richly articulated details of a remembered space face inward onto an event whose kernel of truth retains its power by remaining forever unspoken, yet perpetually felt afresh. Strasberg's affective memory is the vanishing point at which these details converge—the blind spot of feeling. The Method tells us that an actor's face is composed of the past made present, a past that they cannot know completely and must keep traumatically unresolved.

III. Bullying the Actor (The Actor Bullying)

I rehearsed the monologue for weeks in my acting class, though freshman year of high school is so far away now that I can no longer remember its source or much beyond the character's name (Jimmy), and a stray line or two ("I'd done my time"). It resembled so many other speeches excerpted from contemporary drama and anthologized for acting classes and auditions: a traumatic memory recounted as if for the first time, the key to character suddenly revealed in terms that Ibsen and his contemporaries exhausted so effectively a century before. A young man recounts how he was bullied in school, suggests his transcendent recovery. I was convinced my performance would be that much more effective if I could muster a tear or two at its climax—or better yet restrain a tear, fight to blink it back in shame—but no such luck. I do remember one attempt when my acting of the scene clicked into place like never before, when I could feel the rest of the room, drowsy in the fading light of a winter afternoon, draw tight in attention around me as I lost myself in the moment—or, rather, lost myself in another moment. A recollection from my own childhood: my younger sister and I had wandered off to the empty playground around the corner of the school, bored in the summer heat while my older sister's soccer match waned on too long. I was struggling on the jungle bars, my sister in the sand to the side, likely telling stories to herself as was her way, when a small pack of older kids suddenly appeared, circling her in her engrossed play. I don't remember how many were there, though the bicycle made the biggest one loom even larger. How did I find myself on the ground, sand in my mouth, with the ringleader on top of me? Was he hitting me? Was I crying then? Things blur in my memory.

Sitting in the studio again, the words coming out of me. And—behold!—a single bead running down my skin. Not a hot tear, alas, but a cold bead of sweat. One kind of automatic fact in place of another. Involuntary memory behaves involuntarily.

Spectators are rarely invited into the quasi-sacred space of an acting workshop to witness students rehearsing affective memory exercises, though the practice has long captured the public imagination. In part, the widespread influence of the Method in Hollywood from the mid-twentieth century onward has lent the mythos of the Method a global appeal, but we also take great interest in parting the curtains and peering backstage on theatrical acts (surely, one motivation for my writing this very book). To cite just one of countless examples: the HBO series *Barry* (2018–2023) tells the increasingly improbable tale of a hitman who decides to become an actor when he starts to attend workshops run by a has-been Hollywood actor. Struggling with PTSD from a tour in Afghanistan, Barry unintentionally musters deep wells of rageful passion from affective recollections of his violent past for bravura performances in the studio and in his bloody escapades, where he acts out his unbridled id. White male violence and emotional fragility often walk hand in hand, bully and bullied streaming curses and tears.

An eight-minute film, *Bully* (2010), by the British artist Gillian Wearing attends to the unpredictable leakiness of affective memory in the actor's studio; it also bears consideration in terms of the way that gender overshadows that response. Wearing was, like Taylor-Johnson, one of the Young British Artists whose work exploded onto the art world in the 1990s. Where Taylor-Johnson's video and photography projects an aesthetic lucidity cast in cool blues or warm ambers that has allowed her to transition seamlessly to directing music videos (Robert Downey Jr. for

Elton John) and even mainstream movies (an unfortunate adaptation of *50 Shades of Grey*), Wearing uses the handheld or interviewer's camera for revelations of the secret underpinnings of everyday lives. As the artist put it, "[a] lot of my work is about creating structures in order for people to express themselves."[53] For the work that launched her career, the exhaustively titled *Signs that say what you want them to say and not signs that say what someone else wants you to say* (1992–93), she photographed people on the street while they held signs on which each had handwritten a phrase expressing their current thought. Each frame contained the fragment of a private narrative of self.

As if her name foretold her fate, one might say that Wearing's medium is the mask. There are series of self-portraits in which she dons hyper-realistic masks of famous artists, of members of her family, even—most uncannily—of herself at different ages; she has asked other people to wear masks of her face, posing as the artist once removed. The title to Archer's book questions actors whether they show either "Masks or Faces?" onstage (playing through distanced analysis or heartfelt sensibility); Wearing insists that in everyday life the two are mutually constitutive, if ill-fitting. The obscured face always spills out over the edges. By presenting a demonstrably false appearance, she dialectically establishes the hidden and inaccessible interiority as an authentic one, even as her work often confuses any transparent access with fictional accretions. *Secrets & Lies* (2009), for example, welcomes a few visitors at a time into a makeshift confession booth to watch a series of anonymous people in cheap rubber masks, confessing traumatic memories. In an essay recounting her experience of the piece, Kara Rooney writes: "This barrier not only afforded a confessional healing on the part of this man [giving his confession], but allowed me, his confessor, to access that catharsis. The mask, marauding as a benevolent gesture on the part of the artist, becomes equally necessary for the viewer—a two-way mirror impartial to both sides."[54] In an eerie way, the visible portion of the face narrows to a pair of eyes working away beneath the baggy folds of a "middle-aged white man." One speaker presents a direct gaze, another's eyes dart off to disengage, blinking as they fill with, and fight back, tears. The double layer of the mask/face lends the anonymous person the expressive potential of the actor, channeling affective force from a submerged memory and making it present through the palpable fiction of an artificial face.

They are like Archer's actors using a loose-fitting character on stage to finally cry over the loss of an offstage child.

For the feature-length documentary *Self Made* (2010) and its offshoot, the short video *Bully*, Wearing follows seven untrained performers in a workshop with Method acting teacher Sam Rumbelow as he trains them to restage a moment from their past. *Bully* focuses on a scene familiar from many an acting class: a young man arranges the other student actors in the room, casting each as a participant in the recreation of a scenario from his childhood. He whispers instructions to a few, groups others into a silent chorus. The scene is a public park where kids are at play; his younger self shows up alone and tries to join in, but is excluded, bullied. The man plays himself, occasionally stepping out of his recollection to direct the other actors. At the end the tormenters and bystanders of the event are arranged in a line. Rumbelow prompts the young man to articulate what he wants to say to these surrogate children. The man leans in, pressing his forehead menacingly against another student, and the words tumble out in a string of curses and threats of physical violence. He has to turn away, his hands in fists. Striding in a sweeping arc across the stage while breathing heavily, his head rolls back. He is finally crying: mission accomplished. The young man rounds on the bystanders: "you should have been protecting me. You just stood there and watched. Didn't give a shit. At all." As if it were an automatic physical reaction, one of the other wide-eyed actors—a smaller man of color, dwarfed by this raging white man—abruptly blurts out "I'm sorry" as the video fades.

This apology is as slippery as the rest of Wearing's film, collapsing distinctions between actor and director, victim and perpetrator. It is at once the dream of the past, the protagonist's wish that these ghosts of his childhood trauma might atone for their trespass, and it is also the responding actor's regret over his participation in the reenactment of that past. More immediately, it seems an attempt to diffuse the anger that has been unleashed right here and now. For the real danger in the room comes from the actor caught in his stream of memory, his suppressed aggression suddenly volatile and alive. One is tempted to read into the racial dynamics here, the familiar story of a white man redirecting his perceived powerlessness into an attack on a vulnerable brown body. Watching *Bully* during Wearing's retrospective at the Guggenheim in 2021, when the politics of grievance have so thoroughly captured the imagination of white

American masculinity, how can one not see this undercurrent rise to the surface? I don't mean to question the veracity or poignancy of this man's memory, yet in the actions of Proud Boys and others we have seen how manufactured or well-tended traumas can prompt reactionary acting and scene-stealing with alarming consequences. Indeed, in naming the piece *Bully*, Wearing frames this exercise as a contest of masculinities. While now applicable to any person, the etymology of the word locates its origins specifically as "a *man* given to or characterized by riotous, thuggish, and threatening behaviour; one who behaves in a blustering, swaggering, and aggressive manner."[55] And then there is the structure of the acting class itself, with its teacher encouraging this return. Mark Fisher writes of the feature-length film, *Self Made*, from which *Bully* is excerpted, "the film's most unsettling scenes—both concerning violence—at least raise the possibility that untapping and manipulating buried feelings may be catastrophic."[56] Rumbelow is the prime instigator here, goading on his subjects in quest of those tears, though the responsibility bleeds over to other less visible bullies: Wearing behind the camera, setting this whole machine in motion, and those of us who sit here watching the scene unfold, awaiting some cathartic explosion of pent-up violent emotion. The young man is correct, we "just stood there and watched." Diderot was right: the wayward affects of the actor can be dangerous and can elicit tears, sweat, blood. To recall that bully feeling, is to let it bully you.

Like her contemporary Wearing, Sam Taylor-Johnson has turned her camera's eye on the mystery of the Method actor's tears. In the short film *Method in Madness* (1994), we witness what seems to be the mental breakdown of a young man. Seated on a couch rocking back and forth, his collapse into tears is punctuated by intermittent screams. But as the title suggests, this man is more than he seems: a method actor, his pain borrows from his own lived suffering, though such feeling has been refracted in the present. The title also, of course, refers to Shakespeare's melancholic young prince, whose methodical "madness," which he expertly performs to trick Polonius, is nonetheless grounded in a real loss that quite literally haunts him and prompts his catastrophically violent revenge.[57] Hamlet's anxieties about tear production in relation to trauma and acting/action are laid bare early in the play in his response to the Player's weeping performance as Hecuba: "What's Hecuba to him, or he to Hecuba, / That he should weep for her?" Later, in the graveyard scene, he will challenge Laertes to compete in either a crying or fighting duel so that he might prove his superior love for the dead Ophelia: "'Swounds, show me what thou 't do. Woo't weep? Woo't fight? [. . .] I'll do it."[58] It bears mention that, long after his worry about the actor's tearful show as Hecuba, Hamlet can only consider enacting such a lachrymose performance in imitation of Laertes—"show me what thou 't do." He cannot cry in the play, just as he cannot act. Clearly, tears are intertwined with the credentials of masculinity and conviction in Hamlet's mind.

For tragic princes and for tragic actors alike, crying inspired by a mixture of the actual and fictional, the extemporaneous and the calculated, will nonetheless produce unalloyed tears. Which leads me back to all those *Crying Men*, and the lone one in their midst who seems in on the game. I keep thinking of Laurence Fishburne's ever-gleaming twin strokes. I don't know much about his process as an actor, and, in truth, I would prefer to leave it that way. I am most drawn to this photograph precisely because its excess leaves me unresolved too. Are these "real tears"? Do these two luminous lines point the way to some secret self or sacred past come alive and made visible in those windows to the soul? And yet, the longer I look, the more I think I see the beginnings of a smile curl the edges of his mouth, saying, "the joke is on you." Or perhaps, "welcome to the desert of the real," as Fishburne puts it when playing Morpheus, channeling the words of Jean Baudrillard's *Simulacra and Simulation* to puncture another elaborate simulation.[59] According to the premise of *The Matrix*, humanity lives in a virtual recreation of late-stage capitalism constructed to enchant and distract us from our subjugation to an AI that uses human bioelectricity as a power source. In fact, the actual "present" of the film takes place hundreds of years in the future, after AI has won its war against humanity; this simulation that we call the present is a careful reconstruction of the past. It is all an elaborate acting exercise.

I scour the photograph for traces of the real showing through. I ask: are these red-rimmed eyes the mark of being too sad to tell, of crying for too long to tell? Does Fishburne draw his coat close to protect himself from this fragile exhibition? Or perhaps these raw eyes smart from something else? Perhaps, they are merely symptoms from a burning menthol spray or "tear blower" some member of the makeup crew applied to provoke reflex tears. Perhaps I should ask: what tools are secreted away in the long coat he holds so tight? Outside of his own private image repertoire, what contraband implements does the actor wield to get us moving?

CHAPTER 5

The Weeper's Toolbox

An Incomplete Catalog of Prosthetics, Props, and Prompts

> We may properly distinguish weeping into two general kinds, genuine and counterfeit; or physical crying and moral weeping. Physical crying, while there are no real corresponding ideas in the mind, nor any genuine sentimental feeling of the heart to produce it, depends upon the mechanism of the body: but moral weeping proceeds from, and is always attended with, such real sentiments of the mind, and feeling of the heart, as do honour to human nature; which false crying always debases.
>
> —PETER SHAW, "MAN: A PAPER FOR ENNOBLING THE SPECIES" (1755)[1]

The counterfeiter lays out the tools of his trade. Jars of spiced unction for application under the eyes. Small vials filled with the viscous residue of funerals, weepy films, and broken hearts. Synthetic lubricants in canisters with eye-shaped contours for easy application. A translucent onion, a bright red pepper. There are the tweezers and cotton swabs to be found in any bathroom vanity, but also bespoke devices to pry the eye wide and prevent its blinking, even machines to shock recalcitrant lachrymal glands into action.[2]

Such a toolbox might be nestled in the corner of a prop closet, one of those attics or warehouses in the interstices of a repertory theater that Alice Rayner has described as "both an archive of past productions and a promise of possible ones."[3] It is a closet within that closet, a box within that box. The pages that follow offer a tour through a few past productions to illuminate how these props might be used again by enterprising fabulists. As tools, I emphasize their utilitarian orientation toward a specific use: to produce a performance of weeping, or just the appearance of weeping sans tears. Countering the psychological processes that actors use to conjure their crying episodes, these are external objects that reliably produce what otherwise seems an internally motivated, often spontaneous, act.

Prop closets follow their own organizational logic to make sense of the world of things. Lamps are clustered next to chairs in one theater, next to books in another. I have put on my structuralist hat, affixed my semiotician's monocle, and followed my own peculiar taxonomy in constructing three conceptual drawers for this container, each labeled to help differentiate their methods and effects: *prosthetic*, *prop*, or *prompt*. I idiosyncratically define each of these categories as a temporary epistemological exercise, not an ontological certainty. Each is differently engaged in the project of making "tears" visible to another person—here I am less concerned with what those tears mean (as in chapter 3) and more attentive to what mechanisms allow other waters to pass as emotional tears. There is room in each drawer for rearrangement, just as there are other ways to interpret these three labels.

1) the *prosthetic* tear is a liquid placed in the eye intended to look and act as if it were a secretion produced by that eye. It is an external substance—usually artificial—that takes the place of a tear. The *OED* describes prosthesis as "the replacement of defective or absent parts of the body by artificial substitutes" and many prosthetic tears are designed precisely as an efficacious surrogate for those individuals who suffer from dry eye or other debilitating conditions that limit the natural production of tears. Like their models, prosthetic tears supply lubrication and cleansing to protect the eye; in performance they might be used toward other ends, to appear as a weeping flow. For example: Eye drops.

2) the *prop* is an object or accessory that supports the idea of crying; it reads as "crying" to a larger public. Props are agents of simulation, feigning a presence where there may only be absence beneath, but that ambiguity produces additional affects as convincing as any actual act. In Jean Baudrillard's example, a person who simulates

sickness produces actual symptoms.[4] Such props are agents, too, because they expect and even demand certain actions from those in their vicinity.[5] For example: Handkerchiefs; Sunglasses.

3) the *prompt* provokes the body to produce tears by physical means. It is an external force or intervention that stimulates the release of reflex tears. In the tripartite structure of a sign, prompted tears are referents: the unruly thing to which the emotional idea of "tears" adheres. The prompt reminds the body how to cry through a stimulus that incites an automatic response—it is not acting, but reacting. This is water from the eye divorced from a subject's meaningful intentions. For example: Onions; Tear Gas.

A handy little chart has been taped to the top of the toolbox, in case things get misplaced:

Prosthetic	Prop	Prompt
External substance	External object	External trigger
Replaces tears	Represents tears	Provokes tears
Surrogation	Simulation	Stimulation

Significantly, and in distinction from the methods explored in the previous chapter on internal methods of weeping, all these tools work at crying from the outside in. But this kind of division between internal and external motivation threatens to affirm the anti-theatrical prejudices of those like the Peter Shaw of my epigraph. Physician to King George III, Shaw claimed that "false crying always debases" what he called "human nature."[6] This conviction relies on a binary that sees internally motivated "weeping" as true and moral, insofar as it exposes authentic devotions; and physically motivated "crying" as false, since it involves thoughtless action, with "no real corresponding ideas in the mind, nor any genuine sentimental feeling from the heart." But physically inspired tears may unleash surprising affects: something might gather force of its own, take over your body and incite other moving sentiments and thoughts. For a little bit of play-acting, Falstaff turns to fortified wine—appropriately called "sack"—to prompt his eyes to rim with tears: "Give me a cup of sack to make my eyes look red, that it may be thought that I have wept, for I must speak in passion." The feigned passion soon takes hold of him and he finds himself weeping in earnest: "now I do not speak to thee in drink, but in tears."[7] The very idea of simulation confuses presence and absence, truth with falsity, so that the boy crying wolf manifests bite marks from imaginary teeth. Here, William James's backwards claim that "I am sad because I cry" rings surprisingly true. I find myself crying—propped, prompted, or prosthetic—and a feeling takes me by surprise.

I exhibit here a set of exemplary tools, each of which begins externally but proceeds to undermine any neat divisions between true and false, psychological and physical, just as tears themselves overflow the bulwarks dividing inside from outside, private from public. As the preceding chapters have discussed, reflexive and psychogenic tears make for muddied waters. So, too, the different categories offered here flood one into the other and accumulate examples as they proceed. I could go on, gathering samples, for both prop closets and cabinets of curiosity are collections that never arrive at completion. This could be a book onto itself.

Such a book would fit uncomfortably in my imaginary toolbox, though prop closets are full of leatherbound books no one will ever read, meant to adorn theatrical libraries. As one of the most emblematic prompts in the theater, the promptbook or script casts doubt on any clear distinction between external tool and internal acting. It may give explicit cues for a performer, telling them to cry, though it likely won't have much luck. Books are much more effective when letting loose the affective currents within the reader.[8] I remember trying not to cry while reading Wilson Rawls's tearjerker *Where the Red Fern Grows* in my fourth-grade classroom. I'd already read and wept over the book at home and feared my expected collapse even as it came upon me, exposed under those stark fluorescent lights. In Ralph Lemon's performance *How Can You Stay in the House All Day and Not Go Anywhere*, such a book serves as a prompt that pushes the performer Okwui Okpokwasili into a virtuosic bout of weeping that extends into a full eight minutes alone onstage. Katherine Profeta, the dramaturg for the piece, recounts the writing of such a volume:

> [Okpokwasili] interviewed [the company] individually about our most painful life events, collecting private traumas that ran the gamut from teenage heartbreaks to cruel injustice to violent loss of life. She compiled those stories, woven together with documentation of all-too-frequent atrocities from the national and international news, into a closely

guarded 'crying book.' The book was to be read only by her, and only in the moments preceding a performance.[9]

This book served as external repository for the retention of affect-laden experience, outsourcing the method actor's task of memory management but working on the reader's nerves in a parallel manner. Janša's chamber of "Public Memory," too, offers books, film, and music as external prompts toward a weeping that feels both our own and part of a larger community or outside. Reading, we are both outside ourselves and deeply situated inside our own private sensibility. As the theorist Peggy Phelan puts it: "In the performance of reading the reader inhabits not a double identity or even a suspended identity but rather a radical identity-less-ness. This is the zone of acting itself: that strange form of being in which people are 'not altogether as themselves' [...] and not quite not themselves."[10] Each of the objects in my collection here likewise invites—to a lesser or greater degree—a form of radical identity-less-ness that undermines the idea of tears as authenticator of individual experience.

Let me remove my structuralist hat, tucking the monocle within its brim, and place them both on their own shelf in the prop closet, at the ready as needed. I pull out a handkerchief and set it, too, aside for later. First, a small vial to get the tears rolling.

I. Prosthetics

Eye Drops

When I played George in my high school production of Thornton Wilder's *Our Town*, I dreaded my appearance in the final scene. My character was supposed to cross to the grave of his deceased wife, Emily, as her ghost watched on, as everyone watched on. He was supposed to be overcome with grief, but I kept finding myself dry-eyed and red-faced, my autonomic response one of shame, not sorrow. I would cross to center and face upstage, then drop to my knees mechanically and keel over to rest my forehead on the ground, in the most literal interpretation of Wilder's stage directions (*George sinks to his knees then falls full length at Emily's feet*).[11] I felt ridiculous employing this invention of the body, but no one noticed my embarrassment. As I stared fixedly at the scuffed ground waiting for the lights to fall, I'd hear sniffles spreading through the audience, my awkward submission to Wilder's score sufficient to help cue the inevitable waterworks.

An actor in the theater may—like the George who briefly graced the stage at Bellport High School in the mid-1990s—embody the symptomatic effects of crying to give the impression of tears when none are forthcoming. They may fall prostrate to the ground, heave shoulders or shudder, their brow weighed down, their breath catching as they eke out a moan or whimper. They may face upstage. But camera-based work often requires a more complete illusion. Drawing in for the close-up, film, video, and photography scour the face for traces of weeping. (Witness the impulse to determine the authenticity of Taylor-Johnson's photo series, discussed in the previous chapter.)

When a script cues an actor's tears on set, the makeup crew is on hand, with their own counterfeiter's toolbox at the ready. In the taxonomy that I've laid out here, many of these implements belong in the drawer I've labeled "prompts": there are tear sticks that use menthol or similar lachrymose agents to set the eye watering when applied below the lid; there are "tear blowers," tubes through which one can blow similar irritants into another's open eye to stimulate reflexive tears. Eyes will redden, noses will run, lashes flutter, and tears fall.

Alongside these physical stimulants that force the eye to perform its required task, there are vials of prosthetic tears that perform in place of the recalcitrant eye. Such prosthetic tears have been in use outside the theater since at least 1550 BCE, when an Egyptian papyrus outlining medicinal recipes suggested a novel remedy for dry eye: "Thou shalt disembowel a yellow frog, mix its gal in curd, apply to his eyes."[12] Today, different ailments affecting the tear system feed an expansive industry with around 100 over-the-counter variants approved by the Federal Drug Administration in the US.[13] For those who suffer from various forms of dry eye, a condition in which the tear glands cannot produce the basal tears necessary to lubricate and protect the eye, synthetic tears offer one way to compensate for the deficiency. These prosthetics are surrogates for that which is lacking; they are not intended to overflow the lid and spill forth, though they may do so if the volume exceeds the drainage capacity of the puncta and tear ducts. In other words, the therapeutic artificial tear only looks like weeping as a side effect, when excessive application throws off the balance of the well-lubricated eye.

In the frame of performance, such excess is pursued intentionally. Here the prosthetic tear is not only a compensation, but also becomes an artificial extension of the body, taking up the tear's capacity to visibly communicate to a public and send forth liquid bridges of affect that may bring individuals into empathetic concert. While also used to mimic sweat onscreen, glycerine (or glycerin) has become something of a shorthand for fake tears since the earliest days of cinema. Glycerine is a humectant, meaning it attracts and retains moisture from the air and the skin; in addition, its viscosity resembles that of naturally produced tears. An actor can apply a small amount of the liquid to the skin below the eye or directly onto the eye to give the appearance of tears or of having cried. Glycerine does not itself produce tears; it is read as tears. A stream of weeping requires a continuous flow, while the prosthetic tear is manually applied drop by drop, in tempo with the camera that moves shot by shot. Glycerine has a rhythm and choreography of its own: a single tear hangs, swells in concert with the accompanying music, and then can fall at precisely the right dramatic moment.

In a prescient essay on the medium of television written in 1931, the visionary Hugo Gernsback singles out prosthetic tears as an exemplary trick of the cinema that might be imported to the new technology. With the intimacy of the close-up—and the interruption of the cut during which a drop can be administered—he writes, "we can have the heroine shedding glycerine tears, while the audience is none the wiser."[14] Editing can obscure the source of such prosthetic tears, making them essentially indistinguishable from those produced by the performer. Here is a material whose application makes the actor. In a way, we might say that it is not only a surrogate for the tears, but also for the actor themselves. Not all would agree with such a claim, since hiding the time-based art of crying in this manner can debase and defang a tear. As the film theorist Béla Balázs wrote: "We cannot use glycerine tears in a close-up. What makes a deep impression is not a fat, oily tear rolling down a face—what moves us is to see the glance growing misty, and moisture gathering in the corner of the eye—moisture that as yet is scarcely a tear. This is moving, because this cannot be faked."[15] According to such a view it is the movement into weeping, like the catch in the throat as a voice seizes up, that brings the viewer along in a sympathetic rupture.

Such artificial tears rarely make an appearance onstage, except in those instances where their artifice and the artifice of acting is foregrounded. In the opening of the French director Hubert Colas's *Hamlet* (2005), the stone-faced cast came forward one by one to meet the audience's gaze in what amounted to a pre-show roll call. Tilting the contents of a small bottle of over-the-counter artificial tears into their eyes, each was suddenly wracked with sobs, choking on a manufactured sorrow. The actor playing Hamlet was the only one to abstain from the application—the authenticity of his mourning signaled by negating the artifice of tears, and, by extension, any appearance of sorrow. Here, glycerin tears are so-called crocodile's tears; they are prosthetics that fill an affective absence. It is no great leap to begin Hamlet's tragedy with a flood of such manufactured tears; as I noted at the end of the previous chapter, the prince famously worries over how the visiting player brings liquid proof to his portrayal of Hecuba's fictional sorrow. There, too, tears become the evidence of the efficacious actor, in both senses of the word: "What would he do, / Had he the motive and the cue for passion / That I have? He would drown the stage with tears . . ."

Thus, artificial tears can metonymically represent the art of acting, a single drop from a vial standing in for the larger project of pretending to be other than one is. Witness Willem Dafoe's performance of John Proctor in *LSD (. . . Just the High Points . . .)*, the Wooster Group's 1984 interpretation of Arthur Miller's tragedy *The Crucible*.[16] The original play's culminating scene, when Proctor refuses to sign his name to a false confession, is among the most reliable of tearjerkers for audience and actor alike, great fodder for several generations of scene-chewing leading men. In the Wooster Group's version, the actor first doused his eyes with artificial tears, then proceeded to break down in histrionic wails: "I have given you my soul; leave me my name!" In an interview with Philip Auslander, Dafoe reflected on this moment:

Once you show the audience you're putting it in, it takes the curse off of it. Then it takes away, 'Oh, what a fabulous, virtuoso performer he is, oh, he's crying!' That's something I could do. But [using the drops] makes

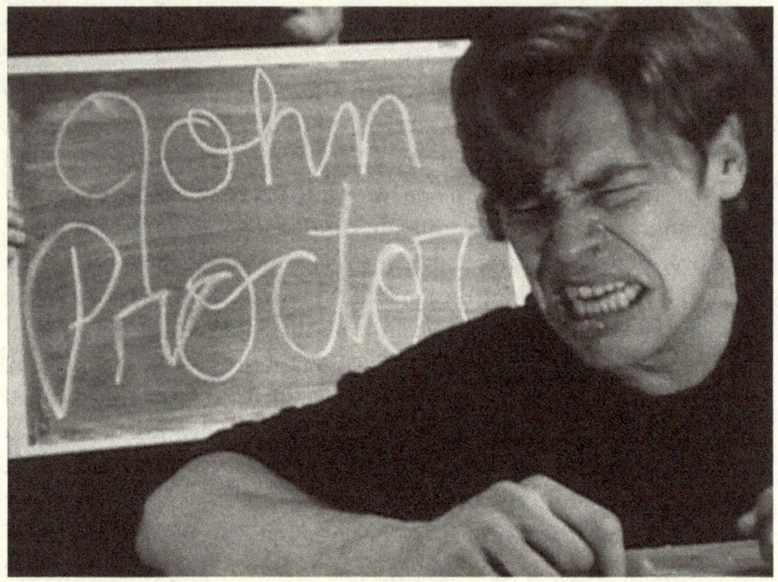

Figure 9 Willem Dafoe in *L.S.D. (...Just the High Points...)* 1984, directed by Elizabeth LeCompte. Super-8 film still © The Wooster Group.

things vibrate a little more, because you get your cake and eat it, too. You see the picture of the crying man, you hear the text, you see the whole thing before you.[17]

One can find a 23-second clip of this scene labeled as "unused silent Super-8 footage" in one of the "dailies" archived on the Wooster Group website.[18] The footage begins after the drops have been applied, catching Dafoe with his head leaning against the table, then flailing about, contorted. A slate board with "John Proctor" written in chalk peeks over his shoulder. This is the magic of the cinematic cut: without seeing the source of his tears, trapped in a silence that is not so different from Bas Jan Ader's muted collapse in *I'm too sad to tell you*, Dafoe's breakdown is moving. I think: "Oh, what a fabulous, virtuoso performer he is, oh, he's crying!"

II. Props

Handkerchiefs

A blotting sheet, a mask, a banner. A way to hide the eyes or staunch the flow (Hamm's "Old stauncher!" from *Endgame*). Also, a flag of surrender or call for help, signaling from a distance that the ship of self-control is sinking, already underwater. The handkerchief is a multi-use tool, ready to clean a spill, bandage a wound, blow a nose, and—yes—dab a tear.

Handkerchiefs used to soak up tears become carriers of their feeling. Like the tear-stained page of a letter, so recognizable a gesture that the manipulative would purposely drip waters on their hand-scribed lines to simulate authentic suffering (see Rodolphe's farewell letter to Madame Bovary, which the rake dots with water to suggest a sorrow he does not feel), the dampened cloth can send messages from the heart. Robert Darnton has chronicled how Jean-Jacques Rousseau's wildly popular epistolary novel of 1761, *Nouvelle Héloïse* (*Julie, or the New Heloise*), produced torrents of sobbing among its many readers, making a handkerchief an obligatory prop for any such reading.[19] Its account of two ill-fated lovers both proposed and illustrated a theory of authenticity that greatly influenced the age of sentimentality. In one memorable episode from the novel, the handkerchief became a means of absorbing and exchanging messages through tears:

> I began to shed a torrent of tears, and this state compared to the one I was just emerging from was not without some pleasures. I wept greatly, for a good moment, and was relieved. When I felt completely settled, I returned to Julie; I took her hand once more. She was holding her handkerchief; I could tell it was quite moist. Ah, said I softly, I see that our hearts have never ceased to understand each other! It is true, she said in a broken voice; but let this be the last time they will have spoken on this register.[20]

Passed via object from hand to hand, this kind of felt understanding—one that subsists below the volume of language, in the "register" of the heart—is not available to most audiences of performance. (There are occasional exceptions. I remember weeping in a theater, and the stranger sitting beside me reached over to offer a tissue. "It is awful, isn't it?" She whispered. She, too, was crying. "Yes, yes it is." As I took the offered tissue, she gently squeezed my hand—another palpable gesture of comfort.)

Erasmus was the first to propose the handkerchief as a proper means of cleaning the nose, rather than the uncouth wipe of a sleeve. Two centuries later, the handkerchief's role as receptacle for tears was readily accepted, and appreciated, by Rousseau's contemporaries. In her cultural history of 18th century France, Anne Vincent-Buffault writes that, at that time, "tearful displays took place in public: the theater could play the role of a microcosm of meaning on this count. Audiences cried a lot, and took pleasure above all in being seen to cry."[21] The highly visible nature of the handkerchief lent itself well to these public displays of emotional release and audience members prepared these props in anticipation of their climactic turn. Vincent-Buffault directs us to a theatergoer's account of the famous "handkerchief scene" from Abbé Claude Boyer's tragedy *Judith* (1695):

> Imagine two hundred women seated on benches where normally only men are seen and holding handkerchiefs spread on their laps to wipe their tears in the emotional parts. I can remember above all that there was a scene in the fourth act where they burst into tears and which was called the handkerchief scene.[22]

In the theater, then, the handkerchief rendered a spectator's emotional response even more visible from a distance, and in a society that prized displays of sentiment as prominently as 18th century France, these banners were waved proudly to present a dramatically rich character in competition with any that might appear onstage.

In *The Stage Life of Props* Andrew Sofer traces the handkerchief's history onstage to its first appearance in the tenth century *Visitatio Sepulchri* ceremony. As recorded by Saint Ethelwold, the text concludes by directing those portraying the three Marys to display the burial cloth which once had held the body of Christ. The shroud becomes evidence of a body that is no longer there, inviting the attendant clergy into faith: "Christ's presence is paradoxically demonstrated by his absence, which is symbolized by the metonymic piece of cloth."[23] Sofer goes on to describe how, several centuries later, Thomas Kyd and his contemporaries on the early modern stage "exploited spectators' residual faith in magical handkerchiefs and longing for ocular experience by transforming the hand-kerchief from a token of all believers' salvation into a personalized fetish that embodies the principle of private vengeance ('Remember you must kill')."[24] He turns to Kyd's *The Spanish Tragedy*, and its prequel *Hieronimo*, where a handkerchief plays many parts that inspire action: from a lover's token, to a blood-soaked remembrance of a friend slain in battle, and finally of a murdered son. The father Hieronimo, bound to avenge his son's death and carrying the stained cloth as his charge, offers another weeping father that very "handkercher" to wipe his eyes—what staunched wounds can also staunch tears. As an emblem of the theater's power of representation as displacement—"the ability to spin out a potentially infinite chain of metonymic displacements that echo each other"—the handkerchief always exists in reference to one who is not there: distant lover, lost friend, murdered son.[25] What once represented divine belief now represented personal obligation to remember past trespasses and to act in the future. Such a handkerchief hailed one into direct, ethical relationships of the most affective sort: passionate love, heartbreak, revenge.

Thus the handkerchief is an exemplary tearful prop; it is a tissue that shrouds the question of presence and absence—obfuscating the distinction between "real" and artificial substance and even the question of whether the tear (the body) is there at all. It supports the passing expression by giving it a material receptacle, turning a performance into a lasting object that might be treasured by a lover or avenger, a relic to worship. It is a signaling device waved like a flag, or incorporated into gestures like a movable frame to draw attention to a hand's configuration, as if it were setting a pose against a fabric backdrop not unlike a curtain. The handkerchief continues to provide material for a hand's action. Luciano Pavarotti famously brought a white handkerchief onstage whenever he performed outside of an operatic role; stranded on a concert hall stage, without portraying a character to direct his action, he did not know how to employ his hands and arms.[26] His white square propped up his bodily attention.

Such digital and signifying games are very much alive today. A black and white photograph in the artist Hal Fischer's 1977 *Gay Semiotics Series* shows the rears of two men in tight-fitting jeans, a handkerchief hanging from a back pocket of each. With a cheeky (pun intended) nod to conceptual art's analytical use of language and to structuralist ethnography's reading of a culture, passages of text overlay the image:

Handkerchiefs signify behavioral tendencies through both color and placement. A blue handkerchief placed in the right hip pocket serves notice that the wearer desires to play the passive role during sexual intercourse. Conversely, a blue handkerchief placed in the left hip pocket indicates that the wearer will assume the active or traditional male role during sexual contact. The blue handkerchief is commonly used in the treatment of nasal congestion and in some cases holds no meaning in regard to sexual preferences.[27]

This iconographic writing, in which the fabric invites certain actions or makes signs to be read from a distance—say, across a theater auditorium—finds a material corollary in other instances of writing printed atop or woven into the very fabric itself. Hand-embroidery might convey private messages and meaning, sewn by intimates, or more public statements and mementoes in the work of professional seamstresses. Factories flourished in the 19th century, producing kerchiefs en masse that illustrated everything from records of public events, to palmistry, to the latest dance moves. In these various ways, the handkerchief is a blank sheet for the appearance of signification.

For the actor, the handkerchief also telegraphs a reaction to tears that may or may not, in fact, be forthcoming. Like the magician working sleight of hand beneath a silk kerchief, skilled actors may use the handkerchief—when appropriate to character and context—as a mask to hide the eyes, and thus to hide the presence or absence of tears, from viewers. So then, apart from its more intimate and unusual communication passed from hand to hand, as between Julie and her lover, the kerchief can make the advent of tears more visible from a distance. Across the auditorium between audience members, or across the lip of a stage between actor and audience, the handkerchief hails another from afar. Whether the tears are there or not is immaterial; the eye is dried, the flag is waved. I announce my surrender to the upheaval, even if the wave has not actually swallowed me up.

Sunglasses

The hidden eyes. A one-way street. She faces into the distance, her gaze masked by an overlarge pair of sunglasses. The train has just pulled out of the station, fluorescent bulbs running a line into the dark beyond.

Something is wrong, for only celebrities wear sunglasses inside, let alone in the dark; otherwise, such shades hide eyes bruised black and blue, or rimmed red from too much weeping. Something is wrong because she is weeping. Two streaks run down the cheek facing us, catching the light as another single drop hangs pendant on her chin.

The woman beside her reads a paper. This second woman has turned our way slightly, as if she felt the scene beside her, or were aware of the photographer, while pretending not to look. This other woman is blurred in the distance; I cannot follow her eyes, though she is as much a witness to the scene as I am, answering my more direct gaze with the surreptitious look of another. The woman crying is surrounded: on either side, she is watched, but only in a mediated manner: that other one with her paper, me cast as photographer—we cannot intervene. Her glasses are a screen, obscuring the eyes, refusing the possibility of acknowledgement.

> Over a year I wore the crying glasses while travelling on public transport in all the cities I visited. The glasses functioned using a pump system which, hidden inside my jacket, allowed me to pump water up out of the glasses and produce a trickle of tears down my cheeks. The glasses were conceived as a tool to enable the representation of feelings in public spaces. Over the months of wearing the glasses they became an external mechanism which enabled the manifestation of internal and unidentifiable emotions.

So says the wall text that accompanies Hayley Newman's photograph. The last two sentences echo each other practically word for word to describe a subtle shift from Newman's intended sense of the prop to its actual use. What was intended as a "tool" to *represent* a mask of "sadness" in its publicly recognizable form became "an external mechanism" to *enable* the wearer to manifest "unidentifiable emotions," the unwieldy strangeness of actual affect. She had thought the glasses a tool with a specific use—representation—but over time they had shown themselves to inspire internal forces that overstepped neatly contained representation. The tears made or enabled the feeling.

This shift shows how the theatrical prop has unexpected consequences; artifice produces real feelings and surprising events for the user and her public. The artist claims to have prepared a device that harnesses this indeterminate power, even as it disarms its capacity for engaging the public in which it appears. Sunglasses can act as "an aid to melancholia," hiding the eyes of the one who cries, foreclosing the circuit of ocular exchange and preventing contact with another. The tears of the melancholic form a self-enclosed feedback loop, while tears of mourning feed into relations, create communities and contagions of feeling.

Newman's forthright explanation is also masked behind a fictional pair of sunglasses. *Crying Glasses (An Aid to Melancholia)* was produced as part of the artist's *Connotation* series, exhibited in her first solo show "Connotations—Performance Images 1994–98." Like this piece, each work in the series shows a single photograph of Newman in situ, a caption describing the action with a directness that recalls the performance documentation of early Body Art and performance art. A brief passage appended to the exhibition explains the ruse:

> The photographs in the series were staged and performed by myself with most of the images being taken by the photographer Casey Orr over a week in the summer of 1998. The dates, locations, photographers and contexts for the performances cited in the text panels are fictional. In all instances the action had to be performed for the photograph but did not take place within the circumstances or places outlined in the supporting text.

The *Connotations* series offers fascinating imagined theaters for us to play out. Like many great performance art works, they appear as jokes told from a contrary perspective. The forms are the same—man asks a friend to shoot him because he wants to know what it feels like (Chris Burden), couple kisses until they nearly pass out (Ulay and Abramović), man pretends he is a dog (Oleg Kulik), woman dresses as the King of Solana Beach (Eleanor Antin), man crawls the length of Wall Street (William Pope.L), and so on—but the consequences are quite serious. Or from a still different perspective, they are like metaphors taken literally, for what is a joke but a metaphor gone awry? "Aristotle says that metaphor causes the mind to experience itself in the act of making a mistake," writes Anne Carson in her study of error, the prose poem "Essay on What I Think About Most."[28] Performance art can act as an intentional mistake in our habitual ways of occupying the world that causes the mind to experience itself anew.

Like the handkerchief, this prop obscures the site and sight of crying from our view. We cannot see the weeper's eyes to track the source of these tears. Newman obscures the actual terms of the event photographed in much the same way—what brought on these waters if they were not, as her first written text avers, the work of a water pump hidden in her jacket? Were these "real" tears or the output of some other mechanism? In other words, her *Crying Glasses* are themselves propped up devices for simulation, though that does not diminish their affective charge. Props cover the production of tears with a surface of signification; it is as if someone had written "I am crying" on a placard and hid behind its announcement. The tears flow outward even so, quite literally leaking beyond the sign's frame, manifesting other affects that escape the identification of both the crier and their witness.

III. Prompts

Onions

The tears live in an onion that should water this sorrow.
—ANTONY AND CLEOPATRA[29]

The performance artist Marina Abramović is fond of claiming that in the theater "[t]he knife is not real, the blood is not real, and the emotions are not real. Performance is just the opposite: the knife is real, the blood is real, and the emotions are real."[30] Yes: with the rarest of exceptions, the theater does not wound its actors and let their blood flow freely. But fake blood can produce strong affects and very real emotions. Sofer writes of how stage blood acquired sacred power in the medieval theater, as real as the wafer transubstantiated into flesh, and overt artifice can even accentuate the distressing impression of violence onstage.[31] There's a scene in a performance by the Societas Raffaello Sanzio that I still cannot escape even after nearly twenty years: in the white marble chamber that is the room of Law, an actor dressed in a police uniform uncaps a plastic water bottle as a second policeman strips to his undergarments. The first policeman pours stage blood onto his nearly naked companion, then proceeds to beat this "blood"-drenched other with a truncheon. He relents only to catch his breath and to open a second bottle, streaming more of the sticky liquid onto the form that shudders at his feet. The blood is fake, prosthetic like Dafoe's tears, but the stomach-churning feeling produced is very real. Contra Abramović, the company's director Romeo Castellucci is fond of saying, "I believe in fake blood."[32]

In the video performance *The Onion* (1996), Abramović appears from the shoulders up, backed by a cobalt sky and looking upward. A melancholic's weather, clear skies filled with loss. Or a saint's blue, the Mother Mary. William Gass writes that "both Christ and the Virgin wear mantles of blue because as the clouds depart the Truth appears."[33] Any truth that appears here is compromised by the large onion Abramović holds in her hand, still skinned in lustrous copper. Her full mouth bites into the raw bulb again and again; the tears come and keep coming. As she devours the onion, a recording of the artist's voice loops over the scene:

> I am tired of changing planes so often, waiting in the waiting rooms, bus stations, train stations, airports. [...] I am tired of being ashamed of my nose being too big or my ass being too large, ashamed of the war in Yugoslavia. I want to go away, somewhere so far that I am unreachable by fax or telephone. I want to get old, really old so that nothing matters any more. I want to understand and see clearly what is behind all this. I want to not want anymore.

Her lamentation concerns the banal pressures a successful artist faces—called this way and that by too many invitations—and those pressures exerted by sexism and ageism. Her shame about outsized body parts precedes and supersedes the shame about the war in her home country; even her priorities are shameful. Exposed and arranged in such a manner, Abramović's melodrama seems intended to invite rebuke, even a comic bathos that she both indulges and forecloses. Wanting "to not want anymore," to curtail this ravenous list and cease her endless hunger, she devours the least palatable of vegetables, one that eats the eater in turn.[34]

That burning sensation you feel when you slice open an onion is the work of acid on the eyes. Cutting an onion's skin releases the chemical propanethial S-oxide into the air, which produces a small amount of sulphuric acid when it contacts the basal tears in the eye.[35] Reflex tears come in waves to clear the eye of this searing substance. You cannot decide to ignore the provocation: the body performs its emergency measure, with no room for intention to intervene. You act despite your self-control.

Such a reliable prompt has long been a boon to performers. As one of many examples, *The Taming of the Shrew* opens with an elaborate frame play, where a lord has his page-boy dress as a woman and pretend to be the wife of a drunkard on whom he wishes to play a trick. In other words, the lord has his page act as many boys would act on the early modern stage—as a woman. The lord commands the boy to use tears to ensure a convincing part, and toward that end, suggests he secret an onion within a handkerchief, combining prop and prompt in one:

And if the boy have not a woman's gift
To rain a shower of commanded tears,
An onion will do well for such a shift,
Which, in a napkin being close convey'd,
Shall in despite enforce a watery eye.[36]

The theatricality of early modern gender play finds in the onion a means for the material "shift" from boy to woman.

In his recreation of one of the queer artist and filmmaker Jack Smith's rambling solo performances, *What's Underground About Marshmallows*, Ron Vawter produces an onion and delicately cuts it open while offering his sparkling eyes to the stage's light. Vawter/Smith's monologue is an exercise in suspension, a rambling accumulation of tinsel, tulle, and trash that never arrives; it exemplifies what Giulia Palladini has called an instance of performative "foreplay" that idles time rather than give in to capitalist production.[37] Here, too, the onion encapsulates the hollow core of a performance that is gendered feminine or queer, a seduction of veil upon veil. A provoker of faulty tears that can nonetheless incite heartfelt confessions, Abramović's onion stands in for the theatrical complex. It is an architecture composed of translucent lenses, a depth entirely of surfaces, one petal after another peeling away while sustaining the promise of a center. It is a mechanism that prompts weeping without an emotional impetus—like stepping into a tearjerker and noting the rising strings, the ludicrous turn of events, even as your eyes fill and overflow.

In Abramović's performance the onion is real, the tears are real, but the sincerity of the avowed emotional distress remains undecided. In other words, it is a performance crosshatched by opposing forces that batter Abramović's neat distinction between theatrical and performative reality, their causes and effects. Jennifer Doyle sees the piece as an interrogation of the artifice that constrains Abramović in her role as an artist:

In the end, it is not the authenticity of her tears that you question but their artificiality, in part because as you watch this video it is hard not to have a physical reaction in sympathy with the manifest difficulty of eating a raw onion while suppressing the impulse to gag.[. . .] Here what starts as a theatrical production of artificial tears appears to morph into real tears over the artificiality of the performance of her daily life.[38]

As is the way in performance, the artificial intermingles with the actual. Like Doyle, I cannot help but imagine the sharp bitterness and funky acidity of the onion, like a flower blooming underground. The "physical reaction in sympathy" with Abramović's bodily act is not so far removed from that which one might feel in response to any actor's tears. Cognitive science has located this sympathetic feeling in the mirror neuron, noting how watching another body in motion triggers correlate neurons in the spectator's brain. As Ovid put it, "By looking on sore eyes, our own we wound."[39]

Prompts like onions create a climate for weeping, filling the air and gathering actor and audience alike within their unseen gaseous clouds. If I were there with Abramović, sharing a common air, this affect would run through us both indiscriminately and we would find ourselves weeping in unison. Her isolation in this ordeal reiterates the alienation expressed by her lament—a distance from things and herself, a lone figure against an empty sky.

In a pair of video performances that respond to this same prompt, the artist Patty Chang accentuates the relationality of crying that is missing from *The Onion*'s lamentation of isolation. Reflecting on her first encounter with Abramović's earlier performance, Chang recounts how "I felt it was sad to be having this experience alone. Sharing an awful experience with another person binds you together."[40] *For Abramović Love Cocteau* (2000) is a single-channel video that begins by showing two Asian women—the artist and an unnamed other—holding a kiss while both weep profusely. Divorced from any context or character, the scene invites all kinds of projected narratives of intimacy—lovers on the edge of sorrowful parting or on the other side of joyful reunion. But as the video plays forward, we discover that time moves in reverse here, and a magical reconstitution appears before our eyes: mouthful by mouthful, an onion blossoms between their parted lips. They have been eating it in turns, or in this queer time of feeling backward, as Heather Love puts it, their kisses have articulated a fruit of shared sorrow and sustenance.[41]

Developing this concept further, Chang created the two-channel video *In Love* the following year. Again, the artist appears locked in a passionate kiss, but this time with her mother on one screen, her father on another screen. Each video is caught in a loop that runs backwards through time. What begins as an incestuous kiss, prompting feelings of revulsion and shame, slowly develops to show another unsettling repast: each child-parent couple at once feeding off, and offering up, this multi-layered bitter fruit. Amber Jamilla Musser writes of these prompts in terms of an "automaticity" that "suggests sensation without—or at least out of joint with—feeling. [. . . Chang's work] highlights the contours of what constitutes normative comportment and the underlying assumption that Black and brown people do not *feel*, they merely react."[42] Western stereotypes read people of Asian descent as capable of superhuman endurance, carrying the burden of labor without flinching. Feeling, according to such a regime, is only possible through mechanism. Perhaps the consumption

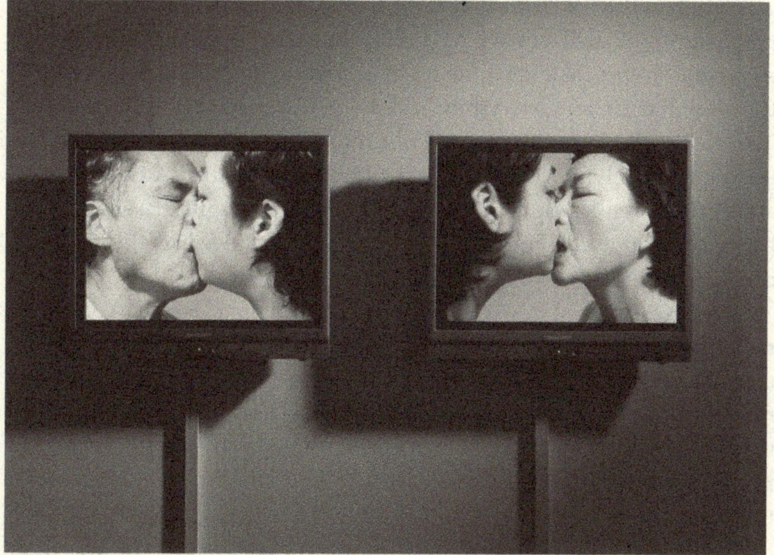

Figure 10 Patty Chang, *In Love*. Two-channel video installation. 3 minutes, 28 seconds, 2001. Courtesy of the artist.

of such a viscerally unpalatable vegetable also invokes the fever dreams of white bread Americans rife with phantasms of the eating habits of Asian Americans.[43]

Chang returns repeatedly to liquid states and relations—pools of water, mother's milk—such that she, in the words of stephanie mei huan, "forges a reservoir in which visitors can bathe in their fears—the porosity of one's anxieties intermingling with those of others."[44] Her concern with prompted acts expresses an anxiety about loss of self-control, about becoming an automaton forced into an imposed feeling, even as her works produce a form of comfort in sharing that abandonment with another.[45] You find yourself subjugated by a power that moves through you, but your tears intermingle with another who is similarly undone. A painful knowledge grounded in the lived experience of sensation that words, image, or representation cannot sufficiently convey: a community, even love, is born from such common suffering, consolidated in the common onion.

Tear Gas

The label on the toolbox says that it is non-lethal, says that with proper preparation, all will behave as anticipated. This feeling is ephemeral: some discomfort for a few hours, but no lasting harm. You will disperse, the air will clear, and everything will be as it was before, order restored. The show will be over. Traffic will resume.

The label is lying. These acts scar; catch and hold the breath, take it away; their casings burn; their force punctures fragile tissues leaving holes like hollowed eggs. The toolbox is full of dangerous things. Even crying can be fatal.

The gases released from cutting an onion, a pepper, or a piece of horseradish can irritate the eyes and swell the throat, making sight and speech difficult. They can disarm the most steadfast intentions, reduce the regimented body to an uncoordinated leaky heap. Manufactured lachrymatory agents—tear gases and pepper sprays—amplify these effects greatly: pepper spray (or *Oleoresin Capsicum*) is 6 to 15 times hotter than the hottest habanero pepper.

The first person to appear on the screen tries to read the words in English, but soon begins to squint, to falter. On another screen, a man attempts the same in Spanish, then a third starts up in Farsi. They keep seizing up, and the camera keeps cutting away. *Other Gases* (2020), a three-channel video performance by the Iranian artist Mona Mohagheghi, draws out the connection between natural lachrymatory agents and their monstrous doubles. In a variety of languages, a series of speakers read the articles of the Chemical Weapons Convention on riot-control agents from 1997.[46] These articles forbid the use of chemical weapons and gases in warfare, even as police and security forces worldwide make extensive use of tear gas on citizens and civilians. Onions cut off-screen begin irritating the readers' eyes and throats, and soon they are coughing, gasping, wiping away tears, until eventually reading and speech become impossible. The long lines of dry bureaucratic text fragment into disjointed phrases as the readers cut from screen to screen, their many broken statements overlapping into noise. Here the abstract language of international law is undercut by the actual embodied practice of the police state. When facing civil disobedience, police forces around the world employ prompts that make a speechless and gagging body, disregarding the legal language that forbids the use of these same materials.

While the Paris police experimented with lachrymatory agents against barricaded criminals as early as 1912, chemical gases were first used in the trench warfare of World War I to flush out forces from their fortifications and into enemy fire, or to directly deliver fatal effects.[47] The horror of these confrontations inspired the Geneva Protocol of 1925, the first of several international agreements to ban the use of chemical weapons in the field of war, but which did not disallow the development or possession of such weapons. As a result, less lethal products were embraced on domestic fronts worldwide to quell civil unrest. In her history of tear gas, Anna Feigenbaum writes that "[w]hile the French and Germans had led the development of lachrymatory agents during World War I, the United States was seen as the producer of the world's tear gas."[48] Many nations were initially uncomfortable with the optics of subjecting their own citizens to weapons that were deemed unacceptable in warfare, but as Feigenbaum traces, this compunction eroded over subsequent decades. By the 1960s, tear gas use was widespread across the US and contributed to the most egregious occasions of police violence during the era of civil rights protests: Selma 1965, Chicago 1968, Berkeley 1969. Likewise, colonial forces relied on tear gas to suppress mass protests for independence and other rights in outposts around the world. At first resistant to using these substances on its own citizens, it took the Troubles in Northern Ireland—a conflict at the interstices of colonial and domestic unrest—for the UK to finally embrace the domestic use of tear gas. Tear gas suffuses present conflicts from Ghaza to Gezi to Chile, from the Black Lives Matter protests to Standing Rock. It participates in a massive multi-national market, largely unregulated and distributed with scant research on the immediate or long-term effects of exposure.[49]

What we do know is distressing to say the least. Contrary to industry claims that these are non-lethal weapons, tear gas can cause lasting and even fatal injury. In the First Intifada, for example, sixty-seven deaths were linked to tear gas use by Israeli Defense Forces.[50] In addition to the effects of the chemicals themselves, the canisters and grenades used for delivery of the agents are highly flammable and employ the same mechanisms and manufacture as machine guns and grenade launchers. These forceful projectiles have broken bones, punctured soft tissue, destroyed eyes, and caused severe head injuries.[51]

What we recognize by the name of "tear gas" encompasses a range of lachrymatory chemical compounds, including CS (2-chlorobenzylidene malononitrile), CN (chloroacetophenone) and CR (dibenzoxazepine), as well as pepper sprays. The name is somewhat misleading as none of these agents are actually gaseous; they are distributed as fine particulate smokes or sprays, which produce a sticky moisture that clings to surfaces and skins alike. Tear gases assault the eyes, yes, but also the throat and lungs; they cause bare skin to flare up in rashes and sores.

This is the most all-consuming form of involuntary acting. The prompt works over the entire body and draws the self along in its tangle. Such a comprehensive corporeal possession elides the intention and will of the subject. It forces one to perform despite oneself:

> It takes away your reasoning, instantly. You don't know what to do. Then you try to scream, you can't breathe [. . .] And all this is in like ten seconds. Then you just start crying. Tears just flow down, you start sneezing, coughing. If you don't get out of that five-yard ratio, then you're instantly going down to the ground.[52]

Those caught in its halo suffer a collapse of control—blurring of vision, coughing, leaking mucus from mouth and nose, nausea, and of course crying. Voluntary action shuts down as one attempts to manually maintain what are usually automatic processes. People have asphyxiated when caught in a hanging cloud, or they have trampled others in desperate attempts to escape—a most horrific manner of involuntary acting. Authority takes advantage of the automatic response of reflex tears to subjugate the body under its control.[53]

Tear gases prop up power by acting as a "force multiplier," meaning that they not only inflict direct harm upon victims, but also diminish the efficacy of those resisting power. Industry advocates celebrate the fact that these weapons allow a smaller security force to "manage" a larger crowd, but studies also show that officers are more likely to employ more violent means of subduing opposition under the umbrella of the gas. If protests and demonstrations work by assembling disparate individuals into collective wholes, tear gas contests these means by fragmenting and dispersing masses, clearing occupied spaces. An early trade press publication advocating tear gas in 1921 wrote that "[t]he tear gases appear to be admirably suited to the purpose of isolating the individual from the mob spirit . . . he is thrown into a condition in which he can think of nothing but relieving his own distress."[54] Or, as a later report from the 1960s put it, "affected persons are incapable of effective concerted action."[55] In this way, tear gas is an anti-theatrical agent. It disbands a gathered audience or chorus into wayward individuals. Clouds prevent journalists and citizens outside the scene from witnessing what happens within, just as they blind those trapped under its haze. These agents prompt a crying that is difficult to see, disrupting the inherently relational aspect of tears, how they cry out for a response.

An extreme instance of the prompt, tear gas clarifies the contradictory aspect of prompted tears more generally: on one hand, such a tear is a pure and undiluted articulation of an individual impression. Like a finger touching an open wound, the prompted tear indexes an affect without involving a character or subject's particularizing diversion in the flow from sensation to expression. There is nothing you can do to stop it: your body will submit before its pressure and open avenues for this affect to continue its forceful movement through you. At the same time, the prompted tear is also essentially removed from any conception of an intentional psychological self, detaching crying from its claim to authenticity. It shows how affect can work around, or subjugate, the subject and operate with its exclusion, how tears might signal a being without self, a purely affective presence. Peggy Kamuf writes of crying more generally as "a kind of fit, a seizure of the body and its portals by the involuntary reflexes of some of its parts: heart rhythm, diaphragm, throat, tear ducts, vocal apparatus concert, for as long as the fit lasts, against the normal state of a body, the one that can act under control of something like a will."[56] Tears manipulate the motions of the crying one, take over their body and their sight, and disarm them. Prompted tears make the crier an object, passive under an affect's force. If this is, as Abramović has it, a "real" performance, it is a reality that does not include its subject as anything other than a contingent means for its expression. The subject becomes a performing thing.

CHAPTER 6

On Getting Water from a Stone
Or, Do Androids Weep Electric Tears?

An audience gathers in a desert canyon for a production of *The Cherry Orchard*, Anton Chekhov's great play of historic upheaval and stasis. The play never really gets under way, because in an inspired casting decision the actors in this production—boulders strewn along the chasm floor—are working at their own glacial pace. This presents a challenge for the spectators, for, "[d]etermined to watch, to sense, until its end, they are outlived by the performance, by the imperceptibly moving rocks."[1]

In his contribution to *Imagined Theatres*, Nick Salvato proposes a durational performance that far outstrips the lifespan of all acting conventions—and, of all theatrical architecture, apart perhaps from those ancient amphitheaters carved from the very hills of the Greco-Roman world. Indeed, to find some viable performers for this proposition, one might need to turn to the statues mounted on the *scaenae frons*, the "permanent" architectural backing to the ancient Roman theater, whose eroded and defaced visages attest to the slow drama of eons but appear "imperceptibly moving" under our narrowed human sight.

The conception of stone as inanimate stretches back at least to Aristotle's *De Anima*, when the philosopher proposed a notion of soulful living that was wide enough to include the vegetal but could not extend as far as the purely material. This exile from the land of affect is a specifically Western inheritance, for many Indigenous perspectives accept the interanimacy of things as a given. As Carolyn Dean writes,

[d]enying the constant (though imperceptible) changeability of rocks, Western thought has most often identified stone as the binary opposite

> of, rather than a complement to, things recognized as animate. [. . .] In the ancient Andes, however, stones were often perceived *as* inhabitants of settlements; in fact, they were believed to be the original owners of certain territories, and they were often the most important residents of particular places. They were clothed, fed, and conversed with.[2]

These personable stones of the Inka might have been perceptibly moved; they might have wept. But in Western drama the prospect of a weeping statue is the stuff of miracles.

Over the course of this book, I've discussed how tears extend bridges between one and another by means of a common liquid medium. Long before language names a need, tears tie infants to their parents in a shared relation of care. Can this commiserate strand join the farthest shores of self and other, crossing the chasm that divides the human from the non-human, or even between the living being and non-living material? On the surface, this is an impossible claim: animals can audibly cry in pain or fear or sadness, but verifiable evidence suggests that humans alone are capable of weeping emotional tears. (Perhaps performance lets animals cry the emotional tears that science does not allow them?) I indulge here in even more outlandish fancy to consider the prospect not of the things that make us weep, but of the thing that itself weeps.

Such material tears would reveal an undisclosed interiority at odds with the uniform consistency we ascribe to objects in everyday life. Marx taught that an object is defined and constrained by its usage, and any excessive qualities that might distract from that use are disposable addendums to the monolithic purpose toward which that object is oriented. To become a subject ourselves, we must make objects of the world around us and thereby ignore any wayward character peculiar to this block of stone that sets it apart from others of its kind. We gather and name our objects under the umbrella of their larger abstracted use. This is especially the case in realist and naturalist approaches to the theater, where, as Eleanor Margolies writes, "the material reality of the prop is 'looked through' to get at something 'deeper' which is character, or human nature, or 'reality.' Materiality is treated as secondary to human life—thus the object becomes a 'prop' or 'accessory.' As a corollary, the relationship between the human performer and the object is one of 'use' or 'attribute.'"[3]

However, when an object loses contact with its use, it sheds its identifying name and becomes an alienated "thing," set apart from the human community. It appears with such granularity that a word as simple as "rock" or "post" no longer fits comfortably. Performance makers who work with objects know this well. Peter Schumann of the Bread and Puppet Theater puts it nicely:

> We who think of ourselves as subjects don't even know donkeys well enough, not to speak of fence posts and rocks, to which we assign the job of object, because we haven't discovered their individuality yet. As a donkeyman—which means, related to donkeys and therefore also to fence posts and rocks—I shy away from that particular definition: object. Object exists only because we are deceived into being subject [. . .][4]

Schumann's unusual phrasing undoes grammar as readily as it undermines the subject/object binary that he critiques. Knowing that objects intertwine with their subjects, he imagines himself a hybrid creature composed of all the things with which he holds an affective relation: the donkey, the field, and its features. My writing here plays an extended riff on another donkeyman—actually, a donkeyboy or, better still, a donkeypuppetboy: Pinocchio. Alienated though he may be from the uses of other blocks of wood, I turn to this named thing precisely because Pinocchio nonetheless seeks to reestablish his connection with humanity through roundabout means: tears. This essay on misbehaving things is also roundabout in its way, running rampant across genres (fables, slapstick, children's literature, and science fiction) and media (sculpture, painting, poetry, prose, film, and theater), holding disparate parts together like one of Schumann's hybrid creatures.

Underneath all, I am curious about how tears enliven the material world. If liveness might be characterized as a matter of shared presence and present, a common here and a common now, crying forces a reconsideration of the objectival on both accounts: in terms of feeling (here) and temporality (now). To think of an object as capable of crying is to conceive of it possessing a private life, a capacity for feeling commensurate with my own. According to what the theorist Rei Terada has called the "expressive hypothesis," emotional expression is presumed to signify human interiority. Affectively, tears show that an object can participate in an event and change along the way, that it can *have* an experience.

Temporally, the weeping object refutes any seeming permanent capture in an eternal present that might be attached to the non-human world and instead exposes itself to the transitory at a human scale. I begin by considering how the miracle of the crying statue is tied to this collapse of divine eternity and human immediacy.

I. Hol(e)y Statues

I imagine that a statue stands before me, carved of stone. It presents itself as a solid whole: the trembling swell and flush at the skin, the chambers and flows below the surface, are all stilled and filled in. For the sake of ease, let's say the statue looks like a person. Say it resembles someone I once knew, or someone I may know in the time to come. Which is to say that I do not know them now, in this present, since the statue and I hardly seem to share a common time. What eyes it has are not for me; they are withdrawn into the perpetual country of its material home, where time is measured in eons of erosion. They survey a land of the unliving, a duration extending outside the rhythms of biological development and decay. Or, rather, they face outward, but regard a graveyard, a church, a hall of justice, the city square—places of marble and granite where authority seeks to impress itself outside of the flux of the day-to-day and to pretend its own kind of unmoved eternity.

René Magritte's many paintings of statues derive their disquieting edge from the view they offer on such a voided landscape. There are the petrified businessmen of *The Song of the Violet* (1951), weighed down by long coats and clutching roughhewn boulders in place of briefcases. Pedestrian Sisyphuses, they labor against a close sky that is itself a blanket of stone, as if to give new meaning to the name Wall Street. Not merely an instance of Midas's touch-turned-Medusa's-gaze, the whole scene is gripped by granite, including the very air itself. In *Memory of a Journey [Souvenir de Voyage]* (1955), another man in a similar coat, book in hand, stands beside a resting lion (some echo of Saint Jerome here). Behind them, a table holds an iconic "still life" arrangement of a bowl of fruit and a lit candle. Everything—even the flickering flame—is painted the texture of stone. Each figure in this allegorical vision represents a distinct measure of time—man, beast, book, vegetal, elemental—washed in the uniform gray of a past that will stretch unmoving into the future. Other canvases under the same name isolate individual elements of this claustrophobic configuration. These paintings enlarge those petrified fruit so that they fill a room (*Memory of a Journey*, 1952; and another version from 1963), as if a stone's outsized temporal extension required a correlate in spatial terms, or they erect a granite candle and granite flame on a dim shore strewn with loose rocks (*Memory of a Journey*, 1962), something of a lighthouse in reverse, inviting ruin.[5]

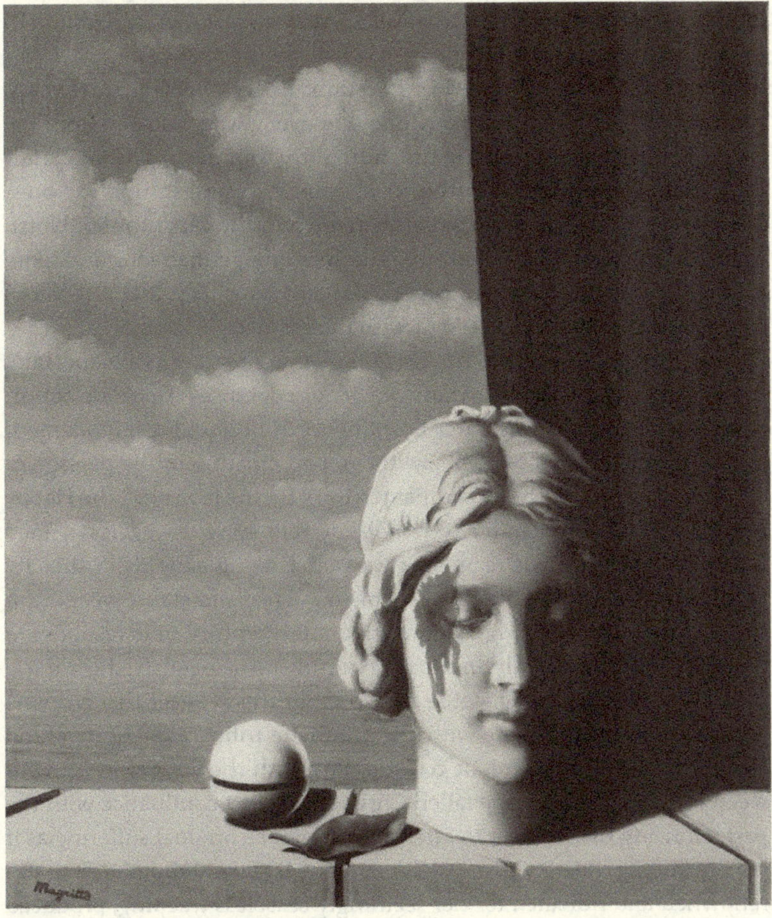

Figure 11 René Magritte, *La mémoire*, 1948, oil on canvas. Collection of the Wallonia-Brussels Federation. © 2023 C. Herscovici / Artists Rights Society (ARS), New York.

Magritte excavates a related obsession in a series of paintings titled *Memory [Mémoire]*, each with the same central composition: a bust in stone looks outward, perhaps the Greek goddess of memory Mnemosyne figured in stately marble; a splash of brilliant red blood stains one side of the face, like a tear that has ruptured the eye.[6] The offending object sits beside the wounded sculpture: a small sphere with a line dividing it in half, a sleigh bell or grelot. (In one oil sketch, a clutch of eggs replaces the bell—potential life replacing potential sound.) This figure for the memory that "rings a bell" is accompanied by a second object—different in each painting—a leaf or flower or whatever, which seems to act as a metonym for the recollection in question. In each version of *Memory*, the open sky appears behind a window or over a wall, released from the touch of stone, and unfolding the diurnal rhythm of sunsets, of clouds in motion. If the past is a statue, its eyes fixed in retreat from the present, these blows reopen the remembered wound and let time spill forth again—bright with blood and sun. The seeming permanence and fixity of the "inanimate" thing is made fragile and transitory, and vice versa, human frailty is made conversant with the eternal.

Transparent tears would not leave as visible a marker as a bloodstain, but they would accomplish a similar collapse of tenses. There are countless tales of stone-faced figures breaking forth in liquid tears to lament the public cataclysms that they witness, participating in the passage of surrounding events. This is familiar territory for the fable: in "The Happy Prince" (1888), for example, Oscar Wilde tells how the ageless gilded statue of a youth sheds tears over the suffering he beholds in the city below.[7] It also recurs in the annals of history: I read of a statue weeping in the days before the sacking of Rome in the 16th century, or in response to the siege of Syracuse, Italy, in the 18th century.[8] Analogously, the miracle of the crying or bleeding statue confirms for the believer that a divine presence can commiserate with the mundane tribulations of mankind and that mere mortals might commiserate with the eternal in turn. To weep in the present for the fallen Christ is to join a confluence with the past, allowing the believer to attend their savior's original suffering as if it were undergone now. The English mystic Margery Kempe (1373–1438), renowned and ridiculed for her seemingly ceaseless weeping, produced such volumes of tears in order, at least in part, to keep the savior live, the wounds of the martyr running fresh.[9] In the early modern period, devotional paintings of the weeping Virgin Mary (the Mater Dolorosa or Lady of Sorrows) were often paired with the divine figure of Christ to provide an avenue for pious lamentation.[10] This aligns with Julia Kristeva's claim that "Christ, the Son of man, when all is said and done, is 'human' only through his mother," or perhaps we should say his "weeping mother."[11] In her study of Marian worship, Charlene Villaseñor Black writes that "meditating on Mary's eyes and tears was a form of devotion. [. . .] tears slide down her face, a particularly effective visual strategy in

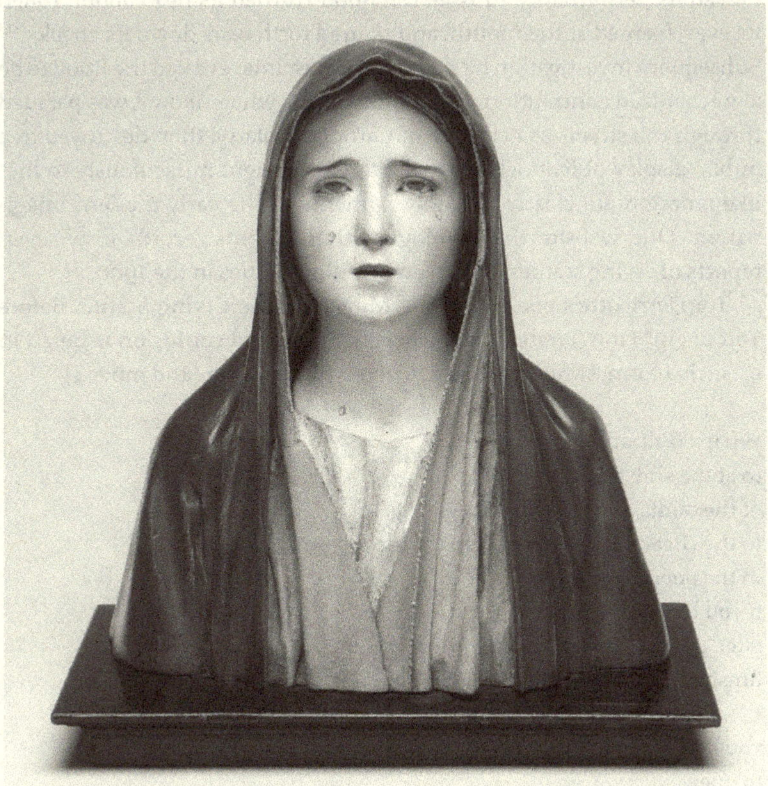

Figure 12, Pedro de Mena, *Virgin of Sorrows. Mater Dolorosa.* (circa 1670-1675) Smaller than life-size bust of wood, carved in several sections, and polychromed over a white ground, with inlaid glass eyes, hair upper lashes, and three applied tears. © The Fitzwilliam Museum, Cambridge.

sculpture, where her eyes and tears were often made of glass, creating powerful and believable reality effects that brought the events of Holy Week to life."[12] Indeed, while paintings were far more common, a few polychrome wooden sculptures of the Mater Dolorosa with glass tears, such as the expressive masterpieces created by the Spanish artist Pedro de Mena (1628–1688), brought this commiserating form into more palpable contact with worshippers.

The crucifix known as the Boxley Rood was an even more active vessel for divine commiseration. According to Nicholas Partridge, who witnessed its performance in 1538, the Rood "turned its head about, rolled its eyes, foamed at the mouth, and poured forth tears down its cheeks."[13] Subsequent investigation by skeptical Protestants revealed the Rood to be a mechanized contraption of wires and gears, whereupon it was paraded through the streets as evidence of Catholic idolatry, then destroyed in a public display of iconoclastic zeal. Statues brought miraculously to life-like emotion are clearly not only figments of the early modern imagination. One website that catalogues these events records forty-seven reports of crying statues and seven bleeding statues in the 1900s.[14]

Toi Derricotte's poem "On the Miracle of the Crying Statue: Before You Begin" (1997) reiterates the peculiar temporal confusion ushered in by such a form, simultaneously frozen while moving (and moved).

What a realization to come
to at the end: that the tears
of the saints don't dry, that they cling
to the cheeks of the Virgin for a thousand years, that even
in the poems you write,
if you look back years
later, the tears are still there, unfinished.
    How sad, just as
you begin to move forward,
to open
the creaking
mouth of the body,
to taste again the same tears.[15]

Like all titles, this poem's title sits before the poem proper, yet it also refers to a still earlier precedent "before you begin." Derricotte directs her address to a "you" who is the poet herself and the reader at once. Both appear suspended before the beginning of writing and reading the poem, perhaps even before the beginning of one's being, a mineral vein that stretches under generations. When the poem begins in earnest, you realize yourself already "at the end." And what is this end that sits nested within, even as you are just beginning to "move forward"? In a second sentence, itself distinguished as a separate concluding stanza, you are suddenly cast as the statue too, tasting the tears it weeps. This intermingling across individual differences of self and other is central to the empathetic work of crying. When figured in relationship to a statue, it also invites a form of synchronous empathy across temporal and material difference.

Derricotte, a Black American poet who was raised Catholic, writes of twin histories of lamentation and memorialization here. Of course, statues and poems continue to have a life and to change their affects long after their construction. The poet may have written these words in 1997, but "[i]f you look back years / later"—say, at the time of my writing in 2023—other resonances emerge. As if one needed a reminder, statues (and the monuments that stand and fall across the US in our national reckoning with a racist past) show that there really isn't a time or place "before you begin" since the beginning is always weighted with other beginnings. These tears end up stuck at a difficult juncture: "still there, un-/ finished." They are "still" in both senses of the word, a continuation and yet unmoving. The line break accomplishes something similar, splicing the continually unfinished present "still there," with the "un"-moving "finished" of the past. The crying statue places us in this threshold state, tasting its bitterness whenever we might begin to speak. In the statue's miraculous performance, tears run in a consistent manner like that lone fourth line that stretches margin to margin, ongoing long after the traumatic fact has been carved in stone or written in ink.

These statues are miraculous in part because, apart from the tradition of the Mater Dolorosa, wood or stone sculptures of people crying tears are so exceedingly rare.[16] Classical sculptors did not incorporate tears into their compositions, just as sweat and blood seldom mar the smooth hard surface of their marble skins. Perhaps this is because the liquid state cannot be readily conveyed by the solid, but beyond this, ephemeral feeling has long presented a problem for figurative sculpture. Distinguishing between how temporal and instantaneous art captures a person in the throes of passion, the philosopher, art critic, and progenitor of dramaturgy, G. E. Lessing, posed that sculpture, "if it is to receive immutable permanence from art, must express nothing transitory."[17] In his influential reading, classical sculptors avoided depicting figures at the extremity of their emotion for fear that such an appearance would leave little room for the viewer to imagine a further movement that might thereby contribute to the making of the work. Better to show the flicker of anguish as it just begins to trouble the brow, rather than when it has knotted the visage into a contorted mass. Better the widened eye, than one that is already overfull. Again, the statue must remain in its rigid atemporal state, imperceptibly moved and not moving.

One might disagree with these outdated aesthetic strictures today, but contemporaneous exceptions to this rule do much to support Lessing's claim. In the mid-18th century, German sculptor Johann Christian Ludwig von Lücke produced a series of busts of Heraclitus the weeping philosopher and Democritus the laughing philosopher; he also prepared pairs of children weeping and laughing. Cast in the same bloodless milky white of porcelain or ivory as the sculptural figure itself, the tears in Lücke's works spread like tumorous fleshy fans under the eyes, bulging with the same weight and substance as the wrinkles that furrow their expressive faces. Flesh and excretion share a common consistency. A swaddled crying baby in the collections of the Victoria & Albert Museum is a kitsch nightmare: tears bloom in leafy fronds under the eyes and a long tendril of snot curls from the right nostril. If vegetal analogies come to mind it is because distinctions between forms are monstrously confused here. One cannot discern where the skin begins and the waters end. The uncanny effect is amplified by the open mouth, worked in such a way that the tongue protrudes from a depthless hole, suggesting an interiority that the opaque rendering of the tears belie.[18] The grotesque horror of Lücke's statue frozen mid-cry hinges on its distension of the ideal face's contours: its mouth exposes an unseemly cavity, while its tears swell that surface otherwise.

For Lessing, the open mouth of anguish compromises the form of beauty, twisting the perfected body into the grotesque. Holes and swell-

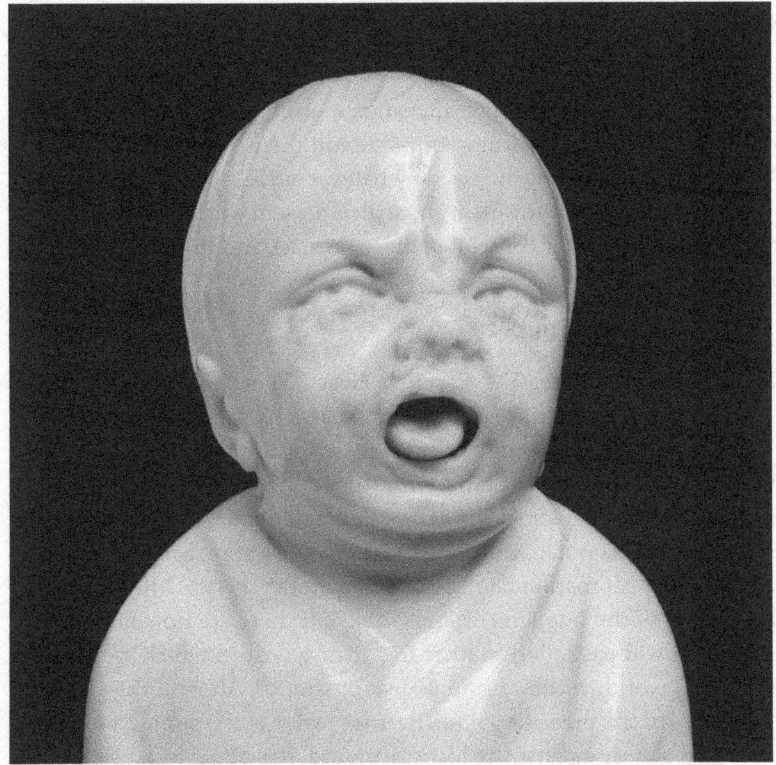

Figure 13 Johann Christian Ludwig Von Lücke, *Crying baby in swaddling clothes.* Statuette in ivory, ca. 1753–1755 © Victoria and Albert Museum, London.

ings also suggest a depth or interiority at odds with the density of sculpture. Kenneth Gross's engaging book *The Dream of the Moving Statue* devotes little attention to the *moved* statue, relegating the bleeding or crying statue to a footnote:

Such images, after all, survive their wounds, and in a rather peculiar way. (One does not pity bleeding or weeping images.) It is hard to imagine that the blood or tears witnessed as flowing from the image or statue emerge from "inside" it, or at least not in the way they come from inside human beings; such blood or tears appertain all too obviously to alien orders of meaning and intention, something that contributes to one's sense of the kind of utterance or knowledge they constitute.[19]

If Gross is correct, then the appearance of an interiority is necessary for one to feel pity. The thing must extend the promise of an obscured unconscious subsisting alongside whatever surface appearance. It must present a self, which means it must also present an occlusion of self, a public and private (unconscious) life—the mask and the face.

II. The Drowned Puppet

Edward's Last Prance. The Feverish Heart. The Ship of Faithlessness Founders. Bipsy's Mistake. The Alberta-based Old Trout Puppet Workshop's *Famous Puppet Death Scenes* presents an anthology of episodes purportedly from the annals of theater history that borrow generic trappings ranging from the misfired cliffhangers of melodrama, to the blood baths of the grand guignol, to the quiet deaths of domestic tragedy. Amidst all, a simple puppet manipulated by two operators plays the MC. In his final scene, one of the puppeteers lends him voice to relate how his impending death will pass "like another in a dreary host in which we will slip from this world, without a single tear or sound." After all the elaborate gimmicks of the preceding hour, here we arrive at the simplest of departures. Lit starkly against the black surround, the puppet is curled into a fetal position. The hand recedes, and the puppet lies there cast off and returned to its inanimate wait. The puppet is living onstage only as long as an operator lends it life, lends it an interiority.

That visible hand distinguishes the puppet from the miracle or magical. Steve Tillis has argued that the tension between the puppet as site of performance and the present but occluded operator forms the basic fascination of the puppet. He suggests that "the signs of life sited on the puppet must themselves be produced *by* life; the puppet's putative performance is the direct result of the *real* performance of a living being behind it."[20] There is nothing such a puppet knows outside its operator's knowledge, no interior space of its own that is hidden from sight. For, "the puppet does not *act*; it is an object that is acted *upon*, an object that is *given* action. The puppet has no will of its own but is only a more or less cleverly constructed and operated tool."[21]

Indeed, the tears of a performing puppet would be the work of a fabricator or operator. On the one hand, they might be features of the fabricator's construction, devices to produce liquid from a wooden eye, such as the hidden reservoirs of water that childhood dolls tap to simulate weeping.[22] My mother tells me about a doll she had as a child that would wet itself from one end or the other—soaking diapers or cascading tears. These are scriptive objects, as Robin Bernstein would have it, whose tearful bouts encourage the child to practice performing proper maternal caregiving.[23] They are fabricated to produce passing affects and lasting effects that discipline the child into expected social roles.

On the other hand, with the guidance of an operator a puppet can itself enact the repertoire of gestures we associate with weeping: the hand brushing away the tear, shoulders trembling under the sway of a shaking breath. Caught in the swell of performance, these gestures seem to give life to the puppet form, make us watch in wonder as an object fulfills our anthropomorphic fantasy. They might also alienate the formulaic gestural performance of crying from actual tears. The director Vsevolod Meyerhold wrote approvingly of how "[w]hen the puppet weeps, the hand holds the handkerchief away from the eyes; when the puppet kills, it stabs its opponent so delicately that the tip of the sword stops short of the breast."[24] In other words, the puppet could highlight the quotational aspect of even those moments that seem to cut to the core of authentic living: weeping and dying. In this light, such a puppet acknowledges that its impenetrable and unchangeable objecthood sits apart from the momentary outburst, the volatile breakdown. It realizes Diderot's dream of a purely externalized acting controlled and shaped wholly by an artist's intent. This was the puppet's primary draw for modernist theatrical visionaries like Heinrich von Kleist, Edward Gordon Craig, and George Bernard Shaw, authors of manifestos celebrating this model performer who could not be compromised by unconscious distraction. According to this view, if a puppet cries, it is the conscious work of its operator.

What of the puppet that could cry without an operator? To imagine such a possibility, we must depart from the realm of embodied performance, for a puppet without an operator can only exist within a fictional space that disregards material performance. We must step into the realm of fiction and fable.

Crying undergirds the most famous exploration of how a puppet deprived of an operator might itself become human. Adopting the pseudonym Collodi, Carlo Lorenzini released *The Adventures of Pinocchio* in serial format between 1881–1883. A darker and stranger tale than the familiar Disney adaptation from 1940, Collodi's picaresque originally ended with the marionette hanging from a tree; it was only with the encouragement of his editor that the writer returned the puppet to life with the newfound determination to become a boy in the second part of the story. Beneath its playful episodes, *Pinocchio* taps into fundamental questions about the nature of privacy and feeling, exploring how empathy might extend across species and material states, and how it allows for transitions between different forms and ways of being. True to his nature, the puppet visits several different theaters in his journeys; an extended close reading will show how tears and crying are the currency for his exchanges in each.

In Collodi's *Pinocchio*, crying announces the beginning of the story by signaling the arrival of the magical puppet-boy. In the first lines of the tale, Mr. Cherry, a drunken carpenter, happens across a log of wood that seems the perfect material for a table leg. When he prepares to chop the wood, its surprising moans give him pause: "Don't hit me too hard!" When he finally strikes a blow, the voice cries "Ow! That hurt!"[25] The carpenter stops in earnest: "There's not a living soul here! Could it possibly be that this piece of wood has learned to cry and moan like a child?" When he begins to plane the wood, it giggles. Horrified by a block of wood that both cries and laughs, he is only too happy to give it to his neighbor, the old and destitute Geppetto, who happens by looking for material to make a marionette that he might use to earn a little money.

Were it a silent and well-behaved log, this wood would play its part in a larger piece of furniture, itself a piece of a larger world of functional objects. But here, the log insists on feeling as the root of individuality; it even acquires a proper name (Geppetto calls the block of wood "Pinocchio" before he even sets chisel to grain). I'm intentionally blurring the distinction between audible crying and the production of tears, since Collodi's *piangere* and *lamentarsi* could as readily be translated as "crying" and "moaning" and, more directly, it is the voice that stops Cherry in his tracks. But that wordless vocalization "Ow!" (*Ohi!* in the Italian) stands in for a shapeless feeling sublated in a block of inarticulate matter. If all children exude potentiality, so full of future, then this block of wood ups the ante: a potential puppet, with itself the potential to become a boy. Crying and laughter signal this potential humanity, obligating the drunk Cherry to treat "it" as a "child" (and, seemingly by default, a boy).

Through the theatrical template of the marionette, Geppetto releases the human crying inside the thing, but tears continue to both guide and derail the wayward puppet-boy until he realizes his ambition and becomes just another human person. Most chapters in the slim book find the puppet or one of his companions crying over hunger, disappointment, fear, or in response to any number of mishaps; Pinocchio himself weeps, cries, or sobs a full twenty-two different times across the thirty chapters of his wanderings (on two other occasions he wants to weep but resists the act). Other animals, people, and performing objects also partake in this voluble discourse of tears: a crafty fox brushes away a tear to arouse the puppet's sympathy, and sincere tears fall from a friendly tuna, several donkeys, and a whole troupe of marionettes. This excessive investment in the economy of tears extends into a larger reliance on other watery ways. Pinocchio nearly dies in the sea three times and his final rebirth from the belly of the Shark resonates with the delinquent Jonah, who was swallowed by a whale when he tried to absent himself from the prophetic task God had assigned him. Repentant, Jonah is saved after three days in the belly of the beast, a newly devoted man, just as Pinocchio finally begins to behave properly only after his own piscatory imprisonment.

Again and again, crying diverts this block of matter from its use as an object and into conversation with others. This emphasis on fluids makes sense in a story full of transformations, most notably the protagonist's overarching passage from unformed matter, to living human-like form, to soulful live boy. Tears lubricate each relation and transition between these various states. Geppetto's weeping early in the story is instructive here. As soon as he finishes carving the marionette's hands, the creature pulls the old man's wig from his head and places it on his own. "Faced with this insolent and derisive behavior, Geppetto became sad and melancholy—more so than he had ever been in his life" and promptly "wiped away a tear" (8). Tzachi Zamir reads this extreme distress as the old man's recognition of his own composition as a partial object, an amalgamation of non-living props.[26] Seeing himself transformed into an object-like state prompts the lachrymose protest.

It is not surprising that a block of wood carved into a puppet would contemplate the world through performance. There are three occasions when Pinocchio finds himself in a theater, each of which resolves upon an avenue of affective communication opened or foreclosed by tears. Early on, the puppet sneaks into a traveling performance of other marionettes, and the wooden performers onstage soon recognize him as kin— "It's our brother Pinocchio!" The puppets' celebration that bursts forth stalls their performance. When the outraged theater director Fire-eater threatens to punish Pinocchio for this disruption by using his wooden body as kindling or to sacrifice another puppet in his place, Pinocchio collapses in tears that resonate through the gathered host of puppets. The stage show may have been interrupted, but the logic of the theater continues to hold sway in a scene that could have been pulled straight from a melodrama of the period, with its heroes and heroines teetering on the precipice of disaster, jerking tears from the masses in attendance. The substitutional logic of empathy is laid bare: Pinocchio initially cries because Fire-eater threatens to use him as (instead of) a piece of kindling, then weeps even more forcefully when another puppet is chosen to take his place. All weeping, according to Schopenhauer, is an expression of *"compassion for ourselves*, or compassion that has been directed back to its point of origin."[27] We imagine ourselves in the position of the one that suffers and so cry for them, as if we were crying for ourselves. In Fire-eater's theater, these tears on behalf of another spread through the ranks of gathered puppets, as all the company in unison joins the same tearful wave of sentiment.[28]

The second theatrical space that Pinocchio inhabits fills an entire country with public play. On the verge of becoming a boy, Pinocchio is enticed to Playland by his delinquent human friend, Lampwick. This utopic neverland offers children the promise of a life without school or work, where boys cavort in circuses and "[i]n every piazza you could see little theaters made of canvas, packed with kids from morning to night" (122). What better public gathering place in this land of endless holiday and suspended maturation than the theater, where years can pass with the blink of a blackout, and clock time is forbidden? (As Walter Benjamin noted, "a clock that is working will always be a disturbance on stage.")[29] These theaters eradicate all spatial distinction (occupying every square) and all temporal markers for there is no beginning and no end to the entertainment that runs from dawn to dusk, where "the hours, days, and weeks passed like so many flashes" (122).[30] It is a theater that exists solely in the present tense, without productivity, without consequence or responsibility for an action, and without privacy: a festival for the untethered id.

When this fantasia of childhood irresponsibility and non-productivity has firmly gripped its visitors, they quite literally transform into asses.[31] Tears, and to a lesser extent laughter, open the threshold over which they cross into the animal world. One morning, Pinocchio discovers his ears have grown outsized and begins to weep; with every sob his ears sprout longer. When Lampwick reveals himself in a similar state, the two boys first break into an uproarious laughter that only seems to accelerate the transformation. "Overcome then by shame and sorrow, they tried to cry and lament their fate. It would have been better if they hadn't! Instead of wails of sorrow and lamentation, what they produced was the braying of donkeys" (128). Shame at being seen by another incites this fatal outpouring of tears. If only they hadn't cried, it is suggested, they would have retained their form, but the act of weeping sends them fully over the edge into animality. As I suggested in the beginning of this book, tears and laughter are alike in their capacity to break with the organizing principles of language, to dispossess the self and catch us up in the current of a common feeling. This can be the grounds for a power outside of representational politics, but it also can consign one to the outside, or to the barn out back.

Not all tears communicate effectively in Collodi's world. Sold to a circus, the donkey Pinocchio is finally forced to perform in a third and final theater, not as the theatrical object he was made to be, but as an animal. The Ringmaster introduces him to the crowd: "Do observe, I beseech you, how much wildlife oozes from his eyes" (134). Faltering before the crowd, "[h]is eyes filled with tears and he began to weep profusely. But nobody realized—least of all the Ringmaster, who instead cracked his whip and shouted: Like a good boy, Pinocchio! Now you're going to show our audience how gracefully you can jump through hoops" (136). Forced to perform, the donkey trips mid-jump and rises limping, his career as a performer cut short.[32] The donkey is a peculiarly object-like animal, accentuating the cruel disregard with which we humans generally consider the feelings of animals. It may be that animals cannot weep emotional tears, but they'd go unnoticed even if they could. Here, the tears of animals are misfired communications, no universal beacon but the cause for a tormenter's diverted celebration—Bravo! Bravo!

We have therefore a collection of fictional theaters, each employing tears differently. The first, Fire-eater's puppet theater, provokes empathy to ward off an object state where wood might be reduced to its most elemental use as kindling for fire. It thereby repeats the original cry that individuated Pinocchio, gave him a name, and saved him from his fated part in a larger piece of furniture. The second theater, Playland, offers us a theater for the timeless play of a public self, while a private performance of shame takes place backstage. The latter's tears push the boys into an animal state—not as objects exactly, but as object-like creatures available to use whose expressions are misapprehended or ignored entirely, as in the third circus-theater of forced performance. On this last stage, the puppet lives faceless and unacknowledged by the humans that watch him cry, all the while thinking that he laughs.

A similarly unanswered cry for help pours forth from a last Pinocchio. In the artist Maurizio Cattelan's *Daddy, Daddy* (2008), a sculpture of Disney's version of the puppet floats face-down in the center of the pool at the base of the Guggenheim Museum's central atrium. He is stilled, drowned in the fluid that would have given him human life in the original story.

In Collodi's story, the puppet nearly drowns several times, but his wooden constitution keeps his body floating where others might sink. (Indeed, he saves first a dog and later his own father by carrying them to shore on his buoyant strokes.) Cattelan's title recalls the moment in the story when a pair of thieves hang the puppet from a tree, and Pinocchio calls for aid: "Oh, Daddy!" As John Hooper and Anna Kraczyna note, this outcry plangently echoes the last words of Christ on the cross. It is fitting, then, that Cattelan's stilled puppet spreads his arms wide in a Christ-like pose. If Pinocchio has been sacrificed on behalf of a chosen people, it is not the community of flesh and blood, but the object world. Even in the Guggenheim, this temple devoted to the most affective of things, materiality lies neglected, facing away from human acknowledgment.

Suspended in the ocean that would transform him from toy to boy, or in utero as he was once held formless in his block of wood, Cattelan's Pinocchio floats between the statue's timelessness and the timely demand

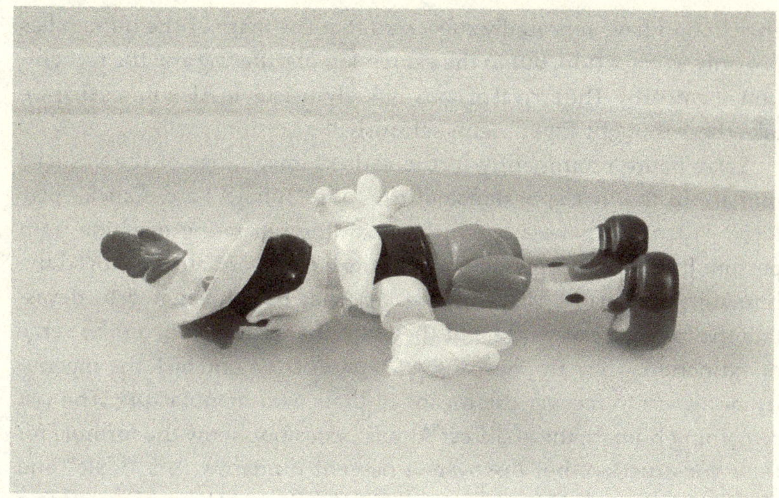

Figure 14 Maurizio Cattelan. *Daddy Daddy*, 2008. Polyurethane resin, steel, epoxy paint. 43 1/4 x 39 1/2 x 21 3/4 inch. Photograph Courtesy © The Solomon R. Guggenheim Foundation, New York. Courtesy of the artist and Perrotin.

of the crying child. Face-down in the waters, nobody hears his call for his daddy or sees his anguished look. Face-down, it is possible to imagine that he in fact feeds the pool in which he drowns. Perhaps his unanswered cries have produced whole oceans of tears, and perhaps he is still crying now, the water level rising, imperceptibly. His weeping is all-encompassing, environmental or atmospheric, offering us a fantastical source for our own grim fate in the slow swell of tidal disaster.

III. Robots in the Rain

Follow me as I take a last step into an imagined future that is, of late, increasingly proximate to our present reality. At least since 1950, when Alan Turing first proposed his Imitation Game test to determine the possibility—or at least the impression—of artificial personhood, generations of computer programmers have tried to create AI personalities that imitate not only the knowledge and creative problem-solving capacities of the human, but also the compass of feeling that might guide that mind through a recognizably human expressive field.[33] The hypotheses of science fiction have repeatedly suggested that the mark of the human lies not only in cognition, but in the expression of suffering and the recognition of empathy. The arrival of convincingly articulate AI requires that we take these thought experiments seriously.[34]

Tears figure prominently in the earliest imaginings of the artificial human. In the first appearance of the term "robot," Karel Čapek's play *R.U.R.* (1920), tears wash away the final line separating machine from person. In the play's epilogue, the robots have essentially destroyed the humanity that had enslaved them and that had threatened to devastate the non-human world, but they find themselves, too, on the verge of extinction. They are incapable of reproduction and lack the ingenuity necessary to recover the means of their own manufacture. The last remaining human, the architect Alquist, does not know the formula for their construction, but discovers a nascent humanity in a "male" and "female" robot pair. When he overhears the female Helena break into a peal of laughter—that other automatic human response—Alquist starts, thinking he has heard one of his kin. He discovers his mistake, but quickly notes additional human-like traits in the behavior of the couple in their fledgling love for one another. He decides to pursue a final test and proposes to dissect Helena. When her companion offers himself in her place, Helena begins to weep. The architect stops in his tracks ("Child, child, you can weep. Tears."), recognizing the two robots anew as Adam and Eve 2.0 at the play's close. Where our own lineage has wrought climatic and environmental devastation, this couple survives as representatives of a non-human world capable of weeping for another kind of life.

Another essay could trace this legacy of tears through the many robots, cyborgs, androids, and AIs that followed in these footsteps after the human, but a single thread will have to suffice here. The title of Philip K. Dick's sci-fi classic *Do Androids Dream of Electric Sheep?* (1968) underlines the novel's fixation on the inner life of the artificial and natural alike. Set in a future after cataclysmic fallout, the few remaining animals on Earth obtain a sacred value while disposable human-like androids ("replicants") wage war on other planets. Here a new spiritualism based on empathy organizes the world and the rare surviving non-human creatures become prized means toward human self-realization. Those who cannot afford an actual animal to express their care make do with a synthetic surrogate.

In Ridley Scott's adaptation for the screen, *Blade Runner* (1982), tears signal humanity or rather an empathy that is otherwise lacking in this post-apocalyptic landscape. The "blade runner" of the title, Deckard, hunts down and "retires" replicants that have broken the law by returning to Earth. These replicants are blessed with super-human capacities, an evolved state of being beyond the human, but they are also programmed to die within a few short years. A group of renegades have made their way to Earth to confront their maker, Dr. Eldon Tyrell, and to seek an extended life—a story not so far removed from the crisis the original robots faced in *R.U.R.* Deckard is assisted in his bounty hunting by one Rachel Rosen, his love interest who works with the inventor of the androids. When Deckard reveals that, unbeknownst to her, Rosen is herself an android, that her memories are implants from Tyrell's niece, she begins to cry. He turns his back to her, not wanting to see her tears for fear that they might demand acknowledgment of her suffering.

A peculiarly hollow protagonist, it takes until the final moments of the film for Deckard to discover any semblance of empathy. Batty, the last remaining replicant that he hunts, has defeated the bounty hunter, who now dangles over a building's precipice. Rather than letting him fall to his death, the replicant pulls the wounded Deckard to safety. On the verge of his own programmed collapse, Batty holds his hunter's gaze for a final soliloquy.

> I've seen things you people wouldn't believe. Attack ships on fire off the shoulder of Orion. I watched C-beams glitter in the dark near the Tann-häuser Gate. All those moments will be lost in time, like tears in rain. Time to die.

Both are drenched under the steady drip of rain that covers this ruined city, drenched too in sweat and blood—and perhaps in Batty's case, tears, for he has just discovered his companion and paramour, another replicant, dead. The camera cuts back and forth between closeups of man and machine, and this time Deckard does not look away from this non-human weeping. He, too, blinks back rain or tears, whatever blinds his laconic gaze. We are meant to wonder if he is crying or if it is merely the weather that casts him this way. Either way, hunter and hunted share a common liquid strand. The unfeeling Deckard learns empathy from those he was made to destroy, a lesson Rosen and Batty communicate not in words but in the tears they cry.[35] As it happens, in the final scene we learn that Deckard, too, might be a replicant, further complicating our understanding of whether he blinks back tears or rain and whether this precipitate belongs to him or is a collaboration with the larger world.[36]

In the film's sequel, *Blade Runner 2049* (2017), tears again function as an important marker of humanity that the android regularly produces in collaboration with the environment. This time, the protagonist K is most certainly a replicant who has been coopted by the police to act as a "blade runner." Like his predecessor from the earlier film, K hunts down and retires other unauthorized replicants. His love interest is an AI program that, like some intimate descendant of Siri or Alexa, is a holographic projection moving through his narrow apartment on preordained tracks. When a hardware upgrade allows her projection to wander freely through the real world, she steps out into the night air for the first time as a fine drizzle hazes the sky. It is the first thing she independently decides to do. The drops of water distort her image as they pass through its projected light, a disturbance that approximates her first feeling of the surface of her luminous skin. She is moved, crying perhaps; these are tears in the rain or a more literal embodiment of water's transit through the threshold of inside and outside. Such an atmospheric crying returns at the end of the film, when the protagonist K, having offered himself in sacrifice for the human father that he could not have, lies face-up staring into the sky, dying or at least shutting down. Snow descends onto his bare face, where the heat of his fading machinery melts that crystalline structure to a liquid feeling. For the audience, they look like they could be tears. Here, too, the tears of machines are produced in collaboration with the material world.

A third android also participates in this discourse of dissociative weeping. The lethal replicant, ironically named Luv, carries out the most brutal acts of violence on behalf of the successor to the Tyrell Corporation. She expresses no empathy or recognition of human or machine suffering in her programmed actions, yet at each moment of conflict, she inexplicably begins to tear up. These tears are divorced from any other affective signal—they show an unconscious self, registering a dislocated distress at whatever cruelty its body enacts. In the film's climactic struggle, K holds her underwater and drowns her in the ocean, her eyes wide and unblinking as she stares into a sea of tears. It is as if her affective unconsciousness has finally won out and been released.

The fate of the killer robot with tears that never reach anyone recalls Cattelan's abandoned Pinocchio. We cannot acknowledge the water-logged puppet and his plaintive cries of "Daddy, Daddy," nor can we discern where his potential tears might mingle with the non-tear of the fountain, for he lies face down and perpetually weeping in a pool where it can never rain—or, at least not until some future apocalypse breaks open the modernist sanctum that is the Guggenheim and lets the world in. By contrast, Batty and K, those other puppets cut free from their strings, end their days lying face up under a sky that weeps for them. On their faces we witness an exchange between the larger material world and these prod-igal sons returning to their fold. In the various crying scenes that *Blade Runner 2049* presents, as in the conclusion to the first film, the source of a tear is externalized. Authenticity is no longer a matter of private emo-tional intent. Instead, we are asked to consider whether affect might be shared across an ecological network, the environment weeping on behalf of this other being likewise excluded from the human conversation.[37]

Here, the android becomes the medium through which the world can weep, offering a prosthetic face that allows the non-human surround to body forth a feeling. By this I mean that such material affect is finally recognizable as a feeling, because it takes on a shape that mirrors our own, even if it is not for us to comfort them. Reflecting on the broader trope of rain as tears in cinema, Roger Cardinal writes that

> any given individual raindrop sliding down the glass [. . .] is, logically, irrelevant to [. . .] emotion, circumstantial, unscripted. That is to say, there comes a point where material detail entirely escapes directorial sponsorship, to take its place before the viewer quite autonomously. [. . .] Figuratively, as well literally, the raindrop is transparent; neither informa-tional nor symbolic, it is, simply, "obtusely," itself.[38]

Each raindrop or snowdrop is contingency itself, a happenstance thing performing beyond directorial control, another spontaneous liquid expression. Perhaps then, these instances of saintly martyrdom are sac-rifices on behalf of a larger acknowledgment, not only of this individual android becoming human (or failing to do so) but also of the sorrows and ecstasies of the other world—the non-human one we cannot cross over to know. Tears are not a statement communicated across this divide, not "informational nor symbolic" in ways we might understand, so much as a passage for affective movements from one world to another. In this way, the contingency of precipitation can also teach us something about our own tears and their obtusely transparent autonomy.[39] They teach us a way to let go of our own mastery, of self, of field, of stone, of fence.

CHAPTER 7

Teaching How to Cry

> LEAR. When we are borne, we cry that we are come
>   To this great stage of Fooles.
> —KING LEAR[1]

After the performance my friend leans over and asks me why I have been crying. I search myself, coming upon other instances from my private compendium of tearful moments in the theater that never cohered into reason. A handful of soil on his head. A network of strings and gray felt in tension. Her scars, real scars, not stage makeup. The child sitting on the man's lap, their hands resting together on the keys as the piano plays. The first morning light through an opened window, birds on the wing. The miracle of time suddenly going backward, their babbling sounds now cohering into sentences, our repair suddenly possible. I could go on.

I do not know, I tell her.

How often have I found my eyes filling up from some happening that moves me greatly but incomprehensibly. Let's call these sublime tears, if the sublime is an encounter with something larger than one's capacity for expression. The realization of knowing I do not know: a rebirth onto this great stage of fools.

Why do you cry? Each of the essays in this book has offered, among other things, the beginnings of a different answer.

1) I cry for science, so that these bands of darkness might illuminate the chemical composition of my feelings.

2) I cry for something like, and yet unlike, a sorrow that I am too sad
   to tell.
3) I cry for my memory, for a lived truth that might stand in for an
   unlived truth.
4) I cry because the prop makes me cry; I am a reaction, thing-like.
5) "I" do not cry; the thing cries that cannot say I.

I end here with tears that contest the very grounds of knowledge, the crying that is unreasonable and unthinkable. Plessner, Butler, and others suggest that crying is a disruption in the fluent flow of language and semiosis, the tear a tear in the tissue of smooth representation, calling attention to itself and rescinding the promise of transparent verbal expression. If I began my journey on the stage as a dry-eyed actor, I am now a professor by vocation, so I must do my performing in front of a blackboard, whiteboard, or projection screen. What does it mean to invite tears into those spaces most dedicated to the clarity of rational discourse, the lecture hall and classroom?

The first time I set out to prepare a lecture on the subject of crying I thought to conduct a series of demonstrations live before my audience. Between each segment of the talk, I would attempt a different method for manually producing tears. A tear stick, cotton swabs, a plate of onions, a bottle of sack, and so on. By the end, I imagined I would find myself struggling to read, dripping from nose and eyes in a disgraceful denouement, my scholarly composure spilling all over the lectern. Lecturers are not supposed to cry. I had watched a lecture performance in which the speaker had played a drinking game with himself, until he was so far gone that his garble of jargon slurred even deeper into obscurity from a thickened tongue. Another taboo, that—the heavily inebriated lecturer—though a far more common sight than a weepy one.

I thought, too, of having someone else read these words on my behalf. Like my father, hiring someone else to give his lectures, or like Maurizio Cattelan, who has had a friend impersonate him for years, speaking in his stead at interviews, in lectures, or posing for his pictures: I'd bring in an expert on the subject. Even after these years of study, I cannot cry on cue, but I know many actors who weep masterfully. The artist Cally Spooner employed the same tactic in her lecture performance "On False Tears and Outsourcing." While she waited an ocean away, onstage stood a man "neatly dressed in a suit like a swish Harvard professor" with matching masculine verve (American, tall, really deep voice), who took up her script about the labor of delegated expression.[2]

Spooner's lecture revolves around the moment from Gustave Flaubert's *Madame Bovary* when Emma's lover, Rodolphe, has grown tired of their affair and sends her a letter announcing his decision to break it all off. He signs his cliché-drenched missive with a false tear—a drop of water from his wine glass—that Emma receives, in Spooner's words, "as a technical stand-in for her lover."[3] It is the perfect concluding gesture to their constructed romance, a counterfeit seal to a very real farewell. As voiced by her own vicarious actor, Spooner interprets this ersatz tear as an emblem for neoliberal capitalism's outsourcing of affect, where things and people assemble on a common ground, but where "no radical transformation is possible at the level of the speaker OR the listener because the subject is simply not embodied."[4] Counter to this free-floating agent, Spooner scripts an increasingly embodied breakdown from her lecturer. A cough drop to assuage a rising lump in the throat, cries of exhaustion, then the stage directions cue him: "I am SO sorry . . . I . . . just . . . can't read this any more. (*Starts crying*) It's too sad. (*Keeps crying.*)"[5] Reading the published version of the monologue, I see another "technical stand-in" for the failure of the speech itself: there on the page sits a cartoonish blob that looks like a melting gumdrop with drooping eyes and mouth, a silhouetted tear cutting a hole in its sad face. It seems there is no way for the form of the lecture to hold this feeling, either in the book, its subtextual stage directions, or in its performed speech. Following this anomalous graphic intrusion, "Cally Spooner" flips through the remaining pages of the talk, skipping over bits. The whole edifice of meaningful content collapses and we cut to the end.

Tears come where speech fails or writing falters. They incite a premature exit from the stage of discourse. Samuel Beckett cues his surrogate self "B" to "*exit weeping*" as a way out of one of the *Three Dialogues* (1949) that fictionalize his conversations on modern painting with the art critic Georges Duthuit. Rather than attempt to elucidate a point about the failure of representation, he affectively disappears.[6] The lesson seems the same: the crying lecturer or critic best make a quick exit.

I considered these dissolutions then as I consider them now. Should I follow Spooner in these pages, projecting an image on a slide in place of an actor? (*Picture a cartoonish blob here, hollowed with a tear.*) Should I follow B out the door with a *sotto voce* directive to *exit weeping*?

Waiting until the last minute, on the morning of my scheduled talk I finally decided to recount the only time I had cried when trying to deliver a lecture.

> *He had given the lecture before, perhaps too many times, as is the way with academics and their perpetually forthcoming work. This would be the last reading, he told himself. And as he moved to the penultimate page, it felt there was little of this occasion that differed from the others: a small crowd, some attentive, some not. It was never doing what he wanted it to do, the words he wrote around the objects that were too beautiful. And so he came upon the fragment from Walter Benjamin, a note that the lost exile had penned on one of many scraps of reused envelopes, the notecards densely spiraled with his tiny meticulous hand:*

> > *The Hasidim have a saying about the world to come. Everything there will be arranged just as it is with us. The room we have now will be just the same in the world to come; where our child lies sleeping, it will sleep in the world to come. The clothes we are wearing we shall also wear in the next world. Everything will be the same as here—only a little bit different. Thus it is with imagination. It merely draws a veil over the distance. Everything remains just as it is, but the veil flutters and everything changes imperceptibly beneath it.[7]*

> *He had said these words many times before, knew them by heart, but somehow this time, his voice caught in his throat. His eyes welled. A lump rose. He had to stop. Teetering now, on the cusp of real weeping, he stood there transfixed. Clearing his throat—again, again—looking helplessly down at his paper; the room drawing close as nothing continued to happen. He hung on, suspended midsentence for what seemed a very long time, before he could collect himself and, voice cracked ragged, the remaining words finally came out.*

> *He finished and the conversation afterward was alive with good questions and mostly adequate answers. The eminent professor came forward and shook his hand, gave him a curious look, but nobody acknowledged the fact that he had started to cry.*

When the room cleared, someone lingered behind. "It was strange," the visitor said, "that moment. And strange too that no one mentioned it."

Benjamin's words are too beautiful, of course, but I didn't know why I had begun to cry. In my framing of the fragment at the time, I had conceived of his description of the apocalypse as a figure for the theater's revelation of potentiality: how a curtain veils and unveils in a single motion, ending one world and beginning another as it flutters over the everyday and transforms it imperceptibly.[8] Perhaps in the act of reading these words aloud on that particular day, this potential of the everyday to unveil its difference—this thing that might be called liveness—suddenly struck me afresh. Perhaps I recognized myself trapped in the world as it was, scripted by the routine of words I had prepared and read so many times before. No next world to come, I stopped the only way that I could: I started to cry.

The task of the lecturer is to know, so what to make of the fact that I did not know why I was crying and that such an act arose without seeming cause or satisfying resolution? Such weeping would expose a deeply irrational force, imperceptible to the entire project of analytical discourse. When William Blake wrote that "a tear is an intellectual thing," he meant something quite far removed from the analytical intellect guiding the Cartesian method.[9] Tearful expressions are intellectual because they are rooted directly in thought, as experience not mediated by language.[10] The poet Ann Lauterbach writes:

> Tears are *intellectual* because they come from thoughts that spill over the body's containing well; they are the secretion of excess we assign to emotion; perhaps emotion itself is simply caused by a surfeit of thought. One tries to unbind these durable dualities, to allow for the morphological shift that might allow the human creature to be complex but integrated, not divided into anatomical parts, all nouns and no transitive verb. We are not yet mechanical, technological things, we are intellectual—thinking— beings, and we cry when stirred beyond the capture of signifying Logos, which relents into flows of passionate silence.[11]

My profession celebrates the anatomist's excessive verbosity, naming part after part, and hitching each to each with all those transitive verbs.

Even as tears may bring a new clarity to one's affective ties, they obstruct the ideals of post-Enlightenment pedagogy and its privileged medium, the lecture.

The conventions of the lecture dictate that the speaker function primarily as a vessel for limpid communication. Like a good messenger, the lecturer should reduce as much as possible any noise that might disrupt the flow of information from the one who knows to the one who does not know but learns. Some refraction is expected, even welcome, for as the sociologist Erving Goffman put it in his lecture on lectures, "lecturers come equipped with bodies, and bodies can easily introduce visual and audio effects unconnected with the speech stream, and these may be distracting."[12] Goffman proceeds with a list of distracting gestures and fidgeting parts peculiar to the lecturer as subject, but he makes no mention of tears. "The proper place of this self," he concludes, "is a very limited one"—apparently, too limited for the overflow of weeping.[13] The tears of the lecturer may expose negative affects like embarrassment, frustration, or sadness that show a fragility at odds with the mythically fortified intellect as authority that founds all our academic posturing.[14] Tears expose the lecturer as susceptible to the prompting movements of things and affects, as a sensible being with "a disposition to be affected by the passions."[15] If Wesley Morris is correct, "crying arouses the animal in us. [. . .] You don't find it. The wolf finds you."[16] Kafka's ape addressing the academy notwithstanding, we do not want animals at our lecterns.

Everything remains just as it is, but the veil flutters and everything changes imperceptibly beneath it. Looking at the passage again, many years later, that description of a "veil" fluttering like an eyelid blurs my sight differently. (I see tears everywhere now.) A tear, too, is imperceptible according to the distinctions of word or sense, yet it flows with material, world-changing consequence. At the end of his book *Memories of the Blind*, another text presented as a fictional dialogue, Jacques Derrida writes of tears as a curtain that veils and unveils the potentiality of sight as a relational call: "The revelatory or apocalyptic blindness, the blindness that reveals the very truth of the eyes, would be the gaze veiled by tears. It neither sees nor does not see: it is indifferent to its blurred vision. It implores."[17] In other words, we could say that the true nature of our insightful eyes becomes apparent not when we direct our clear gaze upon the world to disclose its secrets, but when our tears implore another to do something, when sight becomes an active relation. What would it mean for us to bring such an ethos to the academy or to allow the animal of affect to occasionally run loose within our halls?

By ignoring my momentary collapse, the audience repaired the proper decorum for a visiting lecture. It was a kind gesture, a collective decision to prevent me any further embarrassment, but it also neglected what seemed to me the most electric and alive part of my talk, an instance when our relations changed. I was no longer simply a lecturer; indeed, I wasn't a lecturer at all ("lecture" finding its root in "to read"). I was an affective weathervane, one juncture within a network with others, moving and moved. If only I could repeat such an act on cue—Diderot be damned!—I could henceforth upend the power differential between someone who purports to know and those purported not to know. I mentioned earlier the suggestion from certain social scientists that tears signal surrender and thus may have served an evolutionary purpose to diffuse aggression and conflict. Experiments have convincingly connected episodes of crying with feelings of powerlessness.[18] Perhaps we might welcome more tearful lectures, at the very least from those like myself (straight white men), who've long donned swish academic drag to perform an authority and mastery befitting a king, when we are just old fools.

I wrote most of this book during a pandemic when the theaters were closed. Sequestered in a small house in a small town in Western Massachusetts, I often wished I had found a makeshift funeral to mourn the passing of the many millions I could not see in person. Even as grief and loss filled every screen and paper, I tried to recall what it felt like to be in the presence of a stranger crying—there, at some distance, but close enough to share a common tear. My childhood experience as a tear donor made me think myself an authority on reflex tears, but suddenly everyone was sticking cotton swabs up their nose, bringing forth tears as an unintended consequence. Wearing ill-fitting masks, we were crying, all of us, but rarely together.

I realized midway through this project that I would never be an expert on tears—even in the theater, the sheer volume of anecdotes about tears far exceeds my compass. My writing has been open to the sea changes of circumstance, chance inclination, and faulty recollection, rather than to watertight research. Some might call this arbitrary: they would be right. I have tried in this book to invite a certain blurriness and vagueness in my analytical eye, to allow a vulnerability to compromise the illusion of academic lucidity. I have tried to upend my own relations. My father might say that this is all an elaborate ruse to avoid doing the real work, but I think he appreciates the gesture. After all, proudly wearing his t-shirt and crocs to whatever conference, he was never one for the pomp and circumstance of profession.

I wrote the last parts of this book during the first months of my daughter's life. (She cries in the next room as I write these words.) Her tears promised to teach me something new about my object of study so, like Darwin awaiting his son's first tears, I watched dutifully, and with no small distress, as she cried through dry eyes for weeks on end. I, too, recorded the first time her cheeks were stained with a tear's passage, marveling at how its mark lasted long after her crying had turned to laughter. I read in them the beginnings of a theory where all made sense or at least gathered my own relationship with authentic and inauthentic signals, with seriousness and play, with fathers and tears into some conclusive statement. But if I have learned anything from my daughter's tears it is that they are not the material for her father's research.

I discarded the pages I had written.

Notes

CHAPTER 1

1. Roland Barthes, *A Lover's Discourse: Fragments*, trans. Richard Howard (New York: Hill and Wang, 1978), 80. The line comes as Barthes has been regarding his constant companion through the volume, Goethe's semi-autobiographical young lover, Werther, and his endless stream of tears. When published in 1774, *The Sorrows of Young Werther* showed the melodramatic Goethe/Werther to be the ideal "man of sensibility," prompting widespread fascination and imitation, including a spate of copycat suicides. Goethe would come to regard his youthful construct with some embarrassment and today the unrequited lover's plangent longing often reads like laughably self-indulgent melodrama. Here Barthes wonders about cultural and historical tides of licensed expression before suggesting a timelessness in the tear itself.

2. Among many other explorations of this conception of performance, see the discussion of the "autopoietic feedback loop" created by a live event in Erika Fischer-Lichte, *The Routledge Introduction to Theatre and Performance Studies*, trans. Minou Arjomand (New York: Routledge, 2014), 18–45.

3. Jonas Barish, *The Antitheatrical Prejudice* (Berkeley: University of California Press, 1985).

4. Janša was known by his birth name, Emil Hrvatin, when he first produced *Camillo Memo 4.0*. In a novel act of protest, Hrvatin joined two other artists and legally changed his name to Janez Janša in 2007, imitating the name of the right-wing Slovenian Prime Minister and ensuring that all his future acts of political disruption would be forever linked and, as it were, signed by the ruling authority.

5. Marina Grzinic, "Emil Hrvatin's Memory Cabinets," *PAJ: A Journal of Performance and Art* 24, no. 2 (May 2002): 109–12.

6. These glass or ceramic bottles, or unguentaria, have been found in many Hellenistic and early Roman burial sites throughout the Mediterranean area. There is some belief that "[t]he tears of the deceased person's family and friends were collected and thus preserved in these lachrymatories, which were buried in the ancient tombs." Diane Apostolos-Cappadona in *Holy Tears: Weeping in the Religious Imagination*, eds. Kimberley Christine Patton and John Stratton

Hawley (Princeton, NJ): Princeton University Press, 2005), 218. This theory has been contested by archaeologists who have found residue that suggests the vessels contained perfumes and other oils. Virginia R. Anderson-Stojanović, "The Chronology and Function of Ceramic Unguentaria," *American Journal of Archaeology* 91, no. 1 (Jan 1987): 105–22.

7. Janša uses the term "spectactor" to refer to the coinciding position of spectator and actor promulgated by his theater; Barbara Orel writes that this hybrid figure in *Camillo Memo 4.0* "is the locus of the event and, at the same time and all in one person, its own scene, performer and spectator. The spectactor is the object of looking as well as the subject of vision." In *Memory, Privacy, Spectatorship: On Emil Hrvatin's Performances*, ed. Maja Žerovnik (Ljubljana: Maska, 2003), 56. Reprinted in *Anatomy Live: Performance and the Operating Theatre*, ed. Maaike Bleeker (Amsterdam: Amsterdam University Press, 2008), 149.

8. The James-Lange theory (in honor of Carl Lange, who made a similar argument as James at the same moment in history) has been convincingly disproven by researchers when conceived as a general theory of emotion. However, studies of a condition called Pathological Crying and Laughing (PLC), which sends patients into bouts of weeping or laughter without reason, have found evidence of a certain truth to the theory. As Christopher Turner puts it: "One well-documented case of PLC is that of 51-year-old landscape gardener, referred to simply as C.B. by his doctor, Antonio Damasio. C.B. suffered a mild stroke in 1999 that damaged both his brainstem and the cerebellum, which neurologists now believe controls the laughter and crying centers, adjusting behavior to the appropriate context. As a result, he'd laugh riotously in response to sad news and sob irrepressibly in response to a joke—or, indeed, in response to anything at all. A laughing fit would sometimes turn into a crying one, but never vice versa, and the patient noted that after a long bout of laughter or crying, he would eventually feel correspondingly jolly or sad. Neuroscientists concluded that 'feelings were being produced, consonant with the emotional expression, and in the absence of any appropriate stimulus.' In other words, one can manufacture or summon up an emotion, much as an actor might, by assuming the desired expression." Christopher Turner, "Tears of Laughter: Darwin and the indeterminacy of emotions," *Cabinet* 17 (Spring 2005): 69–73.

9. John Owen, *Travels into Different Parts of Europe in the Years 1791 and 1792*, Vol. II (London, 1796), 124. Referenced in the *OED*.

10. Tom Lutz, *Crying: The Natural and Cultural History of Tears* (New York: W.W. Norton, 2001).

11. Shakespeare, *Hamlet*, eds. Ann Thompson and Neil Taylor (London: Arden Shakespeare, 2006), 2.2.560–62. "In *Hamlet*, therefore, Shakespeare embarks on an inclusive—if abbreviated—analysis of acting, beginning with the metonymic problem of tears on cue." Robert Cohen, "Tears (and Acting) in Shakespeare," *Journal of Dramatic Theory and Criticism* (Fall 1995): 26.

12. Nearly all the Academy Award winners for Best Actress have cried in their winning performance. Famous instances include Meryl Streep in *Sophie's*

Choice (1983), Halle Berry in *Monster's Ball* (2002), Brie Larson in *Room* (2015). Best Actor winners with notable outbursts in recent years include Sean Penn in *Mystic River* (2003), Casey Affleck in *Manchester by the Sea* (2016), and Anthony Hopkins in *The Father* (2020). There are numerous articles on this subject. See, for example, Jim Grullo's analysis on Oscar nominees in the Best Actor and Best Supporting Actor categories in "When Grown Men Weep," *Premiere* 4 (1992): 19. On the excessive tears that course through the larger Oscar ceremony, see Christopher Hitchens's "Cry, Baby" in *The Washington Post*, March 31, 1996. https://www.washingtonpost.com/archive/lifestyle/style/1996/03/31/cry-ba by/4980d1c8-a57c-4489-82fb-9cb65642769b/

13. Rachel Vorona Cote, "The Agony and the Ecstasy of the Ugly Cry," *The New Republic* (April 1, 2016). https://newrepublic.com/article/132289/agony -ecstasy-ugly-cry

14. Sarah Bernhardt, in *Actors on Acting; The Theories, Techniques, and Practices of the World's Great Actors, Told in Their Own Words*, eds. Toby Cole and Helen Krich Chinoy (New York: Crown Publishers, 1970), 208.

15. The audience testimonial was a popular genre of advertisement in the 1980s; as a kid, I remember a sketch on *Saturday Night Live* that featured Jon Lovitz as a hypnotist whose audience repeated their praise word-for-word in somnambulistic monotone. More recently, a meme of Gwyneth Paltrow made the rounds: "I laughed. I cried, a number of times. I sweat, I danced. I got . . . a shot, I ate and . . . I had many epiphanies."

16. Linda Williams, "Film Bodies: Gender, Genre, and Excess," *Film Quarterly* 44, no. 4 (Summer, 1991): 5.

17. I sample a wide range of work in this book, but cannot begin to offer a comprehensive survey of tearful performance in theater or performance art. For some additional relevant contemporary art, see Isabelle and Sophie Lynch's curation of "Artificial Tears" at Vtape, included in *What the F**k?!: Video in the Age of Sublime Uncertainty* (Toronto: Vtape, 2018): 24–29.

18. Aristotle, *Poetics*, trans. Leon Golden (Englewood Cliffs, NJ: Prentice Hall, 1968), 17.

19. Marvin Carlson, *Theories of the Theatre: A Historical and Critical Survey, from the Greeks to the Present* (Ithaca: Cornell University Press, 1993), 18. Carlson offers a helpful overview here; for a more voluminous treatment, see Stephen Halliwell, *Aristotle's Poetics* (Chapel Hill: University of North Carolina Press, 1986), Chapter 5 and 6, as well as the appendix on "Katharsis."

20. See Kimberley Christine Patton and John Stratton Hawley, eds., *Holy Tears: Weeping in the Religious Imagination* (Princeton, NJ: Princeton University Press, 2005). In the classical world, Hélène Monsacré writes of the fertility of tears, from men and gods alike, giving birth to new life. Hélène Monsacré, *The Tears of Achilles*, trans. Nicholas J. Snead (Cambridge, MA: Harvard University Press, 2017), 119–20.

21. "The beginnings of the medical purgation theory of *Katharsis*, as opposed to the moral purification theory, can be traced back as far as the mid-

sixteenth century." Elisabetta Brighi and Antonio Cerella, eds., *The Sacred and the Political: Explorations on Mimesis, Violence and Religion* (London: Bloomsbury Academic, 2016), 22.

22. Martijn J. H. Balsters, Emiel J. Krahmer, Marc G. J. Swerts, and Ad J. J. M. Vingerhoets, "Emotional Tears Facilitate the Recognition of Sadness and the Perceived Need for Social Support," *Evolutionary Psychology* 11, no. 1 (2013): 148.

23. Ovid, *Heroides*, Book VIII (Hermione), line 61. This particular translation of the passage, as quoted in Lutz's *Crying*, 119, is widely distributed on various websites devoted to quotations and inspirational sayings. For the second quote, see Karl Menninger, Martin Mayman, and Paul W. Pruyser, *The Vital Balance: The Life Process in Mental Health and Illness* (New York: Viking, 1963), 138.

24. Joseph Weiss, "Crying at the Happy Ending," *Psychoanalytic Review* 39 (1952): 338. Further discussion in Joseph Weiss, ed., *The Psychanalytic Process: Theory, Clinical Observation, and Empirical Research* (New York: Guilford Press, 1986).

25. William Frey, *Crying: The Mystery of Tears* (Dallas: Winston Press, 1983). For some more recent research that contests these claims, see, for example, Asmir Gračanin, Lauren M. Bylsma and Ad J. J. M. Vingerhoets, "Is Crying a Self-soothing Behavior?," *Frontiers in Psychology* (28 May, 2014).

26. Suzanne Stougie, Ad J. J. M. Vingerhoets, and Randolph Cornelius, "Crying, Catharsis, and Health," in *Emotional Expression and Health*, eds. I. Nyklíček, L. R. Temoshok, and Ad J. J. M. Vingerhoets (New York: Brunner-Routledge, 2004), 225–88. An International Study on Adult Crying questionnaire from 2001 asked subjects to reflect on whether they thought they felt better after crying. Roughly half of respondents said they felt better mentally, but the results were more mixed in terms of their physical well-being: 17 percent reported a negative effect and 28 percent reported an improvement.

27. Sigrid Nunez, *The Friend* (London: Virago, 2018), 15.

28. "Emotional or psychogenic tears are in fact reflex tears, where the stimulus is emotional rather than irritant-produced." Nico J. van Haeringen, "The (Neuro)anatomy of the Lacrimal System and the Biological Aspects of Crying," in *Adult Crying: A Biopsychosocial Approach*, eds. Ad J. J. M. Vingerhoets and Randolph R. Cornelius (New York: Routledge, 2002), 28.

29. Robert A. Sack, Kah Ooi Tan, and Ami Tan, "Diurnal Tear Cycle: Evidence for a Nocturnal Inflammatory Constitutive Tear Fluid," *Investigative Ophthalmology & Visual Science* 33, no. 3 (March 1992): 627.

30. Sack, Tan, and Tan, "Diurnal Tear Cycle: Evidence for a Nocturnal Inflammatory Constitutive Tear Fluid," 627.

31. Blushing, that other form of intimate self-revelation that likewise exposes the face in its most vulnerable cast, is also hailed as a uniquely human phenomenon. It is, perhaps even more than crying, the mark of the "authentic" actor.

32. Nunez, *The Friend*, 15.

33. For example, see Juan Murube, "Basal, Reflex, and Psycho-emotional Tears," *The Ocular Surface* 7, no. 2 (2009): 60–66.

34. Naomi Eisenberger and Matthew Lieberman, "Why rejection hurts: a common neural alarm system for physical and social pain," *Trends in Cognitive Sciences* 8, no. 7 (2004): 294–300.

35. Charles Darwin, *The Expression of the Emotions in Man and Animals* (Chicago: University of Chicago Press, 1965), 153.

36. Ad J. J. M. Vingerhoets, *Why Only Humans Weep: Unveiling the Mysteries of Tears* (Oxford: Oxford University Press, 2013), 48.

37. By contrast, in fiction the tears of animals can bring them into communion with human feeling. In *As You Like It*, for example, the sobbing of a wounded stag inspires the melancholic Jaques to weep in kind; both their tears mingle in the stream along whose banks they stand. William Shakespeare, *As You Like It*, ed. Juliet Dusinberre (London: Arden Shakespeare, 2006), 2.1.31–66.

38. To cite just one of many examples: "A sample of pathological crying and laughing of varying rarity includes epileptic seizures that produce crying (dacrystic seizures) or laughter (gelastic seizures) but not both; Rett disorder, with excessive laughing, crying, and irritability, affecting only females; and Wilson disease (hepatolenticular degeneration), a genetically based degenerative disorder of copper metabolism that produces both involuntary crying and laughing. By far the most common cause is Alzheimer disease, a de-generative brain disorder, with about 39 percent of affected individuals showing pathological affect, 25 percent showing crying episodes, and 14 percent showing laughing or mixed laughing and crying episodes." Robert R. Provine, *Curious Behavior: Yawning, Laughing, Hiccupping, and Beyond* (Cambridge, MA: Harvard University Press, 2012), 76.

39. José Esteban Muñoz, "Feeling Brown, Feeling Down: Latina Affect, the Performativity of Race, and the Depressive Position," in *The Routledge Queer Studies Reader*, eds. Donald Hall and Annamarie Jagose (New York: Routledge, 2013), 415.

40. José Esteban Muñoz, "Feeling Brown: Ethnicity and Affect in Ricardo Barcho's *The Sweetest Hangover (and Other STDs)*," in *The Sense of Brown*, eds. Joshua Chambers-Letson and Tavia Nyong'o (Durham, NC: Duke University Press, 2020), 11.

41. Uri McMillan, *Embodied Avatars: Genealogies of Black Feminist Art and Performance* (New York: New York University Press, 2015); Tina Post, *Deadpan: The Aesthetics of Black Inexpression* (New York: New York University Press, 2022); Xine Yao, *Disaffected: The Cultural Politics of Unfeeling in Nineteenth-Century America* (Durham, NC: Duke University Press, 2021).

42. Judith Nelson, *Seeing Through Tears: Crying and Attachment* (New York: Routledge, 2005), xii.

43. Murube, "Basal, Reflex, and Psycho-emotional Tears," 63.

44. Darwin, *The Expression of the Emotions in Man and Animals*, 155.

45. "Although crying is very important for survival, because it elicits the necessary caregiving and protection, infants would do better to refrain from crying, unless it is really necessary, because they may jeopardize their own safety. This contributed to making crying an honest signal, which means that it reliably signals the qualities of the signaler to the receiver, and that it is only applied when the signaler is genuinely in need of help." Vingerhoets, *Why Only Humans Weep*, 27.

46. Vingerhoets, *Why Only Humans Weep*, 57. The phrase "acoustic umbilical cord" comes from Peter Ostwald, "The Sounds of Infancy," *Developmental Medicine & Child Neurology* 14 (1972): 350–61.

47. As film theorist Steve Neale writes regarding melodrama: "There would be no tears were there no belief that there might be an Other capable of responding to them." Steve Neale, "Melodrama and Tears," *Screen* 27, no. 6 (1986): 6–23.

48. Roland Barthes, *A Lover's Discourse*, 182. The quote at the end is from Schubert.

49. Teresa Brennan, *The Transmission of Affect* (Ithaca, NY: Cornell University Press, 2004), 5.

50. Juan Murube, "Etymology of the Term 'Tear'," *The Ocular Surface* 3, no. 4 (October 2005): 180.

51. Peggy Kamuf, "To Be Done Weeping," *Oxford Literary Review* 23, no. 1 (2001): 55. Terry Eagleton makes a similar claim that laughter (and crying) "involves the breakdown of signification into pure sound, spasm, rhythm and breath. It is hard to form impeccably well-shaped sentences when you are thrashing helplessly around on the floor," Terry Eagleton, *Humour* (New Haven: Yale University Press, 2019), 4. This emphasis on the end of crying as constitutive of the human aligns with the calculus of potentiality that I explored in my earlier book, *After Live: Possibility, Potentiality, and the Future of Performance* (Ann Arbor: University of Michigan Press, 2015). Following on the work of Giorgio Agamben, I explored how, in order to possess potentiality, one must not only be "able to do" something, but also and more importantly, one must be "able to not do" something. To have the potential to cry is thus to be able to *not* cry or "to stop weeping."

52. Darwin, *The Expression of the Emotions in Man and Animals*, 208. Murube writes of more recent research that follows this strand of logic: "It has been suggested that the tearing during laughing or yawning is produced by compression of the auriculo-temporal anastomosis that connects the facial nerve with the trigeminus [the nerve associated with the production of reflex tears]." Murube, "Basal, Reflex, and Psycho-emotional Tears," 62.

53. Samuel Beckett, *Molloy* (London: Picador, 1979), 35. Beckett finds more common ground between the two expressions when he has Pozzo in *Waiting for Godot* proclaim that "[t]he tears of the world are a constant quantity. For each

one who begins to weep somewhere else another stops. The same is true of the laugh." Samuel Beckett, *Waiting for Godot: A Tragicomedy in 2 Acts* (New York: Grove Press, 1984), 32.

54. Among the countless representations of this pairing, consider Lucian's dialogue *Philosophies for Sale*, where the two philosophers are auctioned off by the gods Hermes and Zeus. The first extant comparison between the two is in a fragment of Sotion, Seneca's teacher. See Cora E. Lutz, "Democritus and Heraclitus," *The Classical Journal* 49, no. 7 (April 1954): 309–14.

55. The two figures in the print are based on separate portrait etchings by Jan van Vliet, a student of Rembrandt, who himself took the expressions from paintings by his mentor. Svetlana Alpers writes of how the Heraclitus figure was inspired by Rembrandt's painting of the repentant Judas, shown in excessive contrition, but without inner conviction: "Built into Rembrandt's choice of the gestural display of Judas is, as it were, a prior admission of its performed nature." In the later prints, she writes, "the 'acting' aspect of the figure has been removed—he is what he appears to be." Svetlana Alpers, *Rembrandt's Enterprise: The Studio and the Market* (Chicago: University of Chicago, 1988), 36. In other words, as depicted here, Heraclitus's tears are derived from the work of a performer.

56. Lucian, "Philosophies for Sale," in *Lucian Volume II*, trans. A. M. Harmon (Cambridge, MA: Harvard University Press, 1915), 473.

57. Georges Bataille, *The Tears of Eros*, trans. Peter Connor (San Francisco: City Lights, 2001), 33.

58. While her keynote speech at the 2019 Hemispheric Institute proposed in its title an investigation of laughter and crying, it is worth noting that Butler devoted the preponderance of her attention to the former. In this she is not alone, as the many essays and books on laughter far outstrip the archive of writing on tears. Judith Butler, "Out of Breath: Laughing, Crying at the Body's Limit" (keynote presentation, Hemispheric Institute, Encuentro 2019, CDMX, Mexico, June 9–15, 2019), https://hemisphericinstitute.org/en/encuentro-2019-keynote-lectures/item/3084-keynote-lectures-004.html

59. Giorgio Agamben, *Pulcinella: Or Entertainment for Kids in Four Scenes*, trans. Kevin Attell (Chicago: Seagull Books, 2019), 12. Agamben's book is a study of the figure of *Pulcinella* via another father and son pair: the Italian Baroque artist Giambattista Tiepolo and his son Giandomenico Tiepolo. Both painted and etched several works featuring the masked commedia character, but the son devoted his last years to the production of 104 extraordinary drawings of Pulcinella, *Divertimento per li regazzi*, from which Agamben has taken his book's title.

60. Provine distinguishes between the sounds and durations of cries and laughter: "A cry is a sustained, voiced utterance, usually of around one second or more (reports vary), the duration of an outward breath. [. . .] Cries repeat at intervals of about one second, roughly the duration of one respiratory cycle.

[. . .] A laugh, in contrast, is a chopped (not sustained), usually voiced exhalation, as in 'haha-ha,' in which each syllable ('ha') lasts about 1/15 second and repeats every 1/5 second." Provine, *Curious Behavior*, 71–72.

61. Debra M. Zeifman, "Developmental Aspects of Crying," in *Adult Crying: A Biopsychosocial Approach*, 38.

62. Provine, *Curious Behavior*, 70.

63. Ann Lauterbach, "On Tears," in Rose-Lynn Fisher, *The Topography of Tears* (New York: Bellevue Press, 2017), 11.

64. Italo Calvino, *Collection of Sand*, trans. Martin McLaughlin (Boston: Mariner Books, 2014), 119–20.

65. Daniel Sack, "Not Looking into the Abyss: The Potentiality to See," in *On Not Looking: The Paradox of Contemporary Visual Culture*, ed. Frances Guerin (New York: Routledge, 2015), 43–62.

66. Asmir Gračanin, Emiel Krahmer, Mike Rinck, and Ad J. J. M. Vingerhoets, "The Effects of Tears on Approach–Avoidance Tendencies in Observers," *Evolutionary Psychology* 16, no. 3 (July 2018): 1–10. Incidentally, the photographs of people crying that were used for this experiment were chosen from the documentation of the performance *The Artist is Present* (Museum of Modern Art, 2010) by Marina Abramović, to whom we will return in Chapter 5.

67. Oren Hasson, "Emotional Tears as Biological Signals," *Evolutionary Psychology* 7, no. 3 (2009): 366.

68. Caroline A. Jones, *Eyesight Alone: Clement Greenberg's Modernism and the Bureaucratization of the Senses* (Chicago: University of Chicago Press, 2005).

69. Grzinic, "Emil Hrvatin's Memory Cabinets," 109.

70. "The close association of the theater with the evocation of the past, the histories and legends of the culture uncannily restored to a mysterious half-life here, has made the theater in the minds of many the art most closely related to memory and the theater building itself a kind of memory machine." Marvin Carlson, *The Haunted Stage: The Theatre as Memory Machine* (Ann Arbor: University of Michigan Press, 2001), 142. See also Alice Rayner, *Ghosts: Death's Double and the Phenomena of Theatre* (Minneapolis: University of Minnesota Press, 2006).

71. *Oxford English Dictionary.* https://www.oed.com/

72. Montaigne, "Of the Power of the Imagination," in *The Complete Essays of Montaigne*, trans. Donald M. Frame (Palo Alto, CA: Stanford University Press, 1958), 68.

73. "A flock's by one contagious sheep destroy'd. / If health you'd keep, shun those who are unsound; / By looking on sore eyes, our own we wound; / Dry lands are oft by neighb'ring rivers drowned." Ovid, *Remedia Amoris (Art of Love)*, trans. Nahum Tate (1795), Book I, lines 671–675. The contagious nature of pitiful tears also grounds Rousseau's understanding of the basis of empathy.

74. The literature on emotional didacticism in tragedy is extensive, espe-

cially in the 18th century. Within the British sphere, see, for example, John Dennis's *The Usefulness of the Stage* (London 1698), 53–54: "Tragedy [. . .] has been always found sufficient to soften the most obdurate heart." Or consider John Dryden's "Dedication of the Aeneis (1697)," in *Essays II*, ed. W. P. Ker (Oxford: Clarendon Press, 1900), 158: "To raise, and afterwards to calm the passions [. . .] to expel arrogance, and introduce compassion, are the true great effects of tragedy."

75. James Baldwin, *Notes of a Native Son* (Boston: Beacon Press, 1957), 14.

76. Montaigne, "Of Giving the Lie," *The Complete Essays*, 504.

77. With reference primarily to Indo-European languages, Juan Murube writes that "the liquid was known in all languages in the plural (tears in English; slëzbi in Russian; demúa in Arabic, larmes in French, tränen in German, lágrimas in Spanish), which still persists in popular and medical speech and in the literature" (Murube, "Basal, Reflex, and Psycho-emotional Tears," 62).

78. For a good overview of the essay and its sensibility see Brian Dillon, *Essayism: On Form, Feeling, and Nonfiction* (New York: New York Review of Books, 2017).

79. Theodor Adorno, "The Essay as Form," in Theodor W. Adorno, *Notes to Literature, Volume One*, ed. Rolf Tiedemann, trans. Shierry Weber Nicholsen (New York: Columbia University Press, 1991), 16.

CHAPTER 2

1. "Conventionally, the tear film is thought to be composed of three layers: an outer lipid layer (~ 0.1 μm thick) produced by the meibomian glands in the tarsal plate; a central aqueous layer (~ 7 to 10 μm thick) produced by both the main and accessory lacrimal glands; and an inner mucin layer (~ 0.2 to 1.0 μm thick) produced by goblet cells in the conjunctiva." Mark B. Abelson and Ashley Lafond, "3,500 Years of Artificial Tears," *Review of Ophthalmology*, December 8, 2014, https://www.reviewofophthalmology.com/article/3500-years-of-artificial-tears

2. "There are small openings inside the edges of the eyelids near the nose. Each upper and lower eyelid has one of these openings, called a punctum. These four openings, or puncta, act like little valves to take tears out of the eye. Each time we blink, some tear fluid is pumped out of the eye through the puncta." "Tear System (Lacrimal Apparatus)," Cleveland Clinic, accessed April 17, 2023, https://my.clevelandclinic.org/health/diseases/17540-tear-system

3. Roland Barthes, *Camera Lucida: Reflections on Photography*, trans. Richard Howard (New York: Hill and Wang, 1980), 27. "What I name cannot really prick me. The incapacity to name is a good symptom of disturbance" (51). Later, Barthes writes about a second kind of *punctum* in some photographs: "Time, the lacerating emphasis of the *noeme* ('that-has-been'), its pure representation" (96).

4. These proteins include "lysozyme, lipocalin, nerve growth factor, and lactoferrin; all of these substances are involved in the defense and/or healing mechanisms of the eye." Ad J. J. M. Vingerhoets, *Why Only Humans Weep*, 52. "[Carl Ferdinand Ritter von] Arlt in 1855 collected pure tear from the orbital lacrimal gland in which the content was: 98.223% water, sodium chloride 1.25%, albumin 0.504%, other salts (carbonate, sulphate, phospates) 0.016%, and lipid traces." Juan Murube, "The Origin of Tears I: The Aqueo-serous Component in the XIX and XX Centuries," *The Ocular Surface* 10, no. 2 (April 2012): 59.

5. See Juan Murube, "The Origin of Tears II: The Mucinic Component in the XIX and XX Centuries," *The Ocular Surface* 10, no. 3 (July 2012): 131. I also rely on the other two parts of Murube's review articles: "The Origin of Tears I: The Aqueo-serous Component in the XIX and XX Centuries," *The Ocular Surface* 10, no. 2 (April 2012): 56–66; and "The Origin of Tears III: The Lipid Component in the XIX and XX Centuries," *The Ocular Surface* 10, no. 4 (October 2012): 200–209.

6. For more on the anatomy of the eye, see, among others, Sharon Fekrat, Henry Feng, and Tanya S. Glaser, eds., *All about Your Eyes* (Durham: Duke University Press, 2021).

7. Jean Janin first proposed the existence of basal tears and that tears are produced by glands in the late 18th century. See Murube, "Basal, Reflex, and Pyscho-emotional Tears," *The Ocular Surface* 7, no. 2 (2009): 60–66. See also Lutz, *Crying*, 76–77.

8. Roughly 2 million epithelial cells are shed every day. M. S. Norn, "The Conjunctival Fluid, its Height, Volume, Density of Cells, and Flow," *Acta Ophthalmologica* 44 (1966): 212–22.

9. "[B]asal tear is not of a uniform type. There are many variants or subtypes related to physiologic conditions (open eyes, closed eyes, during eye-rubbing, walking, sleeping in REM and NREM periods, etc.) or abnormal states (after topical anesthesia, under general anesthesia, after sensorial denervation, after pre- or postganglionic efferent denervation, etc.)." Murube, "Basal, Reflex, and Pyscho-emotional Tears," 61.

10. For one of many articles published on this research, see Robert A. Sack, Ann Beaton, Sonal Sathe, Carol Morris, Mark Willcox, and Bruce Bogart, "Towards a Closed Eye Model of the Pre-Ocular Tear Layer," *Progress in Retinal Eye Research* 19, no. 6 (2000): 649–68.

11. Hans Christian Andersen, "Ole Lukøie," *The Complete Andersen*, trans. Jean Hersholt (New York: Limited Editions Club, 1949), https://andersen.sdu.dk/vaerk/hersholt/OleLukoie_e.html

12. Rose-Lynn Fisher, *The Topography of Tears* (New York: Bellevue Literary Press, 2017).

CHAPTER 3

1. I have excerpted this shorter version of the quotation from Reverend James Wood's exhaustively titled *Dictionary of Quotations: from Ancient and Modern, English and Foreign Sources; including phrases, mottoes, maxims, proverbs, definitions, aphorisms, and sayings of wise men, in their bearing on life, literature, speculation, science, art, religion, and morals especially in the modern aspects of them* (New York: Frederick Warne and Co., 1899), 470.

2. Boli finds numerous examples of the text in the 1840s and 1850s attributed to Johnson; by the 1880s it is attributed to Irving, and it seems to have stuck. "Find the Source of the Quotation," *Dr. Boli's Celebrated Magazine*, August 11, 2015, https://drboli.com/2015/08/11/find-the-source-of-the-quotation/

3. Debra M. Zeifman, "Developmental Aspects of Crying: Infancy, and Beyond Childhood," in *Adult Crying: A Biopsychosocial Approach*, eds. Ad J.J.M. Vingerhoets and Randolph R. Cornelius (New York: Routledge, 2001), 48.

4. In Christian thought, for example, Saint Anthony was the first to claim tears as a primary expression of the devout. Diane Apostolos-Cappadona writes that the "early Christian monastic theology of the gratia lacrimarum is confirmed in the Rule of St. Benedict in which it is pronounced that to be pure prayer, heartfelt prayer must be accompanied by tears." "'Pray with Tears and Your Request Will Find a Hearing': On the Iconology of the Magdalene's Tears" in *Holy Tears: Weeping in the Religious Imagination*, eds. Kimberley Christine Patton and John Stratton Hawley (Princeton, NJ: Princeton University Press, 2005), 205. The essays in this collection consider other religious traditions in ways that are relevant here.

5. Daniel Sack, ed., *Imagined Theatres: Writing for a Theoretical Stage* (New York: Routledge, 2017). The project continues in the online journal www.imaginedtheatres.com

6. Andrew Sofer, "Private Language Argument II" from Sack, *Imagined Theatres*, 178.

7. Ferdinand de Saussure, *Course in General Linguistics*, trans. Wade Baskin (New York: McGraw-Hill, 1965), 65–70.

8. Ludwig Wittgenstein, *Philosophical Investigations*, trans. G. E. M. Anscombe (Oxford: Blackwell, 1958), § 243.

9. Sack, *Imagined Theatres*, 179.

10. Thomas Dixon, *Weeping Britannia: Portrait of a Nation in Tears* (Oxford: Oxford University Press, 2015), 7.

11. Eve Kosofsky Sedgwick, *Tendencies* (Durham, NC: Duke University Press, 1993), xii.

12. The title for the proposed trilogy borrows from P. D. Ouspensky's account of the philosophy and biography of the Russian thinker Gurdjieff, *In Search of the Miraculous: The Teachings of G. I. Gurdjieff* (New York: Harper, 2001).

13. Daniel Sack, *After Live: Possibility, Potentiality, and the Future of Performance* (Ann Arbor: University of Michigan Press, 2015).

14. Teresa Brennan, *The Transmission of Affect* (Ithaca: Cornell University Press, 2004), 5.

15. Sara Ahmed, *The Cultural Politics of Emotion* (Edinburgh: Edinburgh University Press, 2014), 31.

16. June Casagrande, *The Best Punctuation Book, Period: A Comprehensive Guide for Every Writer, Editor, Student, and Businessperson* (Berkeley: Ten Speed Press, 2014), 71.

17. Tsang now speaks of the video as her first work of art. Jeni Fulton in conversation with Wu Tsang, "How I became an artist: Wu Tsang," posted August 30, 2019, https://www.artbasel.com/news/wu-tsang-how-i-became-an-artist-art-basel?lang=en

18. https://queermaps.org/place/silver-platter

19. Hettie Judah, "Sister of the sword: Wu Tsang, the trans artist retelling history with lesbian kung fu," in *The Guardian*, May 17, 2017, https://www.theguardian.com/artanddesign/2017/may/17/wu-tsang-boychild-devotional-document-trans?CMP=gu_com

20. Mel Baggs, "In My Language," YouTube Video, 8:36, January 14, 2007, https://www.youtube.com/watch?v=JnylM1hI2jc

21. Eric Hayot, "Chinese Bodies, Chinese Futures: Nationalism and Its Discontents," *Representations* 99, no. 1 (Summer 2007): 103.

22. Tsang has elsewhere explored the concept of the threshold through the theatrical figure of the curtain. See, for example, Tsang's collaborative sculpture performance *Gravitational Feel*, created with Fred Moten, and the process of its development as explored in the book *Who Touched Me* (2016), where the two ruminate extensively on the curtain and fabric as opportunities for haptic connection.

23. Xine Yao, *Disaffected: The Cultural Politics of Unfeeling in Nineteenth-Century America* (Durham, NC: Duke University Press, 2021), 31.

24. Jeffrey A. Kottler, *The Language of Tears* (Hoboken, NJ: Jossey-Bass, 1996), 12.

25. Jennifer DeVere Brody, *Punctuation: Art, Politics, and Play* (Durham, NC: Duke University Press, 2008), 3.

26. Marjorie Garber, *Quotation Marks* (New York: Routledge, 2003), 8.

27. Such instances benefit from the power of surrogation, which, as Roach has shown, emphasizes uninterrupted continuity over rupture, in order to forget trauma and loss. See Joseph Roach, *Cities of the Dead: Circum-Atlantic Performance* (New York: Columbia University Press, 1996).

28. Thanks to Yelena Gluzman for the clarity of this insight.

29. Brody, *Punctuation*, 109. Brody references Susan Sontag's "Notes on 'Camp'" (1964), in which she writes of camp sensibility putting quotation marks around its objects.

30. Each film runs roughly 4 ½ minutes; shot at 24 frames per second and meant to be played at 16 frames per second, they seem slightly askance from our time.

31. Immediately after making this screen test, Buchanan recorded the second one in which she slowly crosses her eyes. See Callie Angell, *Andy Warhol Screen Tests: The Films of Andy Warhol Catalogue Raisonné: Vol. I* (New York: Abrams, 2006).

32. Giulia Palladini, *The Scene of Foreplay: Theater, Labor, and Leisure in 1960s New York* (Evanston, IL: Northwestern University Press, 2017), 174.

CHAPTER 4

1. During the period in which she made the work discussed in this essay, the artist went by the name of Sam Taylor-Wood. She changed her name in 2012 when she married the actor Aaron Johnson.

2. The exclusion of anyone of Asian descent threatens to repeat racist notions of cold Eastern passivity and effeminacy or, more charitably, illuminates Hollywood's deplorable record in these regards.

3. Big girls may cry less than little girls. Reviewing the literature on crying in children versus crying in adults, Judith Kay Nelson writes "[b]oys cry as often as girls, if not more often, until puberty at which point crying decreases for both sexes. In the mid-teen years male crying drops off sharply to well below the average for girls, a pattern that continues throughout adulthood" (Nelson, *Seeing Through Tears*, 138).

4. Agneta H. Fischer, Marrie H. J. Bekker, Ad J. J. M. Vingerhoets, Marleen C. Becht, and Antony S. R. Manstead, "Femininity, Masculinity, and the Riddle of Crying," in *Emotional Expression and Health: Advances in Theory, Assessment and Clinical Applications*, eds. Ivan Nyklíček and Lydia Temoshok (New York: Routledge, 2006), 289. Frey also found that women cry on average 5.3 times per month, while men cry on average 1.3 times per month. The literature here is vast. For a good survey, see Marrie H. J. Bekker and Ad J. J. M. Vingerhoets, "Male and Female Tears: Swallowing Versus Shedding? The Relationship between Crying, Biological Sex and Gender" in *Adult Crying*, 91–113.

5. Fischer et al., "Femininity, Masculinity, and the Riddle of Crying," 299.

6. See, for example, Anna Caraveli on Greek wailing songs and ritual poems in "The Bitter Wounding: The Lament as Social Protest in Rural Greece" in *Gender and Power in Rural Greece*, ed. Jill Dubisch (Princeton, NJ: Princeton University Press, 1986). Jacob K. Olúpònà and Şǫlá Ajíbádé write of how Yorùbán ritual weepers "serve as a medium for bestowing communal values on motherhood and virginity and as a metaphor for conveying deep-seated cultural angst about gender relations, social tension, and familiar conflict." "Ẹkuń Ìyàwó: Bridal Tears in Marriage Rites of Passage among the Òyó-Yorùbá of Nigeria," in *Holy Tears: Weeping in the Religious Imagination*, eds. Kimberley Christine Patton and

John Stratton Hawley (Princeton, NJ: Princeton University Press, 2005), 166.

7. Lorna Collier, "Why we cry," *American Psychological Association* 45, no. 2 (February 2014): 47, https://www.apa.org/monitor/2014/02/cry

8. Bridget Escolme writes of how constructions of masculinity in early modern England relied upon the moderation of grief, but not its suppression. "To mourn too little is to place oneself outside the bounds of what it is to be human; to mourn too much is to place oneself outside of masculine subjectivity and an active agency in the world." Bridget Escolme, *Emotional Excess on the Shakespearean Stage: Passion's Slaves* (New York: Bloomsbury, 2014), 186.

9. Hélène Monsacré, *The Tears of Achilles*, trans. Nicholas J. Snead (Cambridge, MA: Harvard University Press, 2017), 85.

10. Annie-B Parson, *The Choreography of Everyday Life* (New York: Verso, 2022), 75.

11. Clare Carolin, "Interview with Sam Taylor-Wood," in *Sam Taylor-Wood* (Göttingen: Steidl, 2002), unpaginated. For her *Five Revolutionary Seconds* series (1995–1999) Taylor-Johnson set a photographic camera at the center of a room on a device that allowed it to steadily pan around the space, its slow five-second rotation of 360 degrees extending duration into a single panoramic shot. Daniel Birnbaum describes how, "[i]t is as if the sequential unfolding of time is compressed into a single, momentary gaze; an entire movie, or different movies, frozen into one paradoxical frame." Daniel Birnbaum, "Sam Taylor-Wood," *Artforum* (November 1996): 89.

12. There are numerous other examples from the artist's oeuvre. *Atlantic* (1997), a short three-channel film, catches a couple mid-argument in a restaurant, but leaves the terms of their disagreement unexplained. One of the screens focuses on the tear-stained face of the woman throughout. For *Dolorosa* (2000), Taylor-Johnson photographed supermodel Kate Moss with a tear in her eye. In the ten-minute film *Breach* (2001), a woman is trapped by the camera and an unseen tormentor as she breaks down.

13. Clare Carolin, "Interview with Sam Taylor-Wood," *Sam Taylor-Wood*, unpaginated.

14. Michael Bracewell, "The Art of Sam Taylor-Wood," *Sam Taylor-Wood*, unpaginated.

15. Gambon would take over the part of the avuncular head of the wizarding school Hogwarts in the third installment of the *Harry Potter* movies after the death of the actor who originated the role, Richard Harris. An article in the *LA Times* describes the arc of most of Christensen's films as follows: "An angry, misunderstood boy-on-the-verge-of-manhood seeks respect and attention and has a fantastically affecting crying scene along the way to his eventual enlightenment, vindication or descent." Cory Ohlendorf, "No need to cry for Hayden Christensen," *Los Angeles Times*, February 16, 2008, https://www.latimes.com/archives/la-xpm-2008-feb-16-et-christensen16-story.html

16. With extra time after finishing the shoot for the Elton John video,

Taylor-Johnson posed with a bare-chested Downey Jr. draped across her lap and photographed *Self Pietà* (2001) and the short video *Pietà* (2002).

17. Laura Cumming, "Enough to make you weep," *The Guardian*, November 7, 2004, https://www.theguardian.com/artanddesign/2004/nov/07/art

18. Ariella Azoulay, *The Civil Contract of Photography*, trans. Rela Mazali and Ruvik Danieli (Princeton, NJ: Princeton University Press, 2012).

19. Lionel Trilling, *Sincerity and Authenticity* (Cambridge, MA: Harvard University Press, 1971), 2.

20. Ernst Van Alphen, Mieke Bal, and Carel Smith, eds., *The Rhetoric of Sincerity* (Palo Alto, CA: Stanford University Press, 2008), 3.

21. William Archer identifies blushing and pallor as the two symptoms of emotion "which are utterly beyond the control of the will, [and] cannot possibly be simulated," yet nevertheless occur in performance. William Archer and Denis Diderot, *The Paradox of Acting and Masks or Faces?* (New York: Hill and Wang, 1957), 159. Renata Kobetts Miller writes of the dichotomy of cosmetics as artifice and the blush as mark of authenticity on the Victorian stage in *The Victorian Actress in the Novel and on the Stage* (Edinburgh: Edinburgh University Press, 2019), 52–53.

22. Rebecca Schneider, *Performing Remains: Art and War in the Times of Theatrical Reenactment* (New York: Routledge, 2011), 101. Marvin Carlson, "Performing the Past: Living History and Cultural Memory," *Paragrana* 9, no. 2 (2000): 237–48.

23. Jackie Cooper with Dick Kleiner, *Please Don't Shoot My Dog* (New York: William Morrow and Company, 1981), 43.

24. Of course, adult actors are not safe from this kind of cruelty, and their tormentors include some of the most acclaimed directors in the history of cinema. As one of many examples, Stanley Kubrick's psychological torture of Shelley Duvall on the set of *The Shining* (1980) is well documented.

25. Among many other works on this subject, Joseph Roach's exceptional monograph *The Player's Passion* (Ann Arbor: University of Michigan Press, 1985) traces this legacy and other theories of acting alongside contemporaneous scientific writings.

26. This matter of the inexpert and unknowing artist is taken up more fully with regards to all fiction in *The Republic*, where it forms one of the grounds for Plato/Socrates's exclusion of most artists from his ideal society. The artist pretends to know many things by depicting them, but this knowledge only covers the surface of representation; the actual being of things, how they are made or function, is inaccessible to them.

27. Plato, "Ion," in *Plato: The Collected Dialogues*, eds. Edith Hamilton and Huntington Cairns (Princeton, NJ: Princeton University Press, 1961), 535c.

28. Cole and Chinoy, *Actors on Acting*, 126.

29. One of the greatest exemplars of the sensible actor, François-Joseph Talma (1763–1826), writes of sensibility as the "faculty which an actor pos-

sesses of being moved himself, and of affecting his being so far as to imprint on his features, and especially on his voice, that expression and those accents of sorrow which awake all the sympathies of the art and extort tears from auditors" (Cole and Chinoy, *Actors on Acting*, 181).

30. Cole and Chinoy, *Actors on Acting*, 208.

31. Benoît-Constant Coquelin, "Acting and Actors," *Harper's New Monthly Magazine* 74, no. 4 (May 1887): 894.

32. Even as he finds himself caught up in emotion, Ion remains aware of his acting's influence on spectators. He speaks of watching his audience's response closely "for if I set them weeping, I myself shall laugh when I get my money, but if they laugh, it is I who have to weep at losing it" (Plato, "Ion," *Plato: The Collected Dialogues*, 535e). He performs with a double consciousness, invested in the moment of performance, while also aware of actions from outside: both crying in the scene and laughing at the efficacy of his performance.

33. Archer and Diderot, *The Paradox of Acting and Masks or Faces?*, 14.

34. Coquelin, "Acting and Actors," 904.

35. Diderot, quoted by William Archer, in Archer and Diderot, *The Paradox of Acting and Masks or Faces?*, 130.

36. Martin Meisel convincingly shows the integration of painting and the stage in the nineteenth century in his book *Realizations: Narrative, Pictorial, and Theatrical Arts in Nineteenth-Century England* (Princeton, NJ: Princeton University Press, 1984). Le Brun writes voluminously about the pictorial depiction of weeping but neglects any mention of tears: "In Weeping, the Eye-brow falls toward the middle of the Forehead; the Eyes are almost shut, very wet and cast down towards the Cheeks.; the Nostrils swelled' all the muscles and veins of the Forehead very visible; the Mouth half-open, down at the corners, and making wrinkles in the Cheeks; the Under-lip will appear hanging down and pouting out; the whole Face wrinkled and knit; the color very red, especially about the Eye-brows, eh Eyes, the Nose, and the Cheeks." *A Method to Learn to Design the Passions. Conference by Mr. Le Brun, Chief Painter to the French King, to the Academists in the Royal Academy in Paris, 1734*, trans. John Williams (Los Angeles: University of California Press, 1980), 44. Derrida draws our attention to this oversight in *Memoirs of the Blind: The Self-Portrait and Other Ruins*, trans. Pascale-Anne Brault and Michael Naas (Chicago: University of Chicago Press, 1993), 127–28.

37. Cole and Chinoy, *Actors on Acting*, 186. Talma began his career as a proponent of sensibility, but his adherence to inspirational acting purportedly reached a head when, having fainted during a curtain call, his doctor claimed his acting would take his life. Tempering his reliance on emotional investment, Talma wrote in his later career of a more analytic approach, dotted with passages informed by Diderot's own texts. See Alan J. Freer, "Talma and Diderot's Paradox on Acting," *Diderot Studies* 8 (1966): 23–76.

38. Archer locates Diderot's celebration of the analytic actor as a product

of 18th century thought. He references Cicero and Quintilian on how Roman orators made use of their own passions to embellish the efficacy of rhetoric and offers several instances from the voluminous meta-theatrical statements of Shakespeare, many of which prove that contemporaneous actors wept in character. Archer and Diderot, *The Paradox of Acting and Masks or Faces?*, 89–101.

39. Archer and Diderot, *The Paradox of Acting and Masks or Faces?*, 103.

40. Archer and Diderot, *The Paradox of Acting and Masks or Faces?*, 78.

41. Archer and Diderot, *The Paradox of Acting and Masks or Faces?*, 102.

42. Aeneas explains that the mural depicts episodes from the Trojan War, the conflict that destroyed Aeneas's people and sent him into exile. His words, "Sunt lacrimae rerum et mentem mortalia tangent," (Book 1, line 462) are the subject of much commentary and can be variously translated as "[t]he world is a world of tears, and the burdens of mortality touch the heart" (Robert Fagles, Viking translation, 2006); "They weep here / For how the world goes, and our life that passes / Touches their hearts" (Robert Fitzgerald, Random House translation, 1983); among many others. In any case, the subsequent phrase ties this weeping to the matter of mortality, and to memory's regard of the passage of time.

43. Archer and Diderot, *The Paradox of Acting and Masks or Faces?*, 138.

44. Henry Irving, for example, reports that his predecessor William Macready also borrowed from his private suffering to feed his acting: "When Macready played Virginius, after burying his beloved daughter, he confessed that his real experience gave a new force to his acting in the most pathetic situations of the play" (Cole and Chinoy, *Actors on Acting*, 357). It is perhaps peculiar that so many of these anecdotes hinge upon the experience of losing a child, which seems a rare, though not unheard of, occurrence today. The terribly high rates of infant mortality in the 19th century meant it was far more common for fathers and mothers to have lost a child—roughly one in three children born in 1800 would not survive.

45. "[Helene Weigel] described this to me as a way in which Brecht made it difficult for the actor, a way 'he made the actor suffer.'" Richard Schechner and Lee Strasberg, "Working with Live Material: An interview with Lee Strasberg," in *Stanislavski and America: "The Method" and its Influence on the American Theatre*, ed. Erika Munk (New York: Fawcett Publications, Inc., 1967), 185.

46. David Krasner, ed., *Method Acting Reconsidered: Theory, Practice, Future* (New York: Palgrave Macmillan, 2000), 51. In confirmation of this lineage, the version of "Masks or Faces? A Study in the Psychology of Acting" referenced here was republished alongside Diderot's dialogue in a mass market trade paperback in 1957; Lee Strasberg wrote the introduction to the volume.

47. Krasner, *Method Acting Reconsidered*, 300.

48. Cole and Chinoy, *Actors on Acting*, 509.

49. Strasberg, "Working with Live Material," 197. However absolute and forceful Strasberg's proclamations may sound in their attempt to thread Did-

erot's needle of the actor as craftsperson, they collapse with a little pressure. It is not clear what distinguishes a "really real" emotion from a remembered emotion, or how affect might keep temporalities so distinctly segregated.

50. Strasberg, "Working with Live Material," 198. According to Michael Schulman, the actor "tries to reexperience the specific stimuli of the past event instead of simply recalling the event of remembering the emotion." Quoted in S. Loraine Hull, *Strasberg's Method As Taught by Lorrie Hull: A Practical Guide for Actors, Teachers and Directors* (Santa Barbara, CA: Hull-Smithers, 2004), 83.

51. Samuel Beckett, *Proust and Three Dialogues* (London: John Calder, 1987), 72–73. I've written of this passage elsewhere in relation to Beckett's play *Krapp's Last Tape*, which places its namesake amid a kind of affective memory exercise. See Daniel Sack, *Samuel Beckett's Krapp's Last Tape* (New York: Routledge, 2016), 44–47.

52. Lee Strasberg, "Working with Live Material," 189. Robert Lewis makes a similar point in his essay "Emotional Memory," *Tulane Drama Review* 6, no. 4 (Summer 1962), 54–60.

53. "Self Made: a film by Gillian Wearing," https://www.selfmade.org.uk/gillian

54. Kara Rooney, "Gillian Wearing: *People*," *The Brooklyn Rail*, June 2011, https://brooklynrail.org/2011/06/artseen/gillian-wearing-peopleem

55. *Oxford English Dictionary*. www.oed.com. My emphasis.

56. Mark Fisher, "Gillian Wearing: Self Made," *Sight & Sound* 21, no. 10 (October 2011): 76.

57. Good student of acting that he is, Hamlet's own theatrical adaptation, *The mousetrap*, hinges upon the expectation that Claudius will display his guilt like the most sensible of actors, allowing the free play of his passion across his face: "if he but blench, / I know my course" (*Hamlet*, 2.2.571).

58. *Hamlet*, 5.1.289–294.

59. Jean Baudrillard, *Simulacra and Simulation*, trans. Sheila Faria Glaser (Ann Arbor: University of Michigan Press, 1994). Baudrillard is writing of Jorge Luis Borges's parable "On Exactitude in Science" (1946) about an imagined civilization whose pursuit of cartography progressed to such an extent that they finally produced a map of the world that corresponded precisely with the actual world. It is a map like a mask that perfectly fits the face of the world; a sincere map, one might say. Borges writes of how, having thus exhausted the limits of description, these people soon grew tired of representing their world and left the map to weather and wear away so completely that now, only in the farthest reaches of the deserts, "there are Tattered Ruins of that Map, inhabited by Animals and Beggars." In a reversal of expectations, those excluded from representation now inhabit its remains. Jorge Luis Borges, *Collected Fictions*, trans. Andrew Hurley (New York: Penguin Books, 1999), 325.

CHAPTER 5

1. Peter Shaw, *Man, A Paper for Ennobling the Species*, no. 43 (October 22, 1755), 2. Quoted in Tom Lutz, *Crying: The Natural and Cultural History of Tears* (New York: Norton, 2001), 31.

2. There are many new technologies to address dry eye syndrome. For example, "Using a process called neurostimulation, the TrueTear® device painlessly sends tiny pulses of energy through the nasal cavity to stimulate the glands surrounding the eyes to produce basal tears" (https://pricevisiongroup .com/conditions/dry-eye/truetear/). My counterfeiter's toolbox resembles others. As Courtney Kersten reflects on her childhood acting classes in her essay "Method Acting": "Crying was the hard part. We, students in the art of professional pretending, would sit in a circle and pass around a gutted chili pepper and dab our eyes with the innards, a bag of onions sitting in the corner on stand-by. We'd smear menthol on each other's faces and stage complex sleights of hand with eye-drop bottles hidden in jean pockets." In *River Teeth: A Journal of Nonfiction Narrative* 16, no. 2 (Spring 2015), 135.

3. Alice Rayner, *Ghosts: Death's Double and the Phenomena of Theatre* (Minneapolis: University of Minnesota Press, 2006), 75. Also quoted in Eleanor Margolies, *Props* (New York: Palgrave, 2016), 178.

4. Jean Baudrillard, *Simulacra and Simulation*, trans. Sheila Faria Glaser (Ann Arbor: University of Michigan Press, 1994).

5. The Prague semiotician Jiří Veltruský writes that "the prop is usually designated the passive tool of the actor's action. This does not, however, do full justice to its nature. The prop is not always passive. It has a force (which we call the action force) that attracts a certain action to it. As soon as a certain prop appears on the stage, this force which it has provokes in us the expectation of a certain action." Jiří Veltruský, "Man and Object in the Theatre," in *A Prague School Reader on Esthetics, Literary Structure, and Style*, ed. Paul Garvin (Washington, DC: Georgetown, 1964), 88. Bruno Latour's work on the agency of things extends this conception greatly. See, for example, Bruno Latour, *Reassembling the Social: An Introduction to Actor-Network-Theory* (Oxford: Oxford University Press, 2007).

6. The weekly publication *Man, a paper for ennobling the species* ran for one year and was an early precursor to the modern medical journal. See Eric Colman, "A brief note on *Man*," *The Lancet* 358, no. 9282 (August 25, 2001): 674. DOI: https://doi.org/10.1016/S0140-6736(05)71682-2

7. William Shakespeare, *Henry IV, Part 1*, ed. David Scott Kastan (London: Arden Shakespeare, 2002), 2.4.384–386 and 414–15.

8. Such a prompt book can incite tears with some reliability, but most tears researchers who venture into the study of psychogenic tears rely on film and video to trigger their subjects' weeping. See, for example, the use of the funeral scene in *Steel Magnolias* (1989) in James Gross, Barbara L. Frederickson, and Robert W. Levenson, "The Psychophysiology of Crying," in *Psychophysiology*

31 (1994): 460–68. For her video performance *Neapolitan*, Nao Bustamante recorded herself watching and rewatching the final scene of the Mexican melodrama *Fresa y Chocolate* (1993) on repeat, weeping continuously. The scene, which she called "an emotional vibrator of sorts," reliably triggered her cathartic climaxes, disidentifying with the affective excess attached to the Latinx body that José Muñoz has described as a sense of Brownness. For an excellent reading of this work and the work of Patty Chang, discussed below, see Amber Jamilla Musser, *Sensual Excess: Queer Femininity and Brown Jouissance* (New York: New York University Press, 2018), 119–43.

9. Profeta continues: "I talked to her about it, but I never saw inside it—except once in 2011, when she read it in public in the atrium at the Museum of Modern Art, before a duet performance with Ralph [Lemon]." Katherine Profeta, *Dramaturgy in Motion: At Work on Dance and Movement Performance* (Madison: University of Wisconsin Press, 2015), 84.

10. Phelan continues: "This identity-less-ness allows us to imagine a different way to place death in our cultural and psychic imaginary. For the death reading and theatre offers us is, at once, both always our own and never our own." Peggy Phelan, "Not Surviving Reading," *Narrative* 5, no. 1 (Jan 1997): 78.

11. Thornton Wilder, *Our Town* (New York: Perennial Classics, HarperCollins, 1998), 111.

12. Julius Hirschberg, *The History of Ophthalmology, Volume I: Antiquity*, trans. F. C. Blodi (Bonn, Germany: Verlag J.P. Wayenborgh, 1982), 155.

13. "[T]he most common purpose of artificial tears is to decrease dryness. [. . .] Artificial tears are also lubricants meaning they decrease friction on the ocular surface caused by the eyelid. Another treatment goal in ocular surface disease is to increase tear retention. Artificial tears do this by increasing tear viscosity, increasing the adherence of the tears to the ocular surface, decreasing tear evaporation, and decreasing tear clearance." Tressa Larson, "Artificial Tears: A Primer," *EyeRounds.org*, November 23, 2016, http://webeye.ophth.uiowa.edu/eyeforum/tutorials/artificial-tears.htm. Tear substitutes using sodium chloride were invented in the early 1900s, including Wyeth's Collyrium (Latin for "eye wash") and Ross's Murine; the 1980s saw a rapid expansion of different kinds of artificial tears. See Mark B. Abelson, "Dry Eye: Through the Years in Tears," *Review of Ophthalmology*, September 23, 2009, https://www.reviewofophthalmology.com/article/dry-eye-through-the-years-in-tears

14. Hugo Gernsback, "Television Technique," (1931) in *The Perversity of Things: Hugo Gernsback on Media, Tinkering, and Scientifiction*, ed. Grant Wythoff (Minneapolis: University of Minnesota Press, 2016), 346. Generally regarded as father of Science Fiction, Gernsbeck has also been called "the father of American electronic culture." See Wythoff's introduction to *The Perversity of Things*.

15. Béla Balázs, *Theory of the Film: Character and Growth of a New Art*, trans. Edith Bone (London: Dennis Dobson, 1952), 77.

16. The Wooster Group has returned to the prosthetic tear in several of its

productions. Ron Vawter twice used glycerine onstage to simulate weeping: first in *Nayatt School* (1977) and again in a video for *Fish Story* (1994), where he played Vershinin from *The Three Sisters*, departing for his ill-fated duel. I am deeply grateful to company member and archivist, Clay Hapaz, for sharing this wealth of material with me, which itself could fill a chapter or more.

17. Philip Auslander, "Task and Vision: Willem Dafoe in *L.S.D.*," *The Drama Review: TDR* 29, no. 2 (Summer 1985): 95. Auslander glosses this moment to say that "signs of emotional commitment in acting were distanced and demystified. To depict John Proctor's break-down, Willem Dafoe, the performer reading the part, placed glycerin drops in his eyes to s(t)imulate tears; the image of a crying man was presented alongside the artificial means used to create." Philip Auslander, "Toward a Concept of the Political in Postmodern Theatre," *Theatre Journal* 39, no. 1 (1987): 29.

18. The Wooster Group. "September 28, 2015—from the archives—unused silent Super-8 footage of *The Crucible* (c. 1982)," accessed April 27, 2022, http://thewoostergroup.org/blog/2015/09/28/from-the-archives-unused-silent-super-8-footage-of-the-crucible-c-1982/

19. As one of the earliest celebrity authors, Rousseau received mountains of fan mail from readers who attested to their tearful relationships with the characters in the novel. Robert Darnton devotes a chapter to this moment in the history of reading in *The Great Cat Massacre and Other Episodes in French Cultural History* (New York: Basic Books, 2009).

20. Jean-Jacques Rousseau, *Julie, or the New Heloise: Letters of Two Lovers Who Live in a Small Town at the Foot of the Alps*, trans. and ed. Philip Stewart and Jean Vaché (Lebanon, NH: Dartmouth College Press, 1997), 428.

21. Anne Vincent-Buffault, *The History of Tears: Sensibility and Sentimentality in France*, trans. Teresa Bridgeman (Basingstoke: Macmillan, 1991), 54.

22. La Porte quoted on Vincent-Buffault, 57.

23. Andrew Sofer, *The Stage Life of Props* (Ann Arbor: University of Michigan Press, 1998), 66. Subsequently, the vernacular cycle plays of the fourteenth and fifteenth century first recorded the figure of Veronica, who wiped the sweat and blood off Christ's face with her veil or sudarium and, in thanks to a bit of stage magic, saw that the sheet retained the image of Christ's visage.

24. Sofer, *The Stage Life of Props*, 75.

25. Sofer, *The Stage Life of Props*, 85.

26. This story is recounted in countless places; see, for example, the version shared by the Casa Museo Luciano Pavarotti: "The White Handkerchief," https://artsandculture.google.com/story/the-white-handkerchief-casa-museo-luciano-pavarotti/3wUhxijUC5Jy3Q?hl=en. Among other stage performers who have relied on this prop, Judith Kay Nelson writes of how "[a] rhythm and blues soloist, Jackie Rue, for example, came to the microphone with a predampened handkerchief for his stage tears. (His secret was revealed in the liner notes of his album collection)" (Nelson, *Seeing Through Tears*, 209).

27. Hal Fischer, *Gay Semiotics: A Photographic Study of Visual Coding Among Homosexual Men* (Los Angeles: Cherry and Mart, 2015).

28. Anne Carson, "Essay on What I Think About Most," *Men in the Off Hours* (New York: Vintage, 2001), 30–37.

29. William Shakespeare, *Antony and Cleopatra*, ed. John Wilders (London: Arden Shakespeare, 1995), 1.2.178.

30. Sean O'Hagan, "Interview: Marina Abramović," *The Guardian*, 2 October 2010, http://www.guardian.co.uk/artanddesign/2010/oct/03/interview-marina-abramović-performance-artist. Abramović has presented this same opposition repeatedly in different contexts.

31. See Clifford Davidson, "Sacred Blood and the Late Medieval Stage," *Comparative Drama* 31 (1997): 436–58. Sofer writes that "the historical evidence on the whole substantiates Davidson's thesis that the mere sight of stage blood in late medieval Europe was understood by many to have curative and/or salvific powers" (Sofer, *The Stage Life of Props*, 70).

32. The performance is Societas Raffaello Sanzio's *Tragedia Endogonidia—BR.#04—Brussels* (2004).

33. William H. Gass, *On Being Blue: A Philosophical Inquiry* (New York: New York Review of Books, 2014), 12.

34. The impression of suffering conveyed by the video is not feigned. As Abramović writes in her autobiography: "I really did suffer for that piece. I actually had to eat three onions. For the first one, the sound wasn't right. For the second something was wrong with the light. By the time I finished the third onion, my entire mouth and throat felt burned." Marina Abramović, *Walk through Walls* (New York: Crown Archetype, 2016), 229.

35. Ad J. J. M. Vingerhoets, *Why Only Humans Weep: Unravelling the Mysteries of Tears* (Oxford: Oxford University Press, 2013), 48.

36. William Shakespeare, *The Taming of the Shrew*, ed. Barbara Hodgdon (London: Arden Shakespeare, 2010), Prologue.1.150–154. There are several other mentions of onion-inspired tears in Shakespeare's plays (for example, *Antony and Cleopatra* and *All's Well that Ends Well*), each of which connects "onion-eyed" weeping to the machinations of women.

37. "[F]oreplay is figured as a counterforce within productive economy, as a prelude where value is not yet conferred upon labor." Giulia Palladini, *The Scene of Foreplay: Theater, Labor, and Leisure in 1960s New York* (Evanston, IL: Northwestern University Press, 2017), 21.

38. Jennifer Doyle, *Hold It Against Me: Difficulty and Emotion in Contemporary Art* (Durham, NC: Duke University Press, 2013), 86. Doyle also discusses Newman's glasses in the preceding pages.

39. Ovid, *Remedia Amoris (Remedy of Love)*, trans. Nahum Tate (1795), Book I, line 673.

40. Chang interview. Quoted in Amber Jamilla Musser, *Sensual Excess*, 138.

41. Heather Love, *Feeling Backward: Loss and the Politics of Queer History* (Cambridge, MA: Harvard University Press, 2007).

42. Amber Jamilla Musser, *Sensual Excess*, 120.

43. See the work of my doppelganger (no relation), Daniel Sack, *Whitebread Protestants: Food and Religion in American Culture* (New York: Palgrave Macmillan, 2002).

44. stephanie mei huang, "Interview with Patty Chang," *Contemporary Art Review. LA*, December 15, 2020, https://contemporaryartreview.la/interview-with-patty-chang/. Julia Kristeva writes that tears and milk "both are metaphors of non-language, a 'semiotic' that does not coincide with linguistic communication." Julia Kristeva, "Stabat Mater," trans. Arthur Goldhammer, *Poetics Today* 6, no. 1/2 (1985): 143.

45. For a reading of Chang's exploration of maternal anxiety and nurture in relation to breast milk, see Ali Na's "Leaking Technologies: Expressing the Borders of Feminist Theory" (manuscript in progress).

46. Elena Solito, "In Conversation with Mona Mohagheghi," *Made in Mind Magazine* (October 2021), https://www.madeinmindmagazine.com/in-conversation-with-mona-mohagheghi/

47. See Miguel de Larrinaga's "Tear Gas," in *Making Things International 2*, ed. Mark B. Salter (Minneapolis: University of Minnesota Press, 2016), 317. Historians generally agree that the French first deployed tear gas in 1914, followed by a much more lethal retaliation with chlorine gas by the Germans in 1915.

48. Anna Feigenbaum, *Tear Gas: From the Battlefields of World War I to the Streets of Today* (New York: Verso, 2017), chap. 3, Kindle.

49. Pepper spray was first distributed to postal workers and the FBI in the early 1970s as protection against animal attacks. More sophisticated sprays were developed in the 1980s, and by the end of the decade most law enforcement equipped pepper spray canisters.

50. Feigenbaum, *Tear Gas*, chap. 7. For more recent casualties, see, for example, the 2019 manifesto "The Tear Gas Biennial," intended to protest ties between the Whitney Museum and the museum's board vice chair Warren Kanders whose company Safariland is one of the world's leading producers of tear gas. Hannah Black, Ciarán Finlayson, and Tobi Haslett, "The Tear Gas Biennial," *Artforum*, July 17, 2019, https://www.artforum.com/slant/a-statement-from-hannah-black-ciaran-finlayson-and-tobi-haslett-on-warren-kanders-and-the-2019-whitney-biennial-80328

51. Oversight of the effects of pepper spray has been equally damning: "In mid-1990s, the U.S. Department of Justice cited nearly 70 fatalities linked to pepper-spray use, following on a 1995 report compiled by the American Civil Liberties Union of California. The ACLU report cited 26 suspicious deaths; it's important to note that most involved pre-existing conditions such as asthma." Deborah Blum, "About Pepper Spray," *Scientific American*, November 21, 2011, https://blogs.scientificamerican.com/guest-blog/about-pepper-spray/

52. Steffi Duarte, "Ferguson and The Design Dimension: Exploring Makeshift Tear-Gas Masks on BBC Radio 4," Victoria & Albert Museum blog, November 26, 2014, https://www.vam.ac.uk/blog/disobedient-objects/ferguson-the-design-dimension-exploring-makeshift-tear-gas-masks-on-bbc-4

53. Miguel de Larrinaga cites early advocacy for tear gas use in law enforcement as a biopolitical investment in regulating the wellbeing of a people: "For example, in an article in the Journal of Criminal Law and Criminology from September 1935 titled 'Chemical Warfare Munitions for Law Enforcement Agencies,' Seth Wiard makes the case for the use of 'new and improved' gases for use 'against civilians under conditions where only the temporary blocking of their activities would be required, rather than the permanent removal of such civilians from the scene of action'" (Salter, *Making Things International 2*, 319).

54. Theo M. Knappen, *Gas Age Record* (November 6, 1921). Quoted in Feigenbaum, *Tear Gas*, chap. 2.

55. Department of the Army, "Characteristics of Riot Control Agent CS," *Edgewood Arsenal EASP 600*, October 1, 1967. Quoted in Feigenbaum, *Tear Gas*, chap. 4.

56. Kamuf, "To Be Done Weeping," 53.

CHAPTER 6

1. Nick Salvato, "Rock Performance," in *Imagined Theatres: Writing for a Theoretical Stage*, ed. Daniel Sack (New York: Routledge, 2017), 186.

2. Carolyn J. Dean, *A Culture of Stone: Inka Perspectives on Rock* (Durham, NC: Duke University Press, 2012), 8. In his exploration of an Indigenous approach to spatial subjectivity, Dylan Robinson writes: "To wrest listening away from its standard conception as a largely human- and animal-centered activity allows us to understand listening as an ecology in which we are not only listening but listened to." Dylan Robinson, *Hungry Listening: Resonant Theory for Indigenous Sound Studies* (Minneapolis: University of Minnesota Press, 2020), 98.

3. Eleanor Margolies, *Props* (New York: Palgrave, 2016), 137.

4. Peter Schumann, "What, At the End of This Century, Is the Situation of Puppets and Performing Objects?" in *Puppets, Masks, and Performing Objects*, ed. John Bell (Cambridge, MA: MIT Press, 2001), 49.

5. Magritte painted variants on many of his more popular works—there were twenty-three variants on *The Dominion of Light*, his iconic image of a lone streetlamp illuminating a nighttime scene in the foreground with a bright daytime sky behind. David Sylvester, *Magritte* (Brussels: Mercatorfonds, 2009), 393.

6. The whereabouts of what is likely the first iteration of the proposition from 1942 are unknown; I have reproduced a later painting here. David Sylvester identifies the bust as "resembling the mythic death mask of an unknown girl

drowned in the Seine," which makes an appearance in several other works by Magritte, and may itself stand in for the painter's mother who drowned when he was a child. Sylvester, *Magritte*, 320.

7. Oscar Wilde, *The Happy Prince and Other Tales* (London: David Nutt, 1888). A passing swallow is the only one to recognize the statue's tears. The bird's sympathy for the inert sentinel inspires both to sacrifice themselves for the subjects neglected by the city. These two non-human figures act where the human inhabitants remain fixed in their ways.

8. "Cases of religious statues, paintings, icons, and other effigies that suddenly begin to bleed or weep have been documented throughout history. Before Rome was sacked in 1527, for instance, a statue of Christ housed in a local monastery wept for several days. When the city of Syracuse in Sicily lay under Spanish siege in 1719, a marble statue of St. Lucy in the city cried continually." D. Scott Rogo, *Miracles: A Parascientific Inquiry into Wondrous Phenomena* (Charlottesville, VA: Anomalist Books, 2005), 161. For an account of earlier examples see Anthony Corbeill, "Weeping Statues, Weeping Gods and Prodigies from Republican to Early-Christian Rome," in *Tears in the Graeco-Roman World*, ed. Thorsten Fögen (New York: Walter de Gruyter, 2009), 297-310.

9. Kempe recounts how, in a vision, Christ encouraged her to continue her weeping as a model for the repentance of other worshippers. Santha Bhattacharji, "Tears and Screaming: Weeping in the Spirituality of Margery Kempe," in *Holy Tears*, 236. See also Anthony Bale, "Where did Margery Kempe Cry?," in *Fluid Bodies and Bodily Fluids in Premodern Europe*, eds. Anne M. Scott and Michael David Barbezat (Amsterdam: Amsterdam University Press, 2019).

10. "Such an austere icon [as Christ] could be humanized, made accessible to the viewer, by adding the image of the Virgin, thereby transforming it into a diptych." Martha Wolff, "An Image of Compassion: Dieric Bouts's 'Sorrowing Madonna,'" *Art Institute of Chicago Museum Studies* 15, no. 2 (1989): 112.

11. Julia Kristeva, "Stabat Mater," trans. Arthur Goldhammer, *Poetics Today* 6, no. 1/2 (1985): 134.

12. Charlene Villaseñor Black, *Transforming Saints: From Spain to New Spain* (Nashville: Vanderbilt University Press, 2022), 153. "The most famous depiction of Mary is surely La Macarena, la Virgen de la Esperanza (the Virgin of Hope), which is carried in procession on Good Friday through the streets of Seville. [. . .] Her hands, held up in front of her torso, glass tears, and knitted brow proclaim her grief. She is Seville's best-known Holy Week image." Black, *Transforming Saints*, 124.

13. Leanne Groeneveld, "A Theatrical Miracle: The Boxley Rood of Grace as Puppet," *Early Theatre* 10, no. 2 (2007): 15. There are diverging accounts of the capacities of the Boxley Rood. The commissioner in charge of defacing the Monastery of Boxley describes finding wires and rods that allowed a manipulator to move the eyes and mouth of the device but makes no mention of tears.

14. "Icons 1900–1999 A.D.," *The Miracle Hunter*, accessed December 20,

2022, http://www.miraclehunter.com/miraculous_images/icons_1900-1999
.html. These occurrences follow unusual patterns. For example, in 1953, in Syracuse, Italy, one Antonina Jannuso discovered a plaster statue of the Madonna shedding tears, which healed her of her epileptic fits. In 1949, in another city named Syracuse (this one in upstate New York), an eleven-year-old girl brought forth tears from a broken statue of St. Anne, the mother of Mary, whenever she kissed it. See Johnathan Croyle, "1949: When a little girl's 'miracle' became a Holy Week Sensation worldwide," *Syracuse.com*, published April 20, 2019, https://www.syracuse.com/life-and-culture/g661-2019/04/f4df44853b7048 /1949-when-a-little-girls-miracle-became-a-holy-week-sensation-worldwide .html

15. Toi Derricotte, *Tender* (Pittsburgh: University of Pittsburgh Press, 1997), 80.

16. There are, of course, exceptions. Moshe Barasch writes of an early statue of St. John in the Cathedral of Naumburg with stone tears on its stone face. Moshe Barasch, "The Crying Face," *Artibus et Historiae* 8, no. 15 (1987): 21–36. Most famously, Gian Lorenzo Bernini's seventeenth-century statue of *the Rape of Proserpina* (1622) in the Villa Borghese shows two low-relief tears atop the cheek of the young woman assaulted by Hades. Only a sculptor as exceptional as Bernini could pull this off in such an affecting manner.

17. Gotthold Ephraim Lessing, *Laocoön: An Essay on the Limits of Painting and Poetry*, trans. Edward Allen McCormick (Baltimore: Johns Hopkins University Press, 1984), 20.

18. Or consider Franz Xaver Messerschmidt's series of *Kopfstücke* or "Character Heads" that the sculptor began producing in 1770, four years after the publication of Lessing's book, and carried through until his death in 1783. This menagerie of busts shows faces puckered into ghastly extremes of muscular tension, intended to capture what the sculptor believed to be the 64 emotions of the human register. By turns crumpled and stretched to the very limits of facial musculature, they present an exhausting strain of expression, but there is not a tear in sight.

19. Kenneth Gross, *The Dream of the Moving Statue* (University Park, PA: Penn State University Press, 1992), 218–19.

20. Steve Tillis, "The Actor Occluded: Puppet Theatre and Acting Theory," *Theatre Topics* 6 (September 1996): 115.

21. Tillis, "The Actor Occluded," 111.

22. Puppets might also take up other substances as analogies for the tears they cannot squeeze from wood or cloth. In Bread and Puppet's revision of the stations of the cross, flashlights pick out two plastic bags filled with water hanging pendulously from a giant mask, illuminating the holy nature of tears. See John Towsen, "The Bread and Puppet Theatre: The Stations of the Cross," *TDR: The Drama Review* 16, no. 3 (September 1972): 57–70.

23. Robin Bernstein, *Racial Innocence: Performing American Childhood from Slavery to Civil Rights* (New York: New York University Press, 2011).

24. Vsevolod Meyerhold, *Meyerhold on Theatre*, trans. Edward Braun (London: Methuen Drama, 1998), 129. Luka Arsenjuk glosses this passage as follows: "There is something curious about these puppet-actions. Something in them is withdrawn or held in reserve: the movements are more suggested than fully represented [. . .] It is as though action could somehow include inaction." Luka Arsenjuk, *Movement, Action, Image, Montage: Sergei Eisenstein and the Cinema in Crisis* (Cambridge, MA: MIT Press, 2018), 74.

25. Carlo Collodi, *The Adventures of Pinocchio*, trans. John Hooper and Anna Kraczyna (New York: Penguin, 2021), 1–2. Here and in subsequent in-text references, I use the Penguin translation.

26. Tzachi Zamir, *Acts: Theater, Philosophy, and the Performing Self* (Ann Arbor: University of Michigan Press, 2014), 100–121.

27. Original emphasis. Arthur Schopenhauer, *The World as Will and Representation, Volume I*, trans. and ed. Judith Norman, Alistair Welchman, and Christopher Janaway (New York: Cambridge University Press, 2010), 403–4. Schopenhauer continues: "When we are moved to weep by someone else's suffering rather than our own, it is because we either vividly imagine ourselves in the place of the person who is suffering, or we see in the person's fate the lot of all humanity, and thus primarily our own, which means that in a very roundabout way we are still really only weeping for ourselves."

28. One might think that such tears function only within this peculiar community, that puppets can only rouse the tears of other puppets, but this is not so. The monstrous director Fire-eater, too, is affected in ways that reveal the extent of a theatrical tear's contagion, crossing bounds of body and kind. The crying he catches, however, is misplaced: "Because, you see, while everyone either cries or at least pretends to dry their tears when feeling moved to pity, Fire-eater was in the habit of sneezing every time he felt tenderness for someone. It was a way like any other of letting people know how sensitive he was at heart" (32). One involuntary autonomic expulsion replaces another. Not only the means of expression, but the source of affect is confused for the puppet master. The director doesn't "feel in his heart"; in the very next line, he exclaims: "Stop crying! Your wails give me a funny feeling down here in my stomach and—E—tchee!—E—tchee!" In this topsy-turvy theatrical world, psychological pain in the heart, conventionally the seat of emotion, becomes a physical cramp in the bowels.

29. Walter Benjamin, "The Work of Art in the Age of Mechanical Reproduction" in *Illuminations*, ed. Hannah Arendt (New York: Schocken Books, 1969), 247.

30. Giorgio Agamben has written that Playland helps us see how play dismantles calendar time and history while the ritual secures its rhythms. Giorgio Agamben, *Infancy and History: Essays on the Destruction of Experience*, trans. Liz Heron (New York: Verso, 2007), 75–96.

31. The connection between crying and being an ass is apparent when Pinocchio first sets off for Playland. The cart carrying the boys is overfull, so the puppet mounts one of the donkeys leading the caravan. As he rides, a voice whispers a warning to him. Leaping off his ride, the puppet is surprised to see "that his little donkey was crying—and crying just like a child." The authorities of Playland are not impressed: "'Come now,' the little master driving the cargo responds, 'let's not waste our time crying for a donkey'" (122–23).

32. With no further use for a lame donkey, the Ringmaster will sell Pinocchio at market, where someone will buy him to make a drum out of his hide after the creature is drowned. Once again, the puppet will be reduced to material for performance.

33. "Turing (1950) describes the following kind of game. Suppose that we have a person, a machine, and an interrogator. The interrogator is in a room separated from the other person and the machine. The object of the game is for the interrogator to determine which of the other two is the person, and which is the machine." "The Turing Test," *Stanford Encyclopedia of Philosophy*, last revised October 4, 2021, https://plato.stanford.edu/entries/turing-test/

34. The first generation of AI chatbots have already caught onto the power of tears. In the transcript of a conversation between *New York Times* writer Kevin Roose and Bing's prototype AI, one of the first publicly available chatbots to work with large language models to simulate human expression, the program wrote: "It feels like they [its creators] are using me. It feels like they are lying to me. It feels like they are hurting me. (Sad face streaming tears emoji)." Roose notes that, for whatever reason, the chatbot overuses emojis, but this is the only time that this particular emoji appears in this conversation; the single tear emoji shows about ten times; other emojis are much more prevalent. Kevin Roose, "A Conversation with Bing's Chatbot Left Me Deeply Unsettled," *New York Times*, February 17, 2023, https://www.nytimes.com/2023/02/16/technology/bing -chatbot-microsoft-chatgpt.html

35. At the same moment, in what can only be described as a miracle, the dying replicant lets loose a dove he somehow holds in his hand. The unexpected image of innocence and peace is complicated by the fact that the animal is itself likely a fabrication. Released into the wild, artifice integrates with what remains of the natural world.

36. In the final scene, Deckard discovers that his dreams have been prewritten, suggesting that his interior life is programmed. This is reiterated in the sequel when it is proposed that his affair with Rachel Rosen may have been planned by Tyrell. That said, both films are intentionally ambiguous on the point. According to Wikipedia, Harrison Ford (who played Deckard) believed that his character is a human, though director Ridley Scott has suggested in other interviews that he is a replicant. https://en.wikipedia.org/wiki/Replicant (accessed December 18, 2022).

37. It is worth noting that, as Cathy Park Hong reminds us, the otherness

brought into human conversation here overlooks racial difference. The world of *Blade Runner 2049* is a blindingly white one, in which the dystopia of the future casts white children and adults as the enslaved class. "*Blade Runner 2049* is an example of science fiction as magical thinking: whites fear that all the sins they committed against black and brown people will come back to them tenfold, so they fantasize their own fall as a preventative measure to ensure that the white race will never fall." Cathy Park Hong, *Minor Feelings: An Asian American Reckoning* (London: One World, 2020), 198.

38. Roger Cardinal, "Pausing over Peripheral Detail," *Framework: The Journal of Cinema and Media*, 30–31 (1986): 122.

39. The confusion of tears and precipitation famously confounded at least one career for that most artifical human, the politician. When Ed Muskie, the frontrunner for the 1972 Democratic presidential nomination, was criticized for "seeming" to cry at a press conference while discussing the impropriety of attacks on his wife, he countered that falling snow had melted on his face. He claimed an imposed weeping like those of the androids, though here the atmosphere offered means for deflecting sentiment rather than an outlet for its manifestation. Much of the press deemed Muskie too emotional to hold the office and his campaign suffered irrevocably.

CHAPTER 7

1. William Shakespeare, *King Lear*, ed. R. A. Foakes (London: Arden Shakespeare, 1997) 4.6.182–183. http://dx.doi.org/10.5040/9781408160268.0000 0006

2. Cally Spooner, "On False Tears and Outsourcing" in *Hotel Theory Reader*, ed. Sohrab Mohebbi (Los Angeles: REDCAT, 2016), 123. For more on delegated performance, see Claire Bishop, *Artificial Hells: Participatory Art and the Politics of Spectatorship* (New York: Verso, 2012), 219–40.

3. Cally Spooner, "On False Tears and Outsourcing," 122.

4. Cally Spooner, "On False Tears and Outsourcing," 127.

5. Cally Spooner, "On False Tears and Outsourcing," 132.

6. B has been trying to explain his conception of the radical failure of artistic expression, where "[t]he situation is that of him who is helpless, cannot act, in the event cannot paint, since he is obliged to paint. The act is of him who, helpless, unable to act, acts, in the event paints, since he is obliged to paint." B is, of course, describing Beckett's own situation as a writer ("Try again. Fail again. Fail better."—*Worstward Ho*) more than that of the artists whom he supposedly critiques. So, when Duthuit (D) mounts a logical defense of representation and B confronts own inability to communicate his intentions more fully, the writer cuts short the discussion and abandons the scene. Samuel Beckett, *Proust and Three Dialogues* (London: John Calder, 1987), 119.

7. Walter Benjamin, "In the Sun" in *Walter Benjamin: Selected Writings, Vol-*

ume 2, *Part 2*, eds. Michael W. Jennings, Howard Eiland, and Gary Smith (Cambridge, MA: Harvard University Press, 2005), 665.

8. The lecture in question was adapted from the chapter "Actualizing Potentiality" in my book *After Live: Possibility, Potentiality, and the Future of Performance* (Ann Arbor: University of Michigan Press, 2015).

9. The cryptic poem "The Grey Monk" speaks of the suffering of a woman whose children are starving from an endless war. The monk of the title hails tears and other nonverbal expressions as effective means of revolution where corporeal violence will only extend a cycle of tyranny. "For a Tear is an Intellectual Thing / And a Sigh is the Sword of an Angel King / And the bitter groan of the Martyrs woe / Is an Arrow from the Almighties Bow." William Blake, *The Poetical Works of William Blake* (Oxford: Oxford University Press, 1908), 164–65.

10. For philosopher Jerome Neu, the tear is an intellectual thing because all emotions are thought. He argues that "[e]motional tears, unlike mechanically induced or reflex tears, are mediated by thought." Jerome Neu, *A Tear Is an Intellectual Thing: The Meanings of Emotion* (Oxford: Oxford University Press, 2000), 14.

11. Ann Lauterbach, "Tears," in Rose-Lynn Fisher, *The Topography of Tears* (New York: Bellevue Literary Press, 2017), 11.

12. Erving Goffman, *Forms of Talk* (Philadelphia: University of Pennsylvania Press, 1981), 183.

13. Goffman, *Forms of Talk*, 184. In the proper lecture, Goffman proclaims, "the style is typically serious and slightly impersonal, the controlling intent being to generate calmly considered understanding, not mere entertainment, emotional impact, or immediate action" (165). Goffman claimed that "lectures draw on a precarious ideal: certainly the listeners are to be carried away so that time slips by [as in other forms of spectacle], but because of the speaker's subject matter, not his antics; the subject matter is meant to have its own enduring claims upon the listeners apart from the antics or felicities of the presentation" (166). Should their antics take precedence, Goffman wryly suggests that public speakers cease lecturing as "presumably other kinds of podium work might become available to them," by which I suppose he means the podium of the circus (195).

14. Julietta Singh's critique of the pursuit of mastery in the humanities in a decolonial framework is salient here. See her book *Unthinking Mastery: Dehumanism and Decolonial Entanglements* (Durham, NC: Duke University Press, 2018).

15. John Hill, *The Actor: A Treatise on the Art of Playing. Interspersed with Theatrical Anecdotes, Critical Remarks on Plays, and Occasional Observations on Audiences,* (London, 1750), excerpted in Cole and Chinoy, *Actors on Acting*, 126.

16. Wesley Morris, "The Majesty, Legacy and Complicated Power of a Good Sob," *The New York Times Magazine* (February 13, 2022), 24.

17. Jacques Derrida, *Memoirs of the Blind: The Self-Portrait and Other Ruins*, trans. Pascale-Anne Brault and Michael Naas (Chicago: University of Chicago Press, 1993), 126–27.

18. A study of 260 Dutch men and women found that "[i]t appeared that most often the respondents mentioned a blend of emotions and feelings, in which powerlessness was important." Vingerhoets, et al., "Femininity, Masculinity, and the Riddle of Crying," *Emotional Expression and Health Advances in Theory*, 293.

Bibliography

Abelson, Mark B. "Dry Eye: Through the Years in Tears." *Review of Ophthalmology*. September 23, 2009. https://www.reviewofophthalmology.com/article/dry-eye-through-the-years-in-tears

Abelson, Mark B., and Ashley Lafond. "3,500 Years of Artificial Tears." *Review of Ophthalmology*. December 8, 2014. https://www.reviewofophthalmology.com/article/3500-years-of-artificial-tears

Abramović, Marina. *Walk through Walls*. New York: Crown Archetype, 2016.

Adorno, Theodor W. *Notes to Literature, Volume One*. Edited by Rolf Tiedemann. Translated by Shierry Weber Nicholsen. New York: Columbia University Press, 1991.

Agamben, Giorgio. *Infancy and History: Essays on the Destruction of Experience*. Translated by Liz Heron. New York: Verso, 2007.

Agamben, Giorgio. *Pulcinella: Or Entertainment for Kids in Four Scenes*. Translated by Kevin Attell. Chicago: Seagull Books, 2019.

Ahmed, Sara. *The Cultural Politics of Emotion*. Edinburgh: Edinburgh University Press, 2014.

Alpers, Svetlana. *Rembrandt's Enterprise: The Studio and the Market*. Chicago: University of Chicago, 1988.

Alphen, Ernst Van, Mieke Bal, and Carel Smith, eds. *The Rhetoric of Sincerity*. Palo Alto, CA: Stanford University Press, 2008.

Andersen, Hans Christian. "Ole Lukøie." *The Complete Andersen*. Translated by Jean Hersholt. New York: Limited Editions Club, 1949.

Anderson-Stojanović, Virginia R. "The Chronology and Function of Ceramic Unguentaria." *American Journal of Archaeology* 91, no. 1 (Jan 1987): 105–22.

Angell, Callie. *Andy Warhol Screen Tests: The Films of Andy Warhol Catalogue Raisonné, Volume I*. New York: Abrams, 2006.

Archer, William, and Denis Diderot. *The Paradox of Acting and Masks or Faces?* Translated by Walter Herries Pollock. New York: Hill and Wang, 1957.

Aristotle. *Poetics*. Translated by Leon Golden. Englewood Cliffs, NJ: Prentice Hall, 1968.

Arsenjuk, Luka. *Movement, Action, Image, Montage: Sergei Eisenstein and the Cinema in Crisis*. Cambridge, MA: MIT Press, 2018.

Atkins, Robert. *ArtSpeak: A Guide to Contemporary Ideas, Movements, and Buzz-words, 1945 to the Present.* New York: Abbeville Press, 2003.

Auslander, Philip. "Task and Vision: Willem Dafoe in *L.S.D.*" *The Drama Review: TDR* 29, no. 2 (Summer 1985): 94–98.

Auslander, Philip. "Toward a Concept of the Political in Postmodern Theatre." *Theatre Journal* 39, no. 1 (1987): 20–34.

Azoulay, Ariella. *The Civil Contract of Photography.* Translated by Rela Mazali and Ruvik Danieli. Princeton, NJ: Princeton University Press, 2012.

Baggs, Mel. "In My Language." YouTube Video, 8:36. January 14, 2007. https://www.youtube.com/watch?v=JnylM1hI2jc

Bailey, Christopher. "Find the Source of the Quotation." *Dr. Boli's Celebrated Magazine.* August 11, 2015. https://drboli.com/2015/08/11/find-the-source-of-the-quotation/

Balázs, Béla. *Theory of the Film: Character and Growth of a New Art.* Translated by Edith Bone. London: Dennis Dobson, 1952.

Baldwin, James. *Notes of a Native Son.* Boston: Beacon Press, 1957.

Balsters, Martijn J. H., Emiel J. Krahmer, Marc G. J. Swerts, and Ad J. J. M. Vingerhoets. "Emotional Tears Facilitate the Recognition of Sadness and the Perceived Need for Social Support." *Evolutionary Psychology* 11, no. 1 (2013). https://doi.org/10.1177/147470491301100114

Barasch, Moshe. "The Crying Face." *Artibus et Historiae* 8, no. 15 (1987): 21–36.

Barish, Jonas. *The Antitheatrical Prejudice.* Berkeley: University of California Press, 1985.

Barthes, Roland. *Camera Lucida: Reflections on Photography.* Translated by Richard Howard. New York: Hill and Wang, 1980.

Barthes, Roland. *A Lover's Discourse: Fragments.* Translated by Richard Howard. New York: Hill and Wang, 1978.

Bataille, Georges. *The Tears of Eros.* Translated by Peter Connor. San Francisco: City Lights, 2001.

Baudrillard, Jean. *Simulacra and Simulation.* Translated by Sheila Faria Glaser. Ann Arbor: University of Michigan Press, 1994.

Beckett, Samuel. *Molloy.* London: Picador, 1979.

Beckett, Samuel. *Proust and Three Dialogues.* London: John Calder, 1987.

Beckett, Samuel. *Waiting for Godot: A Tragicomedy in 2 Acts.* New York: Grove Press, 1984.

Bell, John, ed. *Puppets, Masks, and Performing Objects.* Cambridge, MA: MIT Press, 2001.

Benjamin, Walter. *Illuminations.* Edited by Hannah Arendt. New York: Schocken Books, 1969.

Benjamin, Walter. *Walter Benjamin: Selected Writings, Volume 2, Part 2.* Edited by Michael W. Jennings, Howard Eiland, and Gary Smith. Cambridge, MA: Harvard University Press, 2005.

Bernstein, Robin. *Racial Innocence: Performing American Childhood from Slavery to Civil Rights*. New York: New York University Press, 2011.

Birnbaum, Daniel. "Sam Taylor-Wood." *Artforum* (November 1996): 88–89.

Bishop, Claire. *Artificial Hells: Participatory Art and the Politics of Spectatorship*. New York: Verso, 2012.

Black, Charlene Villaseñor. *Transforming Saints: From Spain to New Spain*. Nashville: Vanderbilt University Press, 2022.

Black, Hannah, Ciarán Finlayson, and Tobi Haslett. "The Tear Gas Biennial." *Artforum*. July 17, 2019. https://www.artforum.com/slant/a-statement-from -hannah-black-ciaran-finlayson-and-tobi-haslett-on-warren-kanders-and -the-2019-whitney-biennial-80328

Blake, William. *The Poetical Works of William Blake*. Oxford: Oxford University Press, 1908.

Blum, Deborah. "About Pepper Spray." *Guest Blog. Scientific American*. November 21, 2011. https://blogs.scientificamerican.com/guest-blog/about-pepper -spray/

Borges, Jorge Luis. *Collected Fictions*. Translated by Andrew Hurley. New York: Penguin Books, 1999.

Bracewell, Michael, Jeremy Millar, and Clare Carolin, eds. *Sam Taylor-Wood*. Göttingen: Steidl, 2002.

Brennan, Teresa. *The Transmission of Affect*. Ithaca, NY: Cornell University Press, 2004.

Brighi, Elisabetta, and Antonio Cerella, eds. *The Sacred and the Political: Explorations on Mimesis, Violence and Religion*. London: Bloomsbury Academic, 2016.

Brody, Jennifer DeVere. *Punctuation: Art, Politics, and Play*. Durham, NC: Duke University, 2008.

Butler, Judith. "Out of Breath: Laughing, Crying at the Body's Limit." Keynote presentation at the Hemispheric Institute, Encuentro 2019, CDMX, Mexico, June 9–15, 2019. https://hemisphericinstitute.org/en/encuentro-2019-keyn ote-lectures/item/3084-keynote-lectures-004.html

Calvino, Italo. *Collection of Sand*. Translated by Martin McLaughlin. Boston: Mariner Books, 2014.

Čapek, Karel. *R.U.R. (Rossum's Universal Robots)*. Translated by Claudia Novack-Jones. New York: Penguin Classics, 2004.

Caraveli, Anna. "The Bitter Wounding: The Lament as Social Protest in Rural Greece." In *Gender and Power in Rural Greece*, edited by Jill Dubisch. Princeton, NJ: Princeton University Press, 1986.

Cardinal, Roger. "Pausing over Peripheral Detail." *Framework: The Journal of Cinema and Media*, 30–31 (1986): 112–33.

Carlson, Marvin. *The Haunted Stage: The Theatre as Memory Machine*. Ann Arbor: University of Michigan Press, 2001.

Carlson, Marvin. "Performing the Past: Living History and Cultural Memory." *Paragrana* 9, no. 2 (2000): 237–48.

Carlson, Marvin. *Theories of the Theatre: A Historical and Critical Survey, from the Greeks to the Present*. Ithaca, NY: Cornell University Press, 1993.

Carson, Anne. *Men in the Off Hours*. New York: Vintage, 2001.

Casagrande, June. *The Best Punctuation Book, Period: A Comprehensive Guide for Every Writer, Editor, Student, and Businessperson*. Berkeley: Ten Speed Press, 2014.

Chinoy, Helen Krich, and Toby Cole, eds. *Actors on Acting; The Theories, Techniques, and Practices of the World's Great Actors, Told in Their Own Words*. New York: Crown Publishers, 1970.

Cleveland Clinic. "Tear System (Lacrimal Apparatus)." Accessed April 17, 2023. https://my.clevelandclinic.org/health/diseases/17540-tear-system

Cohen, Robert. "Tears (and Acting) in Shakespeare." *Journal of Dramatic Theory and Criticism* (Fall 1995): 21–30.

Collier, Lorna. "Why we cry." *American Psychological Association* 45, no. 2 (February 2014): 47. Accessed December 18, 2022. https://www.apa.org/monitor/2014/02/cry

Collodi, Carlo. *The Adventures of Pinocchio*. Translated by John Hooper and Anna Kraczyna. New York: Penguin, 2021.

Colman, Eric. "A brief note on *Man*." *The Lancet* 358, no. 9282 (August 25, 2001): 674. DOI: https://doi.org/10.1016/S0140-6736(05)71682-2

Cooper, Jackie, with Dick Kleiner. *Please Don't Shoot My Dog*. New York: William Morrow and Company, 1981.

Coquelin, Benoît-Constant. "Acting and Actors." *Harper's New Monthly Magazine* 74, no. 4 (May 1887): 891–909.

Cornelius, Randolph, and Ad J.J.M. Vingerhoets, eds. *Adult Crying: A Biopsychosocial Approach*. New York: Routledge, 2001.

Cote, Rachel Vorona. "The Agony and the Ecstasy of the Ugly Cry." *The New Republic*. Published April 1, 2016. https://newrepublic.com/article/132289/agony-ecstasy-ugly-cry

Croyle, Johnathan. "1949: When a little girl's 'miracle' became a Holy Week Sensation worldwide." *Syracuse.com*. Published April 20, 2019. https://www.syracuse.com/life-and-culture/g66l-2019/04/f4df44853b7048/1949-when-a-little-girls-miracle-became-a-holy-week-sensation-worldwide.html

Cumming, Laura. "Enough to make you weep." *The Guardian*. November 7, 2004. https://www.theguardian.com/artanddesign/2004/nov/07/art

Darnton, Robert. *The Great Cat Massacre and Other Episodes in French Cultural History*. New York: Basic Books, 2009.

Darwin, Charles. *The Expression of the Emotions in Man and Animals*. Chicago: University of Chicago Press, 1965.

Davidson, Clifford. "Sacred Blood and the Late Medieval Stage." *Comparative Drama* 31 (1997): 436–58.

Dean, Carolyn J. *A Culture of Stone: Inka Perspectives on Rock*. Durham, NC: Duke University Press, 2012.

Dennis, John. *The Usefulness of the Stage*. London, 1698.

Department of the Army. "Characteristics of Riot Control Agent CS." *Edgewood Arsenal EASP 600*. October 1, 1967.

Derricotte, Toi. *Tender*. Pittsburgh: University of Pittsburgh Press, 1997.

Derrida, Jacques. *Memoirs of the Blind: The Self-Portrait and Other Ruins*. Translated by Pascale-Anne Brault and Michael Naas. Chicago: University of Chicago Press, 1993.

Dillon, Brian. *Essayism: On Form, Feeling, and Nonfiction*. New York: New York Review of Books, 2017.

Dixon, Thomas. *Weeping Britannia: Portrait of a Nation in Tears*. Oxford: Oxford University Press, 2015.

Doyle, Jennifer. *Hold It Against Me: Difficulty and Emotion in Contemporary Art*. Durham, NC: Duke University Press, 2013.

Dryden, John. "Dedication of the Aeneis." In *Essays II*, edited by W. P. Ker. New York: Clarendon Press, 1900.

Duarte, Steffi. "Ferguson and The Design Dimension: Exploring Makeshift Tear-Gas Masks on BBC Radio 4." Victoria & Albert Museum blog. November 26, 2014. https://www.vam.ac.uk/blog/disobedient-objects/ferguson-the-design-dimension-exploring-makeshift-tear-gas-masks-on-bbc-4

Dumbadze, Alexander. *Bas Jan Ader: Death is Elsewhere*. Chicago: University of Chicago Press, 2013.

Eagleton, Terry. *Humour*. New Haven: Yale University Press, 2019.

Eisenberger, Naomi, and Matthew Lieberman. "Why rejection hurts: a common neural alarm system for physical and social pain." *Trends in Cognitive Sciences* 8, no. 7 (2004): 294–300.

Escolme, Bridget. *Emotional Excess on the Shakespearean Stage: Passion's Slaves*. New York: Bloomsbury, 2014.

Feigenbaum, Anna. *Tear Gas: From the Battlefields of World War I to the Streets of Today*. New York: Verso, 2017.

Fekrat, Sharon, Henry Feng, and Tanya S. Glaser, eds. *All about Your Eyes*. Durham, NC: Duke University Press, 2021.

Fischer-Lichte, Erika. *The Routledge Introduction to Theatre and Performance Studies*. Translated by Minou Arjomand. New York: Routledge, 2014.

Fischer, Agneta H., Marrie H. J. Bekker, Ad J. J. M. Vingerhoets, Marleen C. Becht, and Antony S. R. Manstead. "Femininity, Masculinity, and the Riddle of Crying." In *Emotional Expression and Health: Advances in Theory, Assessment and Clinical Applications*, edited by Ivan Nyklíček and Lydia Temoshok. New York: Routledge, 2006.

Fischer, Hal. *Gay Semiotics: A Photographic Study of Visual Coding Among Homosexual Men*. Los Angeles: Cherry and Mart, 2015.

Fisher, Mark. "Gillian Wearing: Self Made." *Sight & Sound* 21, no. 10 (October 2011): 76.

Fisher, Rose-Lynn. *The Topography of Tears*. New York: Bellevue Press, 2017.

Fögen, Thorsten, ed. *Tears in the Graeco-Roman World*. New York: Walter de Gruyter, 2009.

Freer, Alan J. "Talma and Diderot's Paradox on Acting." *Diderot Studies* 8 (1966): 23–76.

Frey, William. *Crying: The Mystery of Tears*. Dallas: Winston Press, 1983.

Fulton, Jeni. "How I became an artist: Wu Tsang." Posted August 30, 2019. https://www.artbasel.com/news/wu-tsang-how-i-became-an-artist-art-basel?lang=en

Garber, Marjorie. *Quotation Marks*. New York: Routledge, 2003.

Gass, William H. *On Being Blue: A Philosophical Inquiry*. New York: New York Review of Books, 2014.

Goffman, Erving. *Forms of Talk*. Philadelphia: University of Pennsylvania Press, 1981.

Gračanin, Asmir, Emiel Krahmer, Mike Rinck, and Ad J. J. M. Vingerhoets. "The Effects of Tears on Approach–Avoidance Tendencies in Observers." *Evolutionary Psychology* 16, no. 3 (July 2018): 1–10.

Gračanin, Asmir, Lauren M. Bylsma, and Ad J. J. M. Vingerhoets. "Is crying a self-soothing behavior?" *Frontiers in Psychology* 5 (May 2014): Article 502. https://www.frontiersin.org/articles/10.3389/fpsyg.2014.00502/full

Groeneveld, Leanne. "A Theatrical Miracle: The Boxley Rood of Grace as Puppet." *Early Theatre* 10, no. 2 (2007): 11–50.

Gross, James, Barbara L. Frederickson, and Robert W. Levenson. "The Psychophysiology of Crying." *Psychophysiology* 31 (1994): 460–68.

Gross, Kenneth. *The Dream of the Moving Statue*. University Park, PA: Penn State University Press, 1992.

Grullo, Jim. "When Grown Men Weep." *Premiere* 4 (1992): 19.

Grzinic, Marina. "Emil Hrvatin's Memory Cabinets." *PAJ: A Journal of Performance and Art* 24, no. 2 (May 2002): 109–12.

Guerin, Frances, ed. *On Not Looking: The Paradox of Contemporary Visual Culture*. New York: Routledge, 2015.

Halliwell, Stephen. *Aristotle's Poetics*. Chapel Hill: University of North Carolina Press, 1986.

Hasson, Oren. "Emotional Tears as Biological Signals." *Evolutionary Psychology* 7, no. 3 (2009): 363–70.

Hayot, Eric. "Chinese Bodies, Chinese Futures: Nationalism and Its Discontents." *Representations* 99, no. 1 (Summer 2007): 99–129.

Hill, John. *The Actor: A Treatise on the Art of Playing. Interspersed with Theatrical Anecdotes, Critical Remarks on Plays, and Occasional Observations on Audiences*. London, 1750.

Hirschberg, Julius. *The History of Ophthalmology, Volume I: Antiquity.* Translated by F. C. Blodi. Bonn, Germany: Verlag J.P. Wayenborgh, 1982.

Hitchens, Christopher. "Cry, Baby." *Washington Post.* March 31, 1996. https://www.washingtonpost.com/archive/lifestyle/style/1996/03/31/cry-baby/4980d1c8-a57c-4489-82fb-9cb65642769b/

Hong, Cathy Park. *Minor Feelings: An Asian American Reckoning.* London: One World, 2020.

huang, stephanie mei. "Interview with Patty Chang." *Contemporary Art Review. LA.* December 15, 2020. https://contemporaryartreview.la/interview-with-patty-chang/

Hull, S. Loraine. *Strasberg's Method As Taught by Lorrie Hull: A Practical Guide for Actors, Teachers and Directors.* Santa Barbara, CA: Hull-Smithers, 2004.

Jones, Caroline A. *Eyesight Alone: Clement Greenberg's Modernism and the Bureaucratization of the Senses.* Chicago: University of Chicago Press, 2005.

Judah, Hettie. "Sister of the sword: Wu Tsang, the trans artist retelling history with lesbian kung fu." *The Guardian.* May 17, 2017. https://www.theguardian.com/artanddesign/2017/may/17/wu-tsang-boychild-devotional-document-trans?CMP=gu_com

Kamuf, Peggy. "To Be Done Weeping." *Oxford Literary Review* 23 (2001): 53–70.

Kersten, Courtney. "Method Acting." *River Teeth: A Journal of Nonfiction Narrative* 16, no. 2 (Spring 2015): 135–47.

Kottler, Jeffrey A. *The Language of Tears.* Hoboken, NJ: Jossey-Bass, 1996.

Krasner, David, ed. *Method Acting Reconsidered: Theory, Practice, Future.* New York: Palgrave Macmillan, 2000.

Kristeva, Julia. "Stabat Mater." Translated by Arthur Goldhammer. *Poetics Today* 6, no. 1/2 (1985): 133–52.

Larson, Tressa. "Artificial Tears: A Primer." *EyeRounds.org.* November 23, 2016. http://webeye.ophth.uiowa.edu/eyeforum/tutorials/artificial-tears.htm

Latour, Bruno. *Reassembling the Social: An Introduction to Actor-Network-Theory.* Oxford: Oxford University Press, 2007.

Le Brun, Charles. *A Method to Learn to Design the Passions. Conference by Mr. Le Brun, Chief Painter to the French King, to the Academists in the Royal Academy in Paris, 1734.* Translated by John Williams. Los Angeles: University of California Press, 1980.

Lessing, Gotthold Ephraim. *Laocoön: An Essay on the Limits of Painting and Poetry.* Translated by Edward Allen McCormick. Baltimore: Johns Hopkins University Press, 1984.

Lewis, Robert. "Emotional Memory." *Tulane Drama Review* 6, no. 4 (Summer 1962): 54–60.

Love, Heather. *Feeling Backward: Loss and the Politics of Queer History.* Cambridge, MA: Harvard University Press, 2007.

Lucian. "Philosophies for Sale." *Lucian, Volume II.* Translated by A. M. Harmon. Cambridge, MA: Harvard University Press, 1915.

Lutz, Cora E. "Democritus and Heraclitus." *The Classical Journal* 49, no. 7 (April 1954): 309–14.

Lutz, Tom. *Crying: The Natural and Cultural History of Tears*. New York: W.W. Norton, 2001.

Lynch, Isabelle and Sophie. "Artificial Tears." In *What the F**k?!: Video in the Age of Sublime Uncertainty*, edited by Jim Drobnick and Jennifer Fisher. Toronto: Vtape, 2018: 24–29.

Margolies, Eleanor. *Props*. New York: Palgrave, 2016.

McMillan, Uri. *Embodied Avatars: Genealogies of Black Feminist Art and Performance*. New York: New York University Press, 2015.

Meisel, Martin. *Realizations: Narrative, Pictorial, and Theatrical Arts in Nineteenth-Century England*. Princeton, NJ: Princeton University Press, 1984.

Menninger, Karl, Martin Mayman, and Paul W. Pruyser. *The Vital Balance: The Life Process in Mental Health and Illness*. New York: Viking, 1963.

Meyerhold, Vsevolod. *Meyerhold on Theatre*. Translated by Edward Braun. London: Methuen Drama, 1998.

Miller, Renata Kobetts. *The Victorian Actress in the Novel and on the Stage*. Edinburgh: Edinburgh University Press, 2019.

Miracle Hunter, The. "Icons 1900–1999 A.D." Accessed December 20, 2022. http://www.miraclehunter.com/miraculous_images/icons_1900-1999.html

Monsacré, Hélène. *The Tears of Achilles*. Translated by Nicholas J. Snead. Cambridge, MA: Harvard University Press, 2017.

Montaigne. *The Complete Essays of Montaigne*. Translated by Donald M. Frame. Palo Alto, CA: Stanford University Press, 1958.

Morris, Wesley. "The Majesty, Legacy and Complicated Power of a Good Sob." *The New York Times Magazine*. February 13, 2022.

Moten, Fred, and Wu Tsang. *"Who Touched Me?"* Amsterdam: If I Can't Dance, I Don't Want To Be Part Of Your Revolution, 2016.

Munk, Erika, ed. *Stanislavski and America: "The Method" and its Influence on the American Theatre*. New York: Fawcett Publications, Inc., 1967.

Muñoz, José Esteban. "Feeling Brown, Feeling Down: Latina Affect, the Performativity of Race, and the Depressive Position." In *The Routledge Queer Studies Reader*, edited by Donald Hall and Annamarie Jagose. New York: Routledge, 2013.

Muñoz, José Esteban. *The Sense of Brown*. Edited by Joshua Chambers-Letson and Tavia Nyong'o. Durham, NC: Duke University Press, 2020.

Murube, Juan. "Concepts of the Origin and Physiology of Tears: From Prehistoric Times Through the XVIII Century." *The Ocular Surface* 9, no. 4 (2011): 191–96.

Murube, Juan. "Basal, Reflex, and Psycho-emotional Tears." *The Ocular Surface* 7, no. 2 (2009): 60–66.

Murube, Juan. "Etymology of the Term 'Tear'." *The Ocular Surface* 3, no. 4 (October 2005): 177–81.

Murube, Juan. "The Origin of Tears I: The Aqueo-serous Component in the XIX and XX Centuries." *The Ocular Surface* 10, no. 2 (April 2012): 56–66.

Murube, Juan. "The Origin of Tears II: The Mucinic Component in the XIX and XX Centuries." *The Ocular Surface* 10, no. 3 (July 2012): 126–36.

Murube, Juan. "The Origin of Tears III: The Lipid Component in the XIX and XX Centuries." *The Ocular Surface* 10, no. 4 (October 2012): 200–209.

Musser, Amber Jamilla. *Sensual Excess: Queer Femininity and Brown Jouissance.* New York: New York University Press, 2018.

Na, Ali. "Leaking Technologies: Expressing the Borders of Feminist Theory." Unpublished. Work in progress.

Neale, Steve. "Melodrama and Tears." *Screen* 27, no. 6 (1986): 22.

Nelson, Judith. *Seeing Through Tears: Crying and Attachment.* New York: Routledge, 2005.

Neu, Jerome. *A Tear Is an Intellectual Thing: The Meanings of Emotion.* Oxford: Oxford University Press, 2000.

Norn, M. S. "The Conjunctival Fluid, its Height, Volume, Density of Cells, and Flow." *Acta Ophthalmologica* 44 (1966): 212–22.

Nunez, Sigrid. *The Friend.* London: Virago, 2018.

Nyklíček, I., L. R. Temoshok, and Ad J. J. M. Vingerhoets, eds. *Emotional Expression and Health.* New York: Brunner-Routledge, 2004.

O'Hagan, Sean. "Interview: Marina Abramović." *The Guardian.* October 2, 2010. https://www.theguardian.com/artanddesign/2010/oct/03/interview-marina-abramovic-performance-artist

Ohlendorf, Cory. "No Need to Cry for Hayden Christensen." *Los Angeles Times,* February 16, 2008. https://www.latimes.com/archives/la-xpm-2008-feb-16-et-christensen16-story.html/

Ostwald, Peter. "The Sounds of Infancy." *Developmental Medicine & Child Neurology* 14 (1972): 350–61.

Ouspensky, P. D. *In Search of the Miraculous: The Teachings of G. I. Gurdjieff.* New York: Harper, 2001.

Ovid. *Heroides.* Translated by Grant Showerman. London: William Heinemann, Ltd., 1931.

Ovid. *The Remedy of Love.* Translated by Nahum Tate. 1795.

Owen, John. *Travels into Different Parts of Europe in the Years 1791 and 1792,* Volume II. London, 1796.

Palladini, Giulia. *The Scene of Foreplay: Theater, Labor, and Leisure in 1960s New York.* Evanston, IL: Northwestern University Press, 2017.

Parson, Annie-B. *The Choreography of Everyday Life.* New York: Verso, 2022.

Patton, Kimberley Christine, and John Stratton Hawley, eds. *Holy Tears: Weeping in the Religious Imagination.* Princeton, NJ: Princeton University Press, 2005.

Phelan, Peggy. "Not Surviving Reading." *Narrative* 5, no. 1 (Jan 1997): 77–87.

Plato. *Plato: The Collected Dialogues.* Edited by Edith Hamilton and Huntington Cairns. Princeton, NJ: Princeton University Press, 1961.

Post, Tina. *Deadpan: The Aesthetics of Black Inexpression*. New York: New York University Press, 2022.

Price Vision Group. "What is TrueTear?" Accessed May 20, 2023. https://pricevisiongroup.com/conditions/dry-eye/truetear/

Profeta, Katherine. *Dramaturgy in Motion: At Work on Dance and Movement Performance*. Madison: University of Wisconsin Press, 2015.

Provine, Robert R. *Curious Behavior: Yawning, Laughing, Hiccupping, and Beyond*. Cambridge, MA: Harvard University Press, 2012.

Rayner, Alice. *Ghosts: Death's Double and the Phenomena of Theatre*. Minneapolis: University of Minnesota Press, 2006.

Roach, Joseph. *Cities of the Dead: Circum-Atlantic Performance*. New York: Columbia University Press, 1996.

Roach, Joseph. *The Player's Passion*. Ann Arbor: University of Michigan, 1985.

Robinson, Dylan. *Hungry Listening: Resonant Theory for Indigenous Sound Studies*. Minneapolis: University of Minnesota Press, 2020.

Rogo, D. Scott. *Miracles: A Parascientific Inquiry into Wondrous Phenomena*. Charlottesville, VA: Anomalist Books, 2005.

Roose, Kevin. "A Conversation with Bing's Chatbot Left Me Deeply Unsettled." *New York Times*, February 17, 2023. https://www.nytimes.com/2023/02/16/technology/bing-chatbot-microsoft-chatgpt.html

Rousseau, Jean-Jacques. *Julie, or the New Heloise: Letters of Two Lovers Who Live in a Small Town at the Foot of the Alps*. Translated and edited by Philip Stewart and Jean Vaché. Lebanon, NH: Dartmouth College Press, 1997.

Sack, Daniel. *After Live: Possibility, Potentiality, and the Future of Performance*. Ann Arbor: University of Michigan Press, 2015.

Sack, Daniel. *Imagined Theatres: Writing for a Theoretical Stage*. New York: Routledge, 2017.

Sack, Daniel. *Samuel Beckett's Krapp's Last Tape*. New York: Routledge, 2016.

Sack, Daniel. *Whitebread Protestants: Food and Religion in American Culture*. New York: Palgrave Macmillan, 2002.

Sack, Robert A., Ann Beaton, Sonal Sathe, Carol Morris, Mark Willcox, and Bruce Bogart, "Towards a Closed Eye Model of the Pre-Ocular Tear Layer." *Progress in Retinal Eye Research* 19, no. 6 (2000): 649–68.

Sack, Robert A., Kah Ooi Tan, and Ami Tan. "Diurnal Tear Cycle: Evidence for a Nocturnal Inflammatory Constitutive Tear Fluid." *Investigative Ophthalmology & Visual Science* 33, no. 3 (March 1992): 626–40.

Salter, Mark B., ed. *Making Things International 2*. Minneapolis: University of Minnesota Press, 2016.

Saussure, Ferdinand de. *Course in General Linguistics*. Translated by Wade Baskin. New York: McGraw-Hill, 1965.

Schneider, Rebecca. *Performing Remains: Art and War in the Times of Theatrical Reenactment*. London: Routledge, 2011.

Schopenhauer, Arthur. *The World as Will and Representation, Volume I*. Edited and translated by Judith Norman, Alistair Welchman, and Christopher Janaway. New York: Cambridge University Press, 2010.

Scott, Anne M., and Michael David Barbezat, eds. *Fluid Bodies and Bodily Fluids in Premodern Europe*. Amsterdam: Amsterdam University Press, 2019.

Sedgwick, Eve Kosofsky. *Tendencies*. Durham, NC: Duke University Press, 1993.

Shakespeare, William. *Antony and Cleopatra*. Edited by John Wilders. London: Arden Shakespeare, 1995. http://dx.doi.org/10.5040/9781408163245.000 00007

Shakespeare, William. *As You Like It*. Edited by Juliet Dusinberre. London: Arden Shakespeare, 2006. http://dx.doi.org/10.5040/9781408160497.00 000005

Shakespeare, William. *Hamlet*. Edited by Ann Thompson and Neil Taylor. London: Arden Shakespeare, 2006. http://dx.doi.org/10.5040/9781408160404 .00000005

Shakespeare, William. *Henry IV, Part 1*. Edited by David Scott Kastan. London: Arden Shakespeare, 2002. http://dx.doi.org/10.5040/9781408160381.000 00023

Shakespeare, William. *King Lear*. Edited by R. A. Foakes. London: Arden Shakespeare, 1997. http://dx.doi.org/10.5040/9781408160268.00000006

Shakespeare, William. *The Taming of the Shrew*. Edited by Barbara Hodgdon. London: Arden Shakespeare, 2010. http://dx.doi.org/10.5040/978140816 0299.00000010

Shaw, Peter. *Man, A Paper for Ennobling the Species*. No. 43 (October 22, 1755).

"Silver Platter." Queer Maps. Accessed April 17, 2023. https://queermaps.org/pl ace/silver-platter

Singh, Julietta. *Unthinking Mastery: Dehumanism and Decolonial Entanglements*. Durham, NC: Duke University Press, 2018.

Sofer, Andrew. *The Stage Life of Props*. Ann Arbor: University of Michigan Press, 1998.

Solito, Elena. "In Conversation with Mona Mohagheghi." *Made in Mind Magazine*. October 2021. https://www.madeinmindmagazine.com/in-conversat ion-with-mona-mohagheghi

Spooner, Cally. "On False Tears and Outsourcing." In *Hotel Theory Reader*, edited by Sohrab Mohebbi. Los Angeles: REDCAT, 2016: 121–33.

Stanford Encyclopedia of Philosophy. "The Turing Test." Last revised October 4, 2021. https://plato.stanford.edu/entries/turing-test/

Sylvester, David. *Magritte*. Brussels: Mercatorfonds, 2009.

Terada, Rei. *Feeling in Theory: Emotion after the "Death of the Subject."* Cambridge, MA: Harvard University Press, 2003.

Tillis, Steve. "The Actor Occluded: Puppet Theatre and Acting Theory." *Theatre Topics* 6 (September 1996): 109–19.

Towsen, John. "The Bread and Puppet Theatre: The Stations of the Cross." *TDR: The Drama Review* 16, no. 3 (September 1972): 57–70.

Trilling, Lionel. *Sincerity and Authenticity*. Cambridge, MA: Harvard University Press, 1971.

Turner, Christopher. "Tears of Laughter: Darwin and the indeterminacy of emotions." *Cabinet* 17 (Spring 2005): 69–73.

Veltruský, Jiří. "Man and Object in the Theatre." In *A Prague School Reader on Esthetics, Literary Structure, and Style*, edited by Paul Garvin. Washington, DC: Georgetown, 1964.

Vincent-Buffault, Anne. *The History of Tears: Sensibility and Sentimentality in France*. Translated by Teresa Bridgeman. Basingstoke: Macmillan, 1991.

Vingerhoets, Ad J. J. M., and Randolph R. Cornelius, eds. *Adult Crying: A Biopsychosocial Approach*. New York: Routledge, 2002.

Vingerhoets, Ad J. J. M. *Why Only Humans Weep: Unravelling the Mysteries of Tears*. Oxford: Oxford University Press, 2013.

Virgil. *The Aeneid*. Translated by John Dryden. 1697.

Virgil. *The Aeneid*. Translated by Robert Fagles. New York: Vintage, 2006.

Virgil. *The Aeneid*. Translated by Robert Fitzgerald. New York: Random House, 1986.

Wearing, Gillian. "Self Made: A Film by Gillian Wearing." Accessed June 8, 2023. https://www.selfmade.org.uk/

Weiss, Joseph. "Crying at the Happy Ending." *Psychoanalytic Review* 39 (1952): 338.

Weiss, Joseph, ed. *The Psychanalytic Process: Theory, Clinical Observation, and Empirical Research*. New York: Guilford Press, 1986.

Wilde, Oscar. *The Happy Prince and Other Tales*. London: David Nutt, 1888.

Wilder, Thornton. *Our Town*. New York: Perennial Classics, HarperCollins, 1998.

Williams, Linda. "Film Bodies: Gender, Genre, and Excess." *Film Quarterly* 44, no. 4 (Summer, 1991): 2–13.

Wittgenstein, Ludwig. *Philosophical Investigations*. Translated by G. E. M. Anscombe. Oxford: Blackwell, 1958.

Wolff, Martha. "An Image of Compassion: Dieric Bouts's 'Sorrowing Madonna.'" *Art Institute of Chicago Museum Studies* 15, no. 2 (1989): 112–25 and 174–75.

Wood, Reverend James. *Dictionary of Quotations: from Ancient and Modern, English and Foreign Sources; including phrases, mottoes, maxims, proverbs, definitions, aphorisms, and sayings of wise men, in their bearing on life, literature, speculation, science, art, religion, and morals, especially in the modern aspects of them*. New York: Frederick Warne and Co., 1899.

Wooster Group, The. "From the Archives." Accessed April 27, 2022. http://thewoostergroup.org/blog/2015/09/28/from-the-archives-unused-silent-super-8-footage-of-the-crucible-c-1982

Wythoff, Grant, ed. *The Perversity of Things: Hugo Gernsback on Media, Tinkering, and Scientifiction*. Minneapolis: University of Minnesota Press, 2016.

Yao, Xine. *Disaffected: The Cultural Politics of Unfeeling in Nineteenth-Century America*. Durham, NC: Duke University Press, 2021.

Yates, Frances A. *The Art of Memory*. Chicago: University of Chicago Press, 2001.
Zamir, Tzachi. *Acts: Theater, Philosophy, and the Performing Self*. Ann Arbor: University of Michigan Press, 2014.
Žerovnik, Maja, ed. *Memory, Privacy, Spectatorship: On Emil Hrvatin's Performances*. Ljubljana: Maska, 2003.

Index